SURVIVING
KING COTTON

by Robert M. Wade

SURVIVING
KING COTTON

by Robert M. Wade

Harrison House Publishing

Surviving King Cotton
All Rights Reserved
Copyright © 2019 Robert M. Wade
Edited by The Harrison House Publishing Company
Cover Artwork by GenesisPro Designs

PUBLISHER'S NOTE
The opinions expressed in this manuscript are solely the opinions of the author in addition, do not represent the opinions or thoughts of the publisher. The author has represented and warranted full ownership and/or legal right to publish all the materials in this book.
The publisher does not have any control over and does not assume any responsibility for author or third party websites or their content.
This book may not be reproduced, transmitted, or stored in whole or in part by any means, including graphic, electronic, or mechanical without the express written consent of the publisher except in the case of brief quotations embodied in critical articles and reviews. Any reproductions without written permission from the publisher is illegal and punishable by law. Please purchase only from authorized distributors to protect the author's rights.

Harrison House Publishing
www.theharrisonhousepublishing.com
info@theharrisonhousepublising.com
ISBN: 978-0-9996147-5-4
Library of Congress Control Number: 2019905702
Harrison House Publishing and the "HH" logo are trademarks belonging to Harrison House Publishing.

PRINTED IN THE UNITED STATES OF AMERICA

Dedication

This book is dedicated to the loving memory of our beautiful parents: Joseph Harrison Wade and Zelma Maedella Holmes-Wade.

Daddy and Momma, although you are not here to rejoice in our moment of triumph I know you are watching over us and sharing in this dream come true. Thank you for teaching us the power of love, humility, forgiveness, patience, benevolence, and preparing us for the trials of marriage, motherhood, and fatherhood.

We love you and miss you.

Content

Introduction	1
Chapter #1 Parents	9
Chapter #2 Marriage	33
Chapter #3 Mag	39
Chapter #4 Annie	55
Chapter #5 Teenie	65
Chapter #6 Bubba	73
Chapter #7 Sue	89
Chapter #8 Deedie	107
Chapter #9 Biddy	117
Chapter #10 Bobo	135
Chapter #11 Oyce	209
Chapter #12 Wilmer	225
Chapter #13 Pon'k	237
Chapter #14 Margaret	271
Chapter #15 Gene	281

Introduction

Children growing up on the farms in the south in the 1940s, the 1950s and the 1960s were shielded as much as possible from the harsh reality of the racist and segregated conditions in which they found themselves in America. The south was the last stronghold of segregation. Along with this protective shield around them, black children were taught their place in America's society early in life if they were to avoid the white man's wrath; especially the young black male child. It doesn't mean black girls were not mistreated and abused, because they were. But throughout America's history, it is the black male who suffered the most at the hands of the American white man. Early in life, black male children were made to feel their lives were no more important than that of the livestock, mules, cows, hogs, horses, etc., because when black men and boys were murdered, the law didn't care. If the murderer of the black man happened to be black it was one animal killing another. If the murderer of the black man happened to be white, it meant the Negro had to have done something wrong in order for them to kill him.

For centuries the black male was forbidden to look a white person in the eye while talking to them. If he did, it was considered a look of defiance and was punishable by a severe beating or death by hanging. The black male child had to witness the emasculation of their black daddies, and other black men in the community. When white men raped and abused their wives and daughters they were helpless when it came to defending their honor. The black male child grew up swearing if a white man ever touched his wife or daughter, he would kill them; knowing he would probably do no more than his daddy and the other black men in the community had done when faced with the crimes white men committed against black people every day of their lives. Their only recourse was to pray to God to help them live with the humiliation of being treated as less than a man, and look forward to the day they could do unto white folks what white folks did unto them. The white man showed black children on a daily basis what happens to black men who demanded justice against a white man for committing a crime against him. The black accuser was more likely to be beaten if he persisted in trying to get justice for the crime committed against him. Therefore, black girls grew up wondering if they could respect a man who would stand by and do nothing if she, or her daughter, was raped or abused at the hands of a white man. It didn't matter that any retaliation by the black man meant certain death.

Through the eyes of most black children, the injustice committed against them in America must be the way things was supposed to be because this type of treatment went all the way back to slavery and showed no signs of things getting any better during the 1920s thru the early 1960s. Black parents pretended their children were too young to realize to what extent the injustice extended around them; but they knew, especially the little black boys. As in all walks of life, there are those daddies and mommas who lived and taught their children it was better to die as a man, or woman, than to live and be looked upon as being less than a human being. The parents in this story were the latter.

Instead of allowing their children to give in to the hopelessness and despair that surrounded them on a daily basis, they taught their children that the unfair treatment and violence perpetrated against them were the results of growing pains. God was testing their resolve to see if they were willing to suffer as He had suffered and not lose their faith that better days laid ahead for them. After they had proven to God beyond a shadow of doubt that they deserved His grace and mercy, He would put an end to their pain and suffering. He would then allow them to return to as it was in the beginning of time when black people ruled the world. To teach the children any other way would kill their self-esteem and give them no hope for the future. How could their young minds understand the evil that lurked in the hearts of the evil white people who owned the farms and businesses their parents depended on to keep them clothed and fed? So to save the sanity of their children, and maintain their own, it meant the parents had to convince themselves that what they taught their children was the truth. It was through their belief in almighty God and the church, they were able to do just that.

    This book is about one of those black family's struggles to survive the harsh reality of growing up in the American south. It is through the eyes of the children this story is told. They survived on what amounted to slave wages paid by white southern farmers for working in the cotton fields in various southern states in America, from the 1940s to the 1970s. My dear sister who did not contribute her story for inclusion in this book did so for personal reasons. She is no less loved by those of us who did. Though some of the memories are dimmed by time, the brothers and sisters involved in this endeavor give accounts of the hardships they endured while growing up as children in the cotton fields of the south to the best of their recollection. They tell of the whuppings they received at the hand of their momma and daddy, but acknowledge that the whuppings, on most occasions, were well deserved. They tell of never staying put in one place for any length of time. Places like Tiptonville, TN, Hay Tie, MO, Mobile, AL, Yazoo, MS, Corinth, MS, Cow Bayou, Wabash, and finally Lakeview, Arkansas, where most of the Wade children live today. They tell what it was like to chop cotton for $1.50 to $2.00 a day. And pick cotton from "can't see to can't see" for .02 cents a pound, and taking pride in who could pick the most. There was no shame in bragging about who could pick the most cotton because it was an honest day's work; and being children, they had no idea that they were being cheated and underpaid for their labor. They tell of the demands placed on them as children, by their momma and daddy to always do what was right, and to not be afraid to take a stand against what they knew to be wrong. These instilled values were to insure they would grow up strong, independent, and successful adults. The children didn't realize that was their parent's intentions at the time. Instead, they believed their parents were being overly bearing, strict and unbending. Still, they talk of the loving relationship they shared with their parents, and show the respect they had for them.

    They joke easily about sibling rivalry, sibling conflicts,

and unpleasant events that occurred while growing up. They tell of helping themselves to apples they labeled as being community property, being petty thieves, living in haunted houses, experiencing the emotional trauma of losing a sister, an aunt, and even a family pet. The stories are funny, serious, and sometimes plain silly. On a couple of occasions, the revelations may be considered cruel. They understand that what they did as children cannot be changed now that they are grown; so they tell their stories truthfully and let the chips fall where they may in the arena of public opinions, because they have come to terms with each other for what they did as children. The southern drawls are heavy in most of their voices when they talk, as it is with all southerners who carry forward the language, culture, and tradition of their ancestors. Those who moved away from the south and interacted with people from other parts of the country and the world lost their southern accent, but not the beliefs and values instilled in them by their southern parents.

Although the majority of the Wade children grew up during segregation and Jim Crow laws, they reflect mostly on the positive aspects of their lives because as children they didn't delve on the poisonous political system in place at the time. It should not be assumed that they were not affected by the overt racism and daily threats from racist white people, who still believed that black people were nothing more than animals, simply because at one time in America's history they were slaves. They were not immune to the whispers, gossip, and angry outbursts of their parents and neighbors at the reporting of black people being lynched and murdered by racist white people in the south on trumped up charges. But as children, like all other black children in southern communities, they were not burdened with trying to solve or cure the ills affecting the world. One member reflects on his personal feelings of disgust and hatred of a system that dictated that his daddy and momma had to say "Yessuh, yes ma'am or nossuh, no ma'am" to white children no older than themselves; approximately 12 years old and up. Other than the blatant overt racism they experienced, the revelations in this book are about their family and what it was like being a member of such a large family.

The history of the Wade family children is unique because, of the fourteen surviving children born to this family not one was lost due to drugs or alcohol abuse, and none have ever been incarcerated for anything more serious than a DWI. Two of their children preceded them in death, Joe Nathan and Betty Ann. When they tell people the number of siblings in their family, the first question normally asked is, "What was it like growing up with so many brothers and sisters?" Or, "How did y'all survive?" The Wade children say honestly, and with straight faces, that although they had their share of fussing and fighting, it was great growing up in a large family; and as far as surviving, everyone pitched in. When asked if they were offered a chance to live their childhoods over, and with a smaller family, would they? They all say with conviction, they would not change their childhood experiences for any other. They believe their collective belief in God has helped them to remain a close-knit family, who has cared for each other throughout their lives. They agree wholeheartedly that none of them ever went hungry. They didn't always want the food their momma put on the table, but food was always there.

Life was simple living in the country, and they lived in communities that believed in that old African proverb that it takes a village to raise a child. Whoever's house the neighborhood children were playing at in the neighborhood those parents treated them as they did their own children, which meant disciplining them as well as loving them. It was a time if grown-ups told your parents you had misbehaved or did something, wrong the grown-ups reports were not doubted. Of course, questions were asked to clarify the allegations; but the parents in the community knew parents did not go around lying on each other's children. So when children got butt whuppings by a neighborhood parent, the consensus by all parents involved was the child deserved it. And in most cases, the children who got whupped hoped their parents weren't told or didn't find out what they had done, because it usually meant another whipping.

Another great thing about growing up in the country, they say, was the freedom they experienced as children. It was common for them to leave home early in the morning on weekends to go play at a neighbor's house and not return home until late afternoon, or evening, without any worry that something may have happened to them. Or the boys took their daddy's shotguns to go hunting whenever they liked; and they would stay gone all day without their parent worrying whether they had shot each other or someone else. The same held true when they went hunting with friends. The only tension between friends was who would kill the most rabbits or squirrels. On lazy days, evening and weekends, during the summer months, fishing on the banks of the river served a two-fold purpose. One, it was relaxing and gave them time to think about what life had to offer them. Second, it was a means of helping to put food on the table. So imagine if you can, fourteen children living under one roof, each unique in their own way; but at the same time, sharing common beliefs and values taught by caring parents. This is their story.

Chapter #1
PARENTS

In order to understand the attitudes of the children, you must understand the parents from where their teaching and guidance came from.

The head of the family was Joseph Harrison Wade [Better known as Joe Wade]. He was born April 11, 1907 in Corinth, Mississippi to Lars and Ada Wade. He died September 15, 1984 in Lakeview, Arkansas. Joe Wade was born just 42 years after slavery ended.

Although he did not experience slavery first hand, the stench from the open wound caused by that shameful period in America's history was strong in the nostrils of every freed slave. The white southerners were still angry because they felt they had been betrayed by the Northern Yankees for taking away their human chattel, which had provided free labor for hundreds of years. Some white southerners were trying to devise a system through violence and intimidation that would enable them to re-enslave black Americans. Meanwhile, black people were doing everything within their power to prove to white America they posed no threat to them or the nation, and would try their best to be good neighbors.

Joe Wade talked constantly about how mean and ornery white people were when he was growing up in Mississippi, but he refused to elaborate so his children could get an idea of what he was talking about. He said he was twelve years old when he had sworn to almighty God that he would die rather than allow a white man to touch his wife or daughter, or abuse him because they thought they could. He did tell one of his children why he felt that way, which will be explained later. Another subject that was off limits to talk about was his parents and grandparents. As far as the children could tell, it was because he wasn't close to his parents. His grandparents were born into slavery and freed along with the other millions of slaves after the passage of the Thirteenth Amendment to the constitution. He confirmed this information about his grandparents being born into slavery, but would never say if they ever told him what it was like to be enslaved. Also, he never talked about his parents other than to make it known he knew their names and they raised him. The children took this limited information Joe Wade provided and attempted to re-construct as much of his early childhood as possible. It's no secret that during slavery, and for many years afterward, black Americans did not keep birth records of their children births, so it was difficult for them to know for sure when they were born or how old they were. Joe Wade believed his daddy was born around 1879, and his momma around 1881 because she was two years younger than his daddy.

His momma and daddy, Lars and Ada, had a firsthand taste of what it was like to be slaves as children living in Mississippi. The black codes were still firmly in place since President Andrew Johnson let the southern politicians back in congress and gave them power to regulate how the freed slaves in their states could be treated.

If Joe Wade knew his grandparents names, he never told anyone in the family what they were, or how long they lived in bondage before being freed. His children concluded that the stories his grandparents told him about their time in bondage was either too painful for him to repeat, or they were victims of the slave saga where his grandparents were sold away and the family torn apart and he never knew them. The children believed by their daddy and momma staying together, it broke the slave cycle of the Wade family being scattered to the four corners of the world. When pressed by anyone to talk about his past, he would always say he didn't have time to worry about the past; his mind was on what lay ahead for him in the future. Like most slaves, and long after they were freed, the Wade clan didn't keep written histories of their family members because they couldn't read or write. Their daddy was a victim of that era when it was thought educating black people was a waste of time, and violent measures was perpetrated on a daily basis to try and keep that belief intact. Their momma fared better because her momma was not the norm. She insured her daughter got an education. However, being a woman, tradition dictated that their momma abided by whatever daddy said, so her education was used to assist the public educational system in educating her children. As far as their daddy was concerned, putting food on the table outweighed his older children getting an education. Still he encouraged his children to look ahead, not backward. Joe Wades' momma and daddy, Lars and Ada Wade, never learned to read or write either, and they too didn't talk to their children about their painful experiences; also preferring their children to look ahead instead of looking to the past. Therefore, the history of generation after generation of the Wade family history was lost because of illiteracy and painful experiences.

    Although Joe Wade was not born into the legal bondage of slavery, he experienced the new style of slavery that was implemented in its place called Jim Crow. As stated earlier, he didn't talk about his parents, or grandparents, but he did talk about a few of his experiences as a child growing up in Mississippi. He said he never got mad at being called a nigger, because he thought it was normal. That was what he was called by white and black people all the time while he was growing up. Daddy told me stories that I don't know if he told anyone else, or whether they were true or not. According to Joe Wade, his most painful memory while growing up was the time he was playing with his 13 year old female friend by one of the local ponds where they fished. They froze, but not from fear, when they heard a rustle coming from the woods. They expected it was a deer or one of their friends coming to play with them. Otherwise, they would have taken off because of what happened next.

    From the woods stepped two drunken white men with shotguns. They started talking about how pretty his friend was, and asked her if he was her boyfriend. When she told them she wasn't old enough to have a boyfriend, they called her a liar and said they bet she screwed half the black bucks on the farm. Daddy said he and his friend could tell the white men were up to no good, so they tried to walk away. One of the men stepped in their path and pointed his gun at them, and asked why they wanted to leave.

When they told him they just wanted to go home, the other white man laid his gun against the trunk of a tree and approached them saying the girl couldn't leave before giving them a kiss. The girl attempted to run into the woods but was caught and thrown to the ground. Daddy said when he attempted to help her. The white man with the shotgun told him if he took another step, it would be his last.

Knowing what was about to happen, daddy turned his back to the scene where the white man had thrown his friend to ground was now on top of her tearing at her dress, and ripping off her underwear. When she started to scream, the white man struck her across the face and told her she was a lucky black wench to be pleasured by a white man. When the white man violated her, she let out another blood curling scream, only to be punched in the face again. Her screams were reduced to moans of pain and agony. The white man holding the shotgun made daddy turn around and watch as his friend raped the girl. After the first white man was finished with her, he got up and retrieved his shotgun and held daddy at bay while the other one took his turn. The whole time the white men were raping the girl, they were whooping and hollering like animals. After they finished, daddy and the girl were warned if they told anyone what had happened, they would be back that night to get them. Daddy said he tried to comfort her, but she wouldn't let him touch her. After his friend put on her ripped and torn dress and underwear they waited long enough to make sure the white men had left before taking off for home.

When they got to the girl's house and told her parents what had happened, her momma started crying and went into a rage and told her husband to find out who it was that raped their little girl and kill them both. The girl's daddy eyes filled with tears, but he made no commitment to finding out who had raped his child. He said he would report it to the sheriff and let the law take care of them, but he knew the sheriff would blame his daughter for her own rape and nothing would be done. When the girl's momma called him a coward, and being less than a man if he didn't do something about his child being raped he became defensive. He said the girl knew better than to be running around out there in those woods, because there were always drunken white hunters running around out there in those woods looking for trouble. He said they should have run as soon as they saw the white men come out of the woods. Of every unbelievable thing he said, the most memorable to daddy was when he said daddy should have kept the white men from raping his daughter. When the girl's momma reminded her husband that daddy was only twelve years old and the white men had guns, he said it didn't matter. He should have been man enough to protect her. Since he wasn't man enough to protect her, he would not be allowed to ever play with his daughter again. With this, he walked out of the house with the girl's momma at his heel, telling him that he needn't come back because he was a coward and would not protect them anyway.

Daddy said he swore that day that if any white man ever touched his daughter, if he ever had one, he would kill them or die trying. He said he would rather be dead than have to face his daughter day after day, knowing he did nothing to punish her tormenters. He said it was a long time before the girl's screams and the loud noises made as the white men violated her body over and over again stopped haunting him at night. Several weeks after the incident, the family moved and he never saw the girl again. Hearing those stories he told made his children thankful they were not born during that era in America's history.

To understand how Joe Wade survived the hardships he faced during his life we have to study the history of the hardships his momma and daddy before him; and their momma and daddy before them, so on and so on until we reach back to the beginning in the villages of Mother Africa, the origin of his ancestors.

Joe Wade was proud of his African heritage because he said no race of people had ever endured what African people had endured over the hundreds of years in America and survived. He was convinced it was a black God that gave black people the strength and the will to survive their strife and not only survive but prosper. Joe Wade knew he would not live to see the end of racism in the United States, so he encouraged his children to continue working hard, standing up for their rights, demanding their freedom and they would be free someday. African people, he said, were the first people to rule the world and would be the last to rule it before Jesus Christ returned to assume His throne here on the earth. Joe Wade oral history mirrors America's documented historical writings. Both histories reveal that Africa was the first super power in the world, and every nation in existence today has gained from its vast riches, knowledge and inventions, i.e., medical tools, religion, books, astrology, etc. Both document that African men, women, and children were stolen from their homeland and sold into slavery. They document the hardships Africans suffered during the middle passage and as slaves and free men, for hundreds of years in America. So it is appropriate to share some of the history as taught by Joe Wade, before moving on to describing the man himself. It is important to keep in mind that his words are paraphrased here and is not in the first person, therefore it is not exact. And the books he talks about the Preacher referencing he had no idea who wrote them. It was purely memorization of what the Preacher said.

White fo'k wan y'all blak chilluns to b'lieve Afa'ca is dis dep, dark con'try wit vic'ous an'mals fo'min et de mout an runin thru de jung'l killin an eat'n everythin in dey path. An' dat Afa'cans is unciv'lized sav'ges or can'bals, eatin each o'ter an' eny white fo'ks dey kin git dey hans on. Dat lie wuz tarted by de fus' white fo'ks frum Eu'rope, afta dey foun out Afa'ca wuz ful ov di'mons, gol, an udder stuf wuf lot'sa money. So dey tol dem lies to try an skeer offen de udder white fo'ks so dey would'n ave to shar de riches ov de lan.

Un'est white fo'ks who rote de truf in dey his'ry boks bout Afa'ca tel wat dem fo'ks frum Eu'rope foun on dey's ri'val. Dey did'n fin a bac'ward, is'lated con'try dat did'n no wat wuz goin on in udder pawts ov de worl. Et de sane time Eu'rope an dem udder white con'tries in de worl wuz runin round sellin an tradin dey stuf round de worl so wuz de blak fo'ks in Afa'ca. White fo'ks boks say Afa'ca ad de earl'est civ'lizations nown to mane. Co'ple of p'aces I heah tel is in dem boks is E'gyp an Nuby'a. Dey's migh't ole p'aces al'rite. An de blak Afa'cans be proud know'n dey ci'tes wuz de fus' in de worl. Dey bar'ered wit stuf lak salt, irin, pots, surga cane, an udder stuf dat dey gro'ed on dey far'm wit de white fo'ks who trad'd dere. De Afa'cans wuz migh't gud billers too. Dey built dem pyr'mids ova dere in E'gyp, an dat ole ci'ti dey call de ru'ins of de gret city ov Timbuktu. Dem pyr'mids an dat ci't is so wel bilt white fo'ks kan't even figur out ow dey did it. De white fo'ks cum to Afa'ca an mes everythin up. Our ance'tors wuz kilt an o'pressed to de pont dey did'n git a chanc to pas de se'rets on to de nex gen'ration. De pre'cher man down et de church says dem white fo'ks boks say de trans-S'haran trad route link'd Wes Afa'ca to de Medi-ranean See. An ova de Injun Ocean, Afa'cans trad'd frum East Afa'ca to Rabia, Pers'a, an wit Chin'es pe'ple. Afa'cans used de Red See to git frum Afa'ca to Et'opia, an to de Medi-ranean an de Injun Ocean.

Afa'can fo'ks did mo dan jus' trad in dey on lan. Dey wuz sailin round de worl, dat's ow us Afa'cans spred our ra'ligion to udder fo'ks roun de worl, an it wuzn't christ'n ra'ligion e'ther. It wuz Islam. Dem white fo'ks tok dat Islam ra'ligion an chang it to suit deyselves. An' wen dey bougt us ova heah to Amer'ca durin slav'ry, dey beet dat Islam ra'ligion rite outta us an made us orship dey made up God. Ra'ligion wuzn't de onliest ting dem white fo'ks got frum Afa'ca an cla'im dey wuz de fus' to do it. Afa'cans wuz de fus' pe'ple to eva rite a bok. Dat's rite, de fus' bok eva rote wuz by a blak mane. I don kno his name or wat de bok wuz bout, but de white mane's bok say he wuz de fus'. We wuz also de fus' pe'ple to studi de tars to. We tok wat white fo'ks call pen'ils an paper tuday an draw'd de hole uni'verse, becuz we b'lieved de tars, an wat hap'n wit nature ere on earth, wuz ka'nnected sum'ow. We figur'd it out an made a caln'dar, but we don git no cre'it fo it cuz de white his'try riters says white fo'ks made de fus' one dough dey cop'ed it off'n de wals ov caves in Afa'ca. Now dey got voodoo ladies all ova de p'ace lokin at de tars an' talkin bout dey kin tel wat 's gon hap'n to youse by wher dem tars is lo'cated in de sky. If'n youse ast me, we shoul've lef dis tar gazin stuf wit de voodoo pe'ple in Afa'ca. Draw'n pic'ures ov de tars wuzn all de blak pe'ple did fus' e'ther. Wile white fo'ks wuz tryin to figur out ow to docta on dey sick, Afa'cans alre'dy ad med'cal too's use'd by dey doctas to op'rate on dem. An' all'a dese tings I tol youse bout is jus' few ov de tings Afa'cans did fus'. Corse youse lis'en to dese white fo'ks, de Afa'cans wuz too stoopid to eva tink of doin tings lak dat. An'way, it easi to see why Afa'can slavs wuz a'ble to bill mos ov wat youse see in Amer'ca. Dey alre'dy kno'ed ow to sail de seas, ow to wok de lan, ow to mak u'ful stuf to mak life mo' easy fo all'a mankin, an' de Afa'cans alre'dy b'lieved in servin a migh't God.

No one nos ow man'y Afa'cans wuz takin frum dey omes an put in chains. Sum his'try fo'ks says bout 100 mil'ion durin de time ov de awful slav trad. De pre'cher man down et de chur'ch says de white fo'ks bok says de slav trad las'd frum 1619 to 1865. Corse white fo'ks says it wuz on'li bout two thousan Afa'cans takin frum dey omes. An'ways, ov dat 100 mil'ion Afa'cans de bok says wuz tak'n frum dey omes, bout 20 mil'ion died in route to Amer'ca becuz dey did'n wan to be slavs, or wuz kilt by dem mean ship cap'n. De slavs who s'vived an made it to Amer'ca wuz made to wok fo fre all'a dey lives, makin a lot ov white fo'ks in Amer'ca rich. No'bodi nos ow much moni dem white fo'ks made frum slav'ry, but we kno de slavs did'n git eny of dat moni afta dey wuz fre'd.

Durin de C'vil Wa, sum Gen'ral rote a o'der sayin de lan lon de Gaw'gia an South Ca'lina co'asts woul be set side fo de fre'd slavs afta de Wa wuz ova, de so call 40 acras an' de mule. Dere wuz nother white feller name ov Stevens, posedly tol de white fo'ks in con'gress dat de 40 acras an de mule promis'd by dat gen'ral wuz a gud i'de, becuz he know'd wat woul hap'n to de blak fo'ks if'n dey did'n git no lan an de means to fen fo deyselves. He posedly says fo mil'ion blak fo'ks jus' ben turn'd loose frum a co'dition ov depenin on white fo'ks to fe'd and cloth dem. An dey don kno nuthin bout doin bizness. Dey's ben kep ig'nant ov dey rites an de white fo'ks did'n wan dem to be ed'cated. So he wuz fraid bout ow dey wuz goin to earn a livin, an gua'd gainst de cheet'n white fo'ks who ben cheet'n dem all'a dey lives cuz dey kan't read or rite. An las'ly, who wuz goin to teach de ex-slav ow to kno wen dey bein cheet'd wen dey don git a fair wage fo dey laber.

De white fo'ks his'try boks, I is tol, tel us dat feller Stevens made a gud arg'ment to dem white fo'ks in de Ouse of

Rep'sentatives. Dey says ok to dat gen'ral 's o'der to give de fre'd slavs de 40 acras an de use ov a gob'ment mule. De fre'd slav wuz sum hap'p, but dat hap'ness did'n las no lon'ger dan a sno'ball in de summa heat. Pres'dent Andrew Johnson, nother mean white mane who becum pres'dent afta Lincoln wuz kilt, says he wuzn't takin no white mane's lan an givin it to no niggah. Wat dat feller Steven says cum tru, cuz afta Pres'dent Johnson shoot down de bill to give blak fo'ks lan an' de mule de blak coes wuz put in plac.

Dem blak coes try to put blak fo'ks bac' in chains. Dey fix'd tings so de ex-slav massa coul kep de fre'man frum makin a fair wage, an woul'n let dem live wher'eva dey wan'd to. Dat's wen white fo'ks star'd buildin dey white neighbo'hoods an kepin blak fo'ks out. An God hep a blak feller dat would'n wok fo dey fumer slav massa. De feller refusin to wok wuz rested fo not havin a job, jail'd an fo'ce to wok fo fre. It made white fo'ks feel betta cuz it wuz almost lak havin dem coons in slav'ry agin. I don tink I ave to tel youse who made sho dem blak co'ds woked. It sem'd de Klu Klux Klan, an udder white s'premacy groops, wuz re'ly mad wen Mr. Lincoln fre'd us cuz dey git even mean'a dan dey wuz durin slav'ry. Dey convin'ed lot ov po' white fo'ks if'n dey did'n hep o'press blak fo'ks, de blak an'mals woul kill dem all. Dat Pres'dent Johnson wuz a big rac'ist al'right. He made sho de fre'd slavs neva git dey 40 acras an de use of dat gob'mint mule. Stead blak fo'ks wuz cheeted and treeted lak dirt. Tings may not be as bad as wen I wuz growin up in Mis'sippi, but it ain't much betta. Youse chaps got lot'sa wok to do if'n youse wan to be equa to dese mean white fo'ks.

De one ting I coul neva uner'stan, Daddy continued, wuz why white fo'ks feered de fre'd slavs. In de south, blak wimmen raise most ov dey white chiliuns durin slav'ry an afta dey fre'd. White chilluns call'd dem blak wimmen "mammy" til dey git old nough to re'lize dey waren't blak. Den dem white mammies an pappies tol dey white chilluns dey white and better'n de blak wimmen who's teets dey ad suckled fo years. De blak men did'n try to git e'ven gainst dey fo'mer slav massa fo be'n mean to dem eiter. Dey did'n e'ven act lak dey wuz mad at nobodi. Ma'ter ov fac, durin wat dem white fo'ks call re'struction, blak fo'ks an white fo'ks in de north rode in de same railcars sumtines, an et in de same eatin house, an used de same publick to'lets wit'out major pro'lems. Dough blak an white pe'ple got lon pre'ty wel t'gether, white fo'ks still acted lak dey wuz better'n blak fo'ks cause blak fo'ks ad ben slavs, so dey fuse to treet blak fo'ks lak equs. But dey didn go round hangin blak fo'ks fo lookin at dem wrong.

Dat "let git lon" at'tude chan'ed in bout 1896, de pre'cher man says dat wen dem white fo'ks on de S'preme Cote says onli de gob'mint could'n de'crimnate gainst blak fo'ks, but de rest ov de white fo'ks coul. So dat Jumpin Jim Crow, "sep'rate but equal" bull crap, wuz put in p'ace by white fo'ks al'cross Amer'ca. Dis law ad sumthin tuh do wit sum cote kase de pre'cher called Ple'sy v. Ferg'son. Dem S'preme Cote fo'ks ru'ed it wuz ok fo white fo'ks tuh kep blak fo'ks out ov dey's stablishment. Afta dis rulin, dis heah United States ov Amer'ca becum two nations, sep'rate an unequl, wit vi'lence gainst blak fo'ks crankin up. De gob'mint turn' a blin eye tuh de bru'al tings don gainst blak fo'ks. White fo'ks got so car'ied way wit lynchin blak fo'ks dey sol ti'kets as if'n it wuz jus' 'nother day at de carn'val. An' afta de man wuz ded, lot'sa dem white fo'ks ave dey pic'ure takin wit de ded man, or buy greetin cards wit de ded man's pic'ure on it tuh sen tuh dey kinfoks. Sum e'ven tok finga's an ears tuh sho dey friens an' fam'ly. Dem wuz sum sick sum-ov-va-guns. De blak coes an Jim Crow tines in Amer'ca's his'ry wuz mean tuh put de feer ov God in blak fo'ks, an it did. Dem white fo'ks rea'ly enjoy dey white pow'a, an it tickle dem to deat to kno dey's white pow'a is gonna las fo lon tine to cum.

De pre'cher mane says he read dat de murderin and lynchin ov blak fo'ks tarted afta de slavs wuz fre'd. He says if'n de klan ad lynch'd slavs befo dey wuz fre'd, dey woul've ben jail'd fo destroyin de slav massa's proppity. De murderin ov blak fo'ks is still goin strong tuday. B'tween bout 1865 wen de slaves wuz fre'd an 1930, dem white fo'ks ung lot'sa blak men, wimmen, and chilluns. Bout 123 blak fo'ks wuz ung ev'ry yea durin dat 65 yea tine fram. I ere tel de pe'k yea wuz in1892, wen white mobs ung bout 161 blak fo'ks. De h'angin of blak fo'ks did'n end in 1930 dough, it kep goin in tuh de 1950s, even afta de gob'mint says it wuz gainst de law fo dem to h'ang us.

Youse'd tink at leas one white man wuz sen to jail fo murderin all dese blak fo'ks. Nope, not one white man wuz eva put in jail fo murderin blak fo'ks. Dis bruta tine gainst blak fo'ks star'd wit de white s'premacy stanc afta re'struction in de south. We's blak fo'ks ad tuh larn tuh s'vive slav'ry an de blak coes, an wen we thout thangs wuz goin to git betta, lon cum Jim Crow. It wuz ard on blak fo'ks doin de blak co'ds tine but my daddy an momma s'vived, an made a betta lif fo me so I kin mak a betta lif fo youse chilliuns.

It was during the Jim Crow laws Joe Wade was brought into this segregated world that regarded black people as inferior to their white counterparts. It didn't matter that history showed that inventions by black Americans, slaves and free, contributed heavily to make life easier for all Americans, and the world.

Joe Wade was a proud man who, with the grace of God, managed to raise 14 children, first by sharecropping, and later, working for farm wages. Sharecropping was where the farm/plantation owner would rent out a portion of land to an individual, and supply him with the seed and equipment to raise a crop of cotton. At the end of the harvesting season in December, the total amount of money made from the sale of the cotton was added up. From the total amount, the farm owner deducted the rent owed on the land, cost of the seed, and a price for utilizing his equipment, mules, plows, etc. In addition to the rent and use of equipment, he also had to pay for the food and hay he bought on credit during the winter to keep the family and the mules fed. After these deductions, the individual and the farm owner would split the remainder of what was left.

An example of how sharecropping was supposed to work is, the sharecropper made a total of $750.00 from his cotton crop for the year. After the deductions for the seeds, use of equipment and food bought on credit, there would be $250.00 left. The $250.00 would then be split fifty-fifty with the farm/plantation owner, which they each received $125.00. In reality, the farm/plantation owner ended up getting $625.00 and the sharecropper getting $125.00 for a full year of work. Plus, the sharecropper was stuck with the expense of feeding the mules and maintaining the farm equipment between crops.

The example given explains a perfect scenario that very seldom happened. In 99.9% of the cases, the sharecropper's share did not exceed, nor equal, in value the debts owed to the farm/plantation owner for supplies, food, and rent. And since the landlord kept the books, and refused to allow the sharecroppers who could read to look at them, the sharecroppers never knew how much money they were cheated out of. The saddest part about this system was the majority of the black sharecroppers could not even read if the books were shown to them, because they were denied an education. But make no mistake about it, the black sharecroppers knew they were being cheated. When the sharecroppers complained to the local authorities about being cheated out of their share of the profits from that years' crop, nothing was ever done. In fact, it was the local police who ensured the racist system remained intact by threatening to arrest any black sharecropper who complained about being cheated by the white farmers/plantation owners. Then the local white law enforcement personnel would make sure that indebted tenants did not avoid their debt by leaving the farm.

The question can be asked why Joe Wade and other black farmers would enter such an agreement, knowing they were going to be cheated. The majority of these descendants of freed slaves had no professional skills, no land to call their own, and no way of getting any. So they entered the sharecropper agreement with the farm/plantation owner because it gave them a sense of pride to be able to say this wuz their land, although they knew they would never own it. The most they could hope for was to make enough money so their children wouldn't have to suffer as they had. However, entering into the agreement made it impossible for them to avoid dependency and impoverishment. Joe Wade sharecropped for several years before realizing they could make more money, as a family, working as laborers at $1.50 a day chopping cotton during the summer, and earning 2 cents a pound picking cotton in the fall. Because of the un-checked cheating, the black sharecropper fell to the wayside and upset a lot of white farm/plantation owners, because it was the biggest money making game in town for them.

Joe Wade never showed any fear of white men, although he knew that with one wrong step, the white power structure in America could have brought his world crumbling down around him. Still, he never hesitated to confront any white boss he felt had cheated him or his children of their days' labor chopping cotton, or using crooked scales to weigh their cotton sacks during cotton picking season. When asked why he didn't fear the white racist men who could hang him whenever they wanted to, Joe Wade said the only people he ever feared was his momma and daddy, and the powerful God he had never seen but knew would be returning to take His place on earth when this world ended. Joe Wade said he felt sorry for his black countrymen who allowed the 300 + years of beatings, killings, and intimidation by white America to successfully destroy their manhood and their desire to fight for the equality and freedom that was promised to the freed slaves and for the generations to come.

Joe Wade assured his children that he and their ancestors endured the indignities and humiliation of racism, because God showed them the bigger picture of what was to come. The day black men would be returned to their greatness and rightful position here on earth until Jesus returned to unite the world once again. A world not divided by race or ethnicity. An America where white and black would live as one people. The Bible tells us that the first ruler of the earth was a black King named Nimrod. He is the only ruler to have ever ruled such a world. Unfortunately, he challenged God's authority and things have gone downhill ever since.

Until Jesus arrives and regains the throne, black America has to be willing to continue fighting for the rights of all people, believe in their people, believe in their communities, and keep the black family strong and intact. It amazed him that white people thought black people were a broke people, or that black people didn't have roots. Black people's only hope to rise to greatness as a people is to unite, but it is easier said than done. One thing is for sure, black people will never reach their dream if they don't leave a foundation on which future generations can build on. There have always been black people that have risen to greatness individually, but it is the whole that black America should be focusing on. Therefore, the struggle for equality continues with each succeeding generation, he would tell anyone who would listen.

Although Joe Wades' teaching was not lost on us, there were evil forces constantly working against it. The history books in our schools were written by white racist historians who attempted to teach us black history only dates back to slavery. They would have us believe that before being enslaved, our ancestors were nothing more than un-civilized savages running naked through the jungles of Africa, with no history of themselves. It was only after the white man enslaved and Christianized the black heathens did we have a history worth recording. Using these flawed history books, white teachers tried in vain to instill in black children the belief that if not for slavery, they would have no history at all. White racist leaders around the world, who realized the strength and survivability of black Africans, saw them as a threat. Therefore, they convinced there constituents that black people are inferior to them and threatened their way of life, which resulted in the governments being able to pass laws to keep African people in their places. This created belief system took hold throughout the world and united white people against black people worldwide. The visual images of Africa and black people produced and shown by Hollywood has been so convincing, it is almost impossible for black children not to believe they are evil and inferior as the white folks says. If not for radical black parents, black teachers, and black leaders, white people may have succeeded with that underhanded deed. While Hollywood did its part to help discredit black people, it was the recruitment of poor white people who needed to oppress someone so they could feel they were better than them. It was that strategy that worked best. It was also the most effective way for white racist to spread their lies and deceit. Joe Wade was well aware of the methods used by white people to try and keep his children from reaching their potential. In his own way he never missed an opportunity to counter the poisonous teaching of a racist society.

Zelma Maedella Holmes Wade was a very beautiful lady. She was born February 20, 1919 in Corinth, Mississippi to Nancy Holmes and Willie Wilkins. She died February 11, 1996 in Lakeview, Arkansas.

She was often asked if she was part Indian because of her Indian like features. She was light skin, had high cheekbones, and long straight jet black hair. Of course her answer was always no to that question. Being a devout Christian, she did her best to walk in the footsteps of her lord and savior Jesus Christ.

Momma's daddy died in a work related accident when she was very young, so she had very little recollection as to what he did for a living or what he was like. Therefore, she had no grandparents to help guide her while she was growing up. She was shy, easygoing, warmhearted, and did her best to keep the peace in the family, and keep the children fed and dressed. The majority of the time, she would sacrifice her own interests for the sake of the family.

When women took what she considered was a large portion of their family's meager earnings to buy dresses, coats, or other personal items for themselves, at the expense of their children, she viewed it as being selfish on the women's part. When daddy went against her wishes and brought her new dresses, if she felt they were not needed at the time, she would sell it to a neighbor for the price daddy paid for the item in question. Daddy, and most people, thought she felt guilty for having new clothes while her children were wearing hand me downs, but that wasn't the reason. She genuinely believed in the philosophy of waste not, want not. She felt having a lot of dresses that weren't being worn was a waste. She said she didn't go to enough places to have a large wardrobe. This doesn't mean she didn't have the basic necessities of clothing, make-up, and jewelry to wear when she went to town on weekends or to church on Sundays. She just didn't believe in trying to make people believe she was more than she was. She saw no reason to be ashamed of being poor, as long as they had food on the table and clothes on her children's backs.

Her children were in awe of their momma's ability to endure the antics of her husband, their daddy, and the fourteen of them. When they asked her how she kept her sanity among the chaos we caused on a daily basis, and their daddy's drinking and gambling every weekend. She gave them a history lesson on gospel music and the church. Although she only completed the 9th grade in high school, momma was proficient in her use of the English language. Unlike their daddy, slave talk was a small part of her vocabulary. The children never got tired of listening to her talk about gospel music, and the peace of mind being in church gave her.

When I find myself feeling alone, with a heavy heart or a troubled soul, I go to church to pray and listen to the choir sing those old Negro spirituals. Before I realize it, I have forgotten my troubles and find myself swaying in rhythm with the music while the angelic voices of the choir, soothes my soul. As the spirit fills the church, my feet take on a mind of their own and stomp out a beat unknown to me. All I know are the words being sung and the music being played represents beliefs as old as time. They sound like old religious slave songs that originated in the deep, darkest jungles of Africa. Songs the Africans didn't know was in their hearts and would take on a new meaning once they were enslaved in America. They couldn't have imagined in a million years how enslavement would attempt to tear their hearts and souls from their body. The songs were so full of sorrow, yet you knew if you believed in God with all your heart and soul, He would give you whatever your heart desire, in time. You can't help but marvel at the power of the songs and the music as old brothers and sisters with walking sticks or canes get up and dance in the isle. I leave the church with renewed faith and a song in my heart. The spirituality gained this day will sustain me until the devil attempts to claim my soul again, which with the help of God, he never will. After witnessing to her children she would begin her history lesson by saying she didn't believe the slaves would have survived their ordeal if not for gospel music; because it was through the music they could talk to God in the presence of the white slave master without being punished. It was also a way to pass on information to runaway slaves.

Gospel music, Momma said, mirrored the thinking and feelings of the slaves at any given time in their history. So through their songs, the hardships and triumphs they experienced in America could be found in the lyrics the slaves sang. Gospel music crosses the barriers of class, race and nationality, because it speaks from heart to heart and soul to soul. The songs are songs of longing and hope in the face of crisis. Black Gospel Music has been an inspiration to millions of Christians and non-Christians alike, since the first slaves were brought to America from Africa in the belly of slave's ships.

The first Africans to be enslaved in America did not sing black Gospel Music to entertain anyone. There was a deep personal need for hope and inspiration for African people, if they were to survive the ordeal in which they found themselves. It was a way to stay in tune with their roots. So our ancestors' music meant more than just praising God for His blessings. Their music satisfied two main functions in their daily lives: their religion and a sense of relief from the back breaking work they had to endure. For white America, this type of music was fascinating. Not so much so for the Indians, because African music had more in common with Native American music than European music, because it was through songs Indians stayed in harmony with nature and the universe. Africans tribes also used music to celebrate events such as marriages, births, and deaths. Even work, play, and public humor were accompanied by music. The rhythm was important to the music, but the words were primary because they told the story of the particular event. The occasion often dictated the use of specific instruments and hand clapping.

One dominant style of music that was brought to America by Africans during slavery is still retained today. It is the call and response pattern in which the lead singer in the choir sings and the chorus or group answers. These African songs, though similar in nature, were very different because African tribes were stolen and sold from different parts of the continent. It was only after being united in slavery that unified African folk songs emerged.

The original Africans were brought to America, along with their music and songs, from Senegal, Guinea, Gambia, Sierra Leone, Liberia, Ivory Coast, Togo, Dahomey (Benin), Nigeria, Cameroon, Gabon, and the Western Congo. They were members of the Mandingo, Baoule, Fon, Yoruba, Ibo, Fanti, Fulani, Ashanti, Jolof, and Hausa tribes. The mixing of these different African languages produced the greatest gospel music in the history of mankind.

It was during the long ship rides that the Africans realized if they were going to survive their ordeal, they had to learn how to communicate with each other. Since they were from different tribes and spoke different languages, the task was difficult. Upon reaching America, it was through these songs that communication was established and perfected, as can be seen and heard in the recorded slave songs.

These songs were called nigger spirituals, jubilees, folk songs, shout songs, sorrow songs, slave songs, slave melodies, and minstrel songs. The religious songs we sing are most commonly known as Negro spirituals because of the deep religious feeling they express. Many of these spirituals were influenced by the surrounding conditions in which the slaves lived. These conditions were awful and depressing to say the least. The spirituals songs that exist today were handed down from generation to generation. The spirituals that speak of life and death, suffering and sorrow, love and judgment, grace and hope, justice and mercy, were born out of this tradition. They are the songs of a people weary at heart. The Negro spirituals are the songs of an unhappy people, and yet, they are the most beautiful expressions of human experience born this side of the seas.

Spiritual and gospel music is a product of black life in the Americas on plantations in the South during the 246 years when black folks were enslaved. Originating in pain, this outpouring released the deep sense of separation forced upon Africans living on the plantations. They were never given a chance to share in the economic wealth that their labor created in America, which was the nation's first base of wealth. In deep and widespread evil and brutality against a people, there is great opportunity for them to find common threads of deep emotional expression. The "black spiritual", in all of its rhythmic beauty, is one of the gifts that emerged from this painful experience.

To emphasize her point about the type of heart break their slave ancestors song about, Zelma Wade ask her children to imagine they were the momma or daddy in the story passed down in her family from generation to generation; about a slave family being torn apart because their son was being sold, and they knew once he left, they would never see him again.

Imagine if you can, their momma would begin, that you have a six-year-old son, who you are so proud of because he is growing up to be everything you prayed he would be. He is intelligent and hard working. The master is so pleased with his loyalty and willingness to work, he has given him daily chores to do around the big house; which means when he gets older, he will be taught a trade which will keep him out of the cotton and cane fields. The cotton and cane fields were the places no slave in their right mind wanted to work, because it was in the cotton and cane fields where slaves were beaten constantly, and often killed if they didn't produce what the master or overseer thought they were capable of doing. And there was no distinction between men and women, they were both beaten and killed at the whim of their white slave masters.

Your son, being a favorite of the slave master, may even find a way to make enough money to buy the family's freedom someday. You knew to dream of freedom, or having things go the way you wanted them was at best fleeting. Anyway, at the end of a hard day in the field, you come home to your family for supper. Your slave husband who has no say so in anything concerning the family or his own life, comes through the door with tears in his eyes. Right away you know something is wrong, and whatever it is, he has to tell you is not good. But because of the time in history you wait for him to tell you what is wrong instead of asking him right away.

He sit down at the table and place his head in his hands and cusses the day God allowed those White Christian Devils to put you and your ancestors in chains. You cuss yourself for not having the power to protect your family as God gave other men the right to protect theirs. Then reluctantly, you tell your wife your son has been sold to the meanest slave master in Mississippi, which means without a doubt, he is going to end up in the cotton fields. He is going to be worked the same as the horses and mules until he either dies, is killed for resisting his bondage, or trying to run away.

You in turn cuss your man for not standing up for his family as the white man did for his, but you know if he even attempts to protect you or his children, he will be killed on the spot. You ask God why is it your man can do whatever it takes to protect the Master's family and his belongings, but won't fix it so he can protect his own children. You have to deal with the pain of losing a part of you without any say whatsoever. After belittling your husband you run up to the big house and plead with the master not to sell your son because it wouldn't be right to take him away from you. The slave master laughs in your face and reminds you that slaves have no rights. Besides, you can always have another one, he tells you.

What song would you sing after your son was taken away? Thank you God, at least he wasn't killed? No. Like so many of those mommas and daddies before you, you want to escape your bondage after such an ordeal. Would you have sung "Go Down, Moses" because you wanted someone to come and deliver you from your chains? Yes. When you sing about the loss of your son, everyone in the community, and even those who didn't live in the community, would know that something devastating happened to your family. Some families couldn't deal with being broken up, so they killed their children and committed suicide rather than live apart.

"How would you feel if you were that momma or daddy?" Zelma Wade would ask each of her children, overwhelmed with the sadness of the story.

Her children would stare at her blankly because no matter how hard I tried, I couldn't place myself in that scenario because I was so far removed from the days of slavery. As bad as the racial situation was in Mississippi, I couldn't even imagine what it would be like to be a slave. Now if daddy didn't get along with the plantation owner, he could pull up stakes and move on.

After regaining control of her emotions, Momma continued her music lesson. Do you know what the song "Swing Low, Sweet Chariot" meant to the slaves? Her questions were always rhetorical. When they said they looked over Jordan and what did they see coming to carry them home, they were talking about some mode of transportation that would take them up north and out of bondage, where they could live as free men and women. On the surface, you think it's about life and the hereafter. But, all the slaves knew it was about the promise of life in the here and now, devoid of slavery. "Home" in slave songs wasn't necessarily heaven, but freedom instead. When the slaves sang of running away to a free country that they called "my home" or "Sweet Canaan the Promised Land", this country was on the Northern side of the Ohio River that the slaves called the river Jordan.

Some Negro spirituals referred to the Underground Railroad, an organization that helped slaves run away. Take "Wade in the Water" as an example. Those unfamiliar with the song believed the slaves were singing about being baptized, or performing some type of ritual. Actually, it was a message for runaway slaves. They were being told that slave hunters were watching the roads and had dogs to chase them with. If they wanted to avoid the dogs picking up their scent, they should wade in the water so their scent would be washed down stream, thereby avoiding detection, therefore the meaning "God would trouble the water." Regardless of the meaning of the song, the majority of them got started in secret during religious meetings, usually deep in the woods of the slaves states to avoid detection by the white slave masters, who forbid them to worship any God other than the one who taught them to be obedient to their slave master. Only when they were sure the slave master didn't understand the message in the song did they sing it publicly. These spiritual songs were so beautiful, the slave master would sing along with his slaves sometimes, not knowing that he was helping to pass along information that helped a runaway slave to escape to freedom. She used the writings of individuals like W.E.B. DuBois and Thomas

A. Dorsey to make herself clear, which she had memorized from listening to schoolteachers discuss their writings while in school and at church during community gatherings.

　　Black gospel music originated from the souls of black folks during slavery and the black codes, and it continued during the Jim Crow era. Although slavery had been abolished, the cruel treatment of black folks did not end there. The chains had been removed and replaced with laws that allowed white people to be harsher than when black folks were enslaved. Since they were no longer anyone's property, any white man could kill a black person and not be persecuted because black folks were still not considered human. This cruel treatment caused a hurt so deep, it is still felt in black communities throughout America. These are eras in our history we as a people must never forget. Regardless of how painful the memory is for us, we must remember the hardships our ancestors endured, the sacrifices they made to get us to where we are today. Then you have to teach the next generation, so they will know the sacrifices you made for them to get to where they will be a hundred years from now. We must keep our history alive so each generation will know how far we have come as a people. This way, no generation will ever forget the sacrifices their ancestors made to make life better for them. It is important that we insure future generations don't lose this rich history. You won't know where you are going if you don't know where you came from. Unfortunately, it is up to us as black people to keep our history alive because we know white America is not going to put our story in their history books. I want you children to remember black gospel music has had a tremendous impact in America. Not only did black gospel music give black folks hope when it seemed there was none, it gave America hope during its darkest days during the world wars and the stock market crash in 1929.

　　"I want you to know", Zelma Wade continued, "through God black gospel music had an impact throughout the world. I want you to know that God charged black folks with the awful task of showing the world that if you believe in Him, he will see you through. That's why God gave us the ability to convey His words through black gospel music". Her history lesson completed, she kissed me on the forehead and told me to never forget my African ancestry, or what our ancestors gave to America and the world. She then lifted her angelic voice in a song so old, I didn't recognize it, but it was beautiful.

Having a strong disciplinarian and workaholic for a father, and a loving, easy going Christian woman for a momma who also wasn't afraid of work, the Wade children learned early you have to work for what you want. This doesn't mean that white America did not place obstacles in their paths because they did; but the Wade children realized as long as they did things the way their parents taught them, they would be okay.

Chapter #2
MARRIAGE

In 1941, Joseph Harrison Wade and Zelma Maedella Holmes were united in holy matrimony in Corinth, Mississippi. Between the two of them, 16 children were brought into this world. Two of their children preceded them in death, Joe Nathan & Betty Ann. Four of the children were from previous marriages. Joe Wade brought three of the four into the marriage, Vera, Lenora, and Joe Nathan. Their momma Donna died from tuberculosis after being married to Joe Wade for nine years. Zelma Holmes brought Christine into the marriage after splitting up with her daddy, James Davis. Momma had another daughter name Annie. Momma and Mr. Davis agreed that Annie would remain with him.

  The Wade children never got a chance to interact with their grandparents because of unknown reasons as far as their daddy was concerned. He left home at age thirteen and never went home again. If he had any regrets about not mending his relationship with his parents before they died, he never told anyone in the family about it, including their momma.

  As mentioned earlier, their momma's daddy died when she was very young and his family never came forward to embrace her. You could not have had so different a set of personalities if you tried. Joe and Zelma Wade legitimized the saying that opposite attract.

  Joe Wade was a free spirit, a gambler, a boozer, a womanizer, quick tempered, loud, boisterous, and a fighter. His temper was the cause of him having to spend six months in jail. According to the story he told to anyone who would listen he should have served twenty years, but black on black crimes in America at that time were of little concern to local law enforcement officers.

  One a Saturday night while shooting craps (dice) at one of the many gambling houses, Joe Wade said he'd won the majority of everyone money in the house. One of the men who had lost all his money asked to borrow two dollars so he could stay in the game. Being it was the code of most gamblers at the time to never leave a man broke, Joe Wade said he loaned the man the two dollars with the understanding that if the man's luck changed, he would repay the two dollars he borrowed. Well, as luck would have it, the man's luck changed and he ended up winning everyone's money; Joe Wades' included. Joe Wade said he told a friend who was with him that he was going to ask the stranger for the two dollars that he'd loaned him. The friend told him that he had seen other men loan the man money in the past, and he had refused to pay them back. His friend then wished him luck in getting his money back because the man was known for not paying his debts. Joe Wades' response was, "the man is going to pay me or else".

Joe Wade went over to where the man was laughing and joking with other men who had been in the game and asked him for his money. The man looked Joe Wade up and down and said he wouldn't pay if it were his momma he owed. Without arguing, Joe Wade said he pulled out his gun and shot the man dead. Although it was cold-blooded murder, he had no fear of going to jail for any length of time because he was the best sharecropper on the farm where he was sharecropping at the time. What that meant was they lived by the white farm owners' code for their best black sharecroppers, "If you can stay out of the grave, I'll keep you out of jail." So, for that cold bloodied act, Joe Wade received a six-month jail sentence. To show how insignificant black lives were, daddy was allowed to work his land during the day and report to the jail at night. Because of that incident, he instilled in his children that taking the life of another person was never to be taken lightly because when you took it, you could never give it back. He said he learned later that the man he killed had a wife and nine kids. He said he felt so badly about the incident, he never killed another man. He said he shot at a few, but always missed on purpose just to let them know he wasn't to be messed with. Joe Wade said although he never killed another man, it didn't mean he was never at the scene of future shootings. One shooting he witnessed almost cost him his life.

Again, while gambling at one of the local gambling

establishment, Joe Wade said he witnessed the shooting of a rich white farmer's son, by two white men he had seen on several occasions while gambling in various gambling houses. He didn't know their names because he never asked. Nor did he remember ever hearing anyone else mentioning their names. The white rich kid accused the other white men of cheating him and they got into a fight and the white kid was shot and killed. During the investigation, someone told the police that daddy was at the scene the night the boy got killed, so they arrested him. While daddy was in jail, the white boy's daddy came and visited him and offered him $25,000.00 dollars to tell who had killed his son. Everyone knew he was not guilty of the murder because it was known the shooter was a white man, but since Joe Wade was at the scene at the time of the shooting, the police figured he knew who committed the crime. Knowing it was certain death for a black man to squeal on a white man, regardless who they killed, he developed a case of amnesia.

When the police questioned him, Joe Wades' story was he was too drunk to remember what had happened, and he didn't recognize any of the white men who were there at the time of the shooting. He always laughed when he talked about the interrogation he had to endure at the hands of the investigating police officers. When he wouldn't change his story that he was too drunk to remember what happened, or who was there, he was made to pull his pants down around his ankles and sit on a block of ice. He said the initial shock when his bare butt came in contact with the cold ice almost made him forget what would happen to him if he told on the white men who had killed the white boy. For maximum effect, the policemen made sure when he sat on the ice, his testicles and genital came in contact with the ice. He had serious doubts if he would ever be able to produce another child after having his testicles frozen. The fear of death was much stronger than not being able to produce more children, so he suffered through it. Joe Wade said, luckily, after a while his butt became so numb he couldn't feel anything, and that was why he was able to stick to his story. He said as far as he knew, the killers were never captured, and he never saw them again. He figured they skipped town after the murder. Joe Wade said, luckily for him, he suffered no ill effect of having his genital frosted.

As stated earlier, Zelma Wade was shy, warmhearted, and slow to anger. Alcohol did not agree with her because it took very little to get her drunk, so she very seldom drank anything. And she never accompanied daddy on these gambling excursions he took because her religious upbringing would not allow her to openly sin like that. Besides, she didn't want to get shot by some drunken fool or get hit by a stray bullet with someone else's name on it. She didn't even stick around in the room where her husband held crap games at the house, preferring to sit with her children telling stories, and later on watching television.

Zelma Wade was your typical country housewife. She cooked, cleaned the house and bathed the children, washed the clothes, raised the children, kept the peace, wiped runny noises, tended to cuts and scrapes, rocked screaming babies to sleep, satisfied and supported her husband as he did his part to keep the family clothed and fed, worked in the garden, and canned the goods. She never complained about not having fancy clothes and furniture, and she worked outside the home to help support the family on occasions. She took the time to appreciate the simple things in life. Like listening to her babies say their first words or watching them take their first steps. Like picking beautiful wild flowers for the kitchen and thanking God for her being able to see them. Like taking walks with her children and explaining to them that everything they saw and heard; the green grass, the tall sturdy trees, the buzzing bees, the chirping birds, the barking dogs, the meowing cats, the oinking pigs, and the mooing cows, were gifts from God. She wasn't a hell raiser like her husband. Her life was more orderly and simple. However, she had her dislikes as well.

Zelma Wade disliked the situations they found themselves in whenever her children asked for things she could not provide. She disliked having to say, "yes ma'am, no ma'am, yessuh, nossuh" to white children no older than her own children. She disliked the derogatory comments white men directed at her because of her beauty whether her husband was with her or not, and having to restrain her husband from retaliating because he would be risking his life to do so. He would ask them politely not to insult his wife again. They knew how much it upset him when they made those remarks, so they would only laugh and tell him if he didn't want men commenting on her beauty, he had better keep her at home. She disliked the racist Klu Klux Klansmen who paraded around the countryside at night in their white robes, intimidating the black farmers. What she disliked most of all was knowing no matter what black people did to help keep America the best country in the world, white people would never give them their just due. She disliked the thought that the only way black people would ever get their dues was to fight and die for it in the countryside and in the streets of America. She hoped the fight wouldn't claim the lives of her children if they chose to get involved when the time came, but if it did, she would know it was God's will and He would reserve a place in heaven for them. When she needed to get away from the everyday troubles of the world, she went fishing.

  Zelma Wade was one of the most dedicated fishing women in the history of Arkansas. Bamboo cane poles grew almost everywhere trees grew, and made the best fishing poles. At the beginning of each fishing season, she would take one or two of her sons with her to cut her fishing poles. Being future men, the boys would cut the first cane pole that looked good to them and would be ready to go home. Zelma Wade tested pole after pole for its thickness, its length, its strength, and durability prior to it being cut. She didn't believe in destroying nature's gifts if it could be avoided. After choosing the poles she thought would meet her standards, the poles were cut. But the boys knew better than to think the process was complete because more often than not, one or all the poles would not pass her hands on test, and the process would start all over again until she found the right ones. It was no use arguing with her because she would not leave until she had at least five perfect bamboo poles. The poles cut and not chosen, they brought home with them to be used as kindling wood to start fires in the stoves. She didn't believe in leaving anything in the woods to rot if it could be used. When they got home, she would string each pole with care, using twenty-pound catgut nylon fishing line. She said if she caught anything big enough to break twenty-pound catgut line, it was too big for her to eat anyway. She would help her young children string their poles after completing her own.

On fishing days, the boys would dig worms. The majority of the worms found in the dirt around the house were night crawlers. The night crawlers bodies were soft and easy for the fish to snatch off the hook without getting caught. But from time to time, they would find the hard body worms that the fish could not get off to easily. The worms bodies were so tough, after all the innards were torn out the outer skin would still be attached to the hook, reducing the amount of worms needed for that fishing day. Sometimes, in late August and September, when the ground was so dry the worms would be too deep to find, alternative bait had to be used. During these times, they would find weed worms that had bored themselves into the stalk of certain weeds, grubs worms found in old rotting logs, or crickets.

Sometimes it depended on the body of water you were fishing in that decided which type of bait you used. For Zelma Wade, that was not a problem because every body of water she fished in had brims, blue gill perches, and catfish that would bite the big juicy worms she offered them. And she offered the fish the worms during sunshine and even in the rain. When her husband would ask her why she went fishing in the rain, she said because the fish got hungry whether the sun was shining or not.

These two different personalities joined forces and produce fourteen productive American citizens. Their marriage was until death did they part. To the both of them it can be said, "A job well done".

Vera Magaline Wade Tharp
Born: November 5, 1934
Place of Birth: Corinth, Mississippi

Chapter #3
MAG

I was born November 5, 1934, in Corinth Mississippi during a time when black people in America were treated like dirt by white people. We didn't have the rights those school books said we had. Like the right to vote, to live where ever we liked. To be given equal treatment under the law or to have those who commit crimes against us punished. Life on the plantation was so hard, and the treatment by white people so unfair, I felt we must still be in slavery. I say this because black folks were beaten for just saying they wanted to vote. Black folks were not allowed to live wherever they wanted to, and nothing was done to white men when they raped black women and girls, or hung black folks for no reason. When black folks did complain to the police they were threatened with being locked up if they didn't drop the charges, or stop making trouble for the good white citizens on those farms or in town. On top of the hostility and unfairness, we worked like dogs from sun-up to sundown and never got ahead. And being daddy was sharecropping, it meant long days in the summer chopping cotton and picking cotton in the fall. Corinth, Mississippi will always be etched in my mind as one of the most miserable places in the world. It seemed like the harder we worked the more the white man cheated us out of what we had worked for, at least that's what daddy said when he would be fussing and cussing at the end of each sharecropping season. To us children that was hard to understand because daddy always said if we worked hard enough, we would have the money to get what we want. I don't ever remember having enough money to get what we needed, let alone what we wanted.

Beside working like a dog and being broke, there was one particular incident that keeps this era fresh in my mind. During cotton-picking season in the fall, I had a bad habit of standing around watching birds. It wasn't that they were very interesting to me. I used them as a distraction whenever I got tired of bending over those cotton rows. My back would be killing me, so I would take a break. Daddy would warn me to get back to work when he felt I had stretched my back long enough. I would go back to picking, but as soon as my back started hurting again, I would stand around counting the number of birds in the air. Normally he only told us to do something one time before getting physical, but I got several warnings. I should've known I was pushing my luck, but I continued to ignore daddy's warnings. One day, as usual, I straightened up to relieve the tension in my back. When I stood up to stretch, a flock of birds flew overhead. I was standing there counting away when cotton stalks, bows and all, started raining down on my back and behind. When daddy got through with me, the stalks were worn down to nothing. It took a couple of those beatings before it broke me from counting birds; but I continued standing up and stretching my back whenever I got tired of bending over. I just didn't stand as long.

To add to the everyday tension of living in Mississippi daddy was confrontational when dealing with white people when he knew they were trying to cheat him or humiliate him somehow. So when he left home in the morning, we didn't know if he would be coming home that night. Black men were hung all the time for disrespecting white people and daddy had a habit of pushing the envelope. He was also the glue that held the family together. I don't know what we would have done without him. Sometimes I wondered if he shared our concern.

Daddy was one of the biggest bootleggers of moonshine whiskey in the state of Mississippi. People came from all the farms and from town to buy his brew. He was able to get away with making whiskey because he was friends' with a local white man who provided the equipment and split the profits with him. His white friend ended up getting busted and sent to prison for a year. I don't remember for how long, but that ended daddy and the white man's friendship. They tried to get daddy on the same charge for bootlegging but he got away somehow. The plantation owner knew daddy was involved in bootlegging whiskey and didn't like it, but daddy was his best worker so he looked the other way. Daddy's and the white man's problems started when their business got too prosperous. Because they wouldn't share their wealth with the sheriff and the local politicians it was time to shut them down.

While working on that plantation daddy supposedly caught the eye of the missus of the house and rumor had it she was inviting him into their bedroom whenever her husband was out of town.

I don't know whether it was true or not, but a white woman from another farm stopped in front of our house one day and motioned for momma to come to the road. Being it was a white woman naturally I was nosey. I didn't get too close because momma would have shooed me away, so I got within hearing distance and listened to what the woman told momma. She told momma daddy was going to get himself hung because he was sleeping with his boss' wife. That she had stopped by the woman's house one day and caught them in bed. She said she was only telling her that because she was concerned for us children and didn't want to see us without a daddy. After the lady left momma told me she was probably lying because daddy wouldn't mess with her nasty white tail. I didn't believe it because after the sharecropping season ended daddy would go to Sheffield, Alabama to work to keep the family fed. I never knew what type of work he did there in Alabama and I didn't care. My only concern was that I didn't go hungry. When momma told daddy that evening what the white woman had told her, he laughed it off and said that gossipy ole' white woman was always trying to talk to him, but he wouldn't give her the time of day. He assured momma it was nothing but a lie, because he knew what happened to black men who slept with white women in Mississippi.

Another incident that could have gotten daddy in a lot of trouble was when we were sharecropping in the Mississippi Delta and daddy got sick. He was so sick he couldn't work for a couple of months during the height of the cotton-picking season. We were too young to get the crop in by ourselves, so the plantation owner had to pay some of the other sharecroppers to pick the cotton. He was mad as hell because it was costing him a lot of money to get the crop in, plus he was loaning daddy money to pay his doctor bill, for food for us, and for our livestock. The way daddy figured it he would never be able to get out of debt with that white man. Every crop he raised for the next ten years were already owed to the white plantation owner. It was well known if a black man didn't pay his debt, it was grounds for a white man to have him jailed for nonpayment of his debt, or the white man could have him hung.

Daddy, the nonbeliever of following man's rules, told momma he only had one way out. So at 3 a.m. one morning, daddy loaded what little belonging he wanted to take with him, and us, in a borrowed truck and left Mississippi owing that white man at least a thousand dollars. The plantation owner never suspected a thing because daddy kept right on telling the plantation owner he guessed he would be working for him forever, right up to the day we left. Before leaving the plantation he sold everything he didn't need or want to neighbors dirt-cheap so he would have a little traveling money to relocate from the Mississippi Delta to Haiti, Missouri and never looked back. I don't remember who loaned daddy the truck so we could move from the Mississippi Delta to Haiti, Missouri. Everything worked to perfection. When we got to Haiti, Missouri daddy returned the truck to its owner.

* * * *

I never got a break because I was a female. Daddy expected me to carry my weight along with everyone else in the cotton fields. There was even a time when I had to perform the duties of a son instead of a daughter. To my surprise, I did just that. I helped daddy set up the cotton rows and leveled them off so we could plant the cotton. When the cotton came up, I helped chop it; and in the fall, I helped him pick it. After all that hard work, I never knew if we made a profit or not because daddy always said handling the money was the man's job. I do know I never got anything at the end of the year. It was because of an incident that occurred between daddy and my brother, Joe Nathan, which caused me to have to assume the role I was forced to play.

    Joe Nathan befriended a white boy on the plantation and they played together quite often. One day while they were playing, the white boy gave him fifty cents. When Joe Nathan got home and showed us the money, daddy thought he had stolen it. One thing daddy didn't tolerate in his house was a liar or a thief. The truth being told, he was both. Daddy justified his lying and stealing saying he only lied to and stole from white folks, and everyone knew we could never steal enough from them to make up for what they stole from us. He told us we weren't going to be like him; we were going to be better than he was. He wanted to ensure that we broke that chain of lying and cheating that he and his generation had to do sometimes just to make ends meet. Unfortunately, he never told us how we could break the cycle. He only encouraged us to work harder in the cotton fields, so we found ourselves following in his footsteps. We were never encouraged to get an education as a way to get ahead, or encouraged to leave the farm in pursuit of a better life. Anyway, no matter how hard Joe Nathan tried to convince daddy that the white boy gave him the money, daddy didn't believe him. Daddy was so convinced Joe Nathan had stolen the money, and was lying about it, he put Joe Nathan's head on the chopping block in the yard and threatened to chop his head off if he didn't tell the truth about where he got the money. Joe Nathan told daddy he just had to cut his head off because he wasn't changing his story because he was telling the truth. Momma, my older sister Lenora, and me were all hollering, crying, and begging daddy not to do it. After much begging on our part daddy finally let him go.

    The following day, Joe Nathan brought the white boy to the house to tell daddy he had given him the money. Daddy thanked the white boy for clearing things up, but he didn't apologized to Joe Nathan for threatening to cut his head off. Because of this incident, Joe Nathan had had enough of living under daddy's rules. Several days later after the incident, while we were picking cotton, he told us he could no longer live under daddy's roof so he was leaving. We tried to talk him out of it because he was only 16 years old and had no idea where he was going or what he was going to do once he got there. He said daddy left home when he was only thirteen and he survived, and so would he. That night, while everyone was asleep, Joe Nathan left home for good.

After Joe Nathan left, I had to take up the slack and became for all practical purposes, the boy of the family. In addition to the farm work I mentioned earlier, I had to help daddy saw the wood and bust it up for the stoves, I also had to go to the woods with him. Right along with daddy, I had to cut down trees, help load the logs, and haul the wood home. I was mad at Joe Nathan for a long time for leaving because of the added responsibility that was placed on my shoulders.

I didn't see Joe Nathan again until ten years later when he came to visit us in Lake County in Tiptonville, Tennessee. He was living in Missouri when he came to see us, but said he was on his way to New York. Daddy had never said anything to us about how he felt when Joe Nathan left, but upon his return after ten years, daddy was the happiest man in Tennessee. They acted like they were old friends who hadn't seen each other for a long time. I don't know if they talked about the incident that caused Joe Nathan to leave in the first place. If they did, all was forgiven. The only thing I think that daddy may not have liked about the new Joe Nathan was he had changed his name to "Shine." We all knew anyone named Shine couldn't be very dependable or honest. But we all accepted him for what he was, daddy and momma's son and my brother.

Joe Nathan was real black, and he hated it. Daddy tried to tell him not to be ashamed of his black skin, but it didn't do any good. He always said his children were not going to be as black as he was, so he didn't like dark women like himself. He said his kids were going to be light skinned and have long straight hair like white folks so they would have a chance in this racist world. So he only dated high yellow colored women and white women. I don't know about the white women because I never seen him with one. His problem was, he was like his daddy. He always had three or four women he was playing at the same time. Unfortunately, his playing too many women at the same time caught up with him. I don't remember what year it was when we got the word from the local sheriff that Joe Nathan was stabbed to death by two women in New York. Daddy told them he didn't have the money to bring him home to be buried, so members of a church buried him in New York. Again, as he had hidden his feelings when Joe Nathan left home, daddy never said anything to anyone about how he felt about the death of his son. However, daddy did take comfort in knowing he had talked to his son in Alabama before he took off for New York. Joe Nathan had gone with daddy to Mobile, Alabama to help him look for a house because daddy was ready to leave Tiptonville. I never saw Joe Nathan again after that visit in Tennessee.

* * * *

Lenora started working around the age of nine, but she didn't provide much help because she was sick most of the time and daddy had to send her home at least twice a week. When she did chop, or pick cotton, daddy always made sure there were grown folks around to keep an eye on her because she always lagged far behind everyone else. Her lack of work in the field wasn't the only place that annoyed me as far as Lenora was concerned. Me, and Lenora had to get up at 5 a.m., sometimes 4 a.m., to help momma cook breakfast in the mornings prior to going to school or to the cotton fields, depending on what time of year it was. I would be griping and grumbling at having to get out of bed at such an ungodly hour, and Lenora would be griping and grumbling about being made to get out of bed when they knew she was sick.

We knew what we were supposed to do without being told. Every morning it was our job to fry whatever meat we happened to have for that particular morning. Sometimes it would be sausage, sometimes fatback, sometime salt pork, and sometime salmon paddies. Momma's job was to bake the bread and cook the oatmeal or grits, which she cooked every morning. Lenora would let the grease in the skillet get too hot before putting the meat into the skillet. By doing so, when she put the cool meat in the hot grease, it would pop and spew burning her arms and hands. After having a few of the droplets burn her she would be too scared to turn the meat over from that point forward. She would back away from the stove so she wouldn't get burned. So I would have to tend to the meat so it wouldn't burn. On other occasions when Lenora threw the meat into the skillet, momma would get mad and tell us to get out of her kitchen. On those occasions, daddy would get mad at us for not helping momma cook. Sometimes Lenora would stand so far back from the stove she had to throw the meat into the skillet. When she did this, the grease would splash onto the top of the stove and catch fire, sending momma into a panic to put the fire out. I believed she threw the meat in the skillet like that just to get out of having to cook. I just knew Lenora was going to burn the house down one day. Luckily, she never did.

Lenora, and me had other chores in the morning while growing up. We had to milk the cows and churn the milk once it was gathered. It seemed the cow teats were always dirty and we would have to clean them off before doing the milking. We would get out the big wooden churn and slosh and slosh until we could separate the butter, the buttermilk, and skim milk. Those were happy times when we could go in the kitchen and get fresh milk from where it was kept cool sitting in bottles in a bucket of ice. A chore we had to do during the fall was when the corn was harvested. Lenora and me usually when we got home from school on Fridays and on weekends, had to shuck the corn and then shell it off the cob into one of the number 1 tub. When we had shelled enough corn daddy would pour it into a burlap sack and take it to the grinding mill to get it ground into corn meal which momma used to make cornbread.

When we reached our teen years he reluctantlystarted letting boys come to the house at night to see us. Daddy and momma always went to bed early, and he would pretend to be asleep. Me, or Lenora, would stand by momma and daddy's bedroom door and listen for their snoring before getting frisky with our boyfriends. Upon hearing the telltale sound that they were asleep it was fun time. Thinking momma and daddy were asleep, we would do some heavy petting. But as soon as the boy's hand started going places they had no business going, daddy would ask what was going on in there; or he would show up in the doorway and tell the boy it was about time for him to be on his way home. We didn't realize that daddy and momma could hear our heavy breathing, and that was how they knew when to intervene. I don't think daddy ever slept when there was a boy in the house anyway.

* * * *

While living in Mississippi, we would cook our daily meals on the regular wood stove, but at suppertime daddy put a long iron rod with hooks on it across the center of the fireplace. We would make a fire and hang the big iron cook pots on the hooks, and that was how we cooked beans and greens, and anything else that had to be boiled. We sat iron skillets on the coals in the fireplace to bake our bread. I don't remember how long we had to cook that way, but I looked at it as just another phase of life we had to endure.

There is one period in my life that was completely without a silver lining. I don't remember why or what years they were, but momma and daddy had to have government stamps in order to buy shoes and meat, and for reasons unknown to me, the stamps never lasted through out the whole year. A couple of years in a row, in the latter part of March when it got warm enough, daddy made us go barefoot when we got home from school so we wouldn't wear out our shoes before he got more stamps. We would run around in the woods and through the bottom playing barefoot. Sometimes we would step on a sharp object of some sort and cut our feet. We would go home bleeding and crying. Momma or daddy would clean the wound, put some type of salve on it, wrap a piece of cloth around the foot and send us on our way, still without shoes. Most mornings in March it would be pretty cold, so we had to wait until it warmed up before going outside to play. When the weather got a little warmer in April, daddy would run us outside to play shortly after breakfast on weekends. If an unexpected cold front came through and we complained about it being cold outside, he told us to tough it out until it got warm. When the stamps ran out, momma and daddy couldn't buy meat at the store in town. During this period of time, we ate a lot of possums, coons, rabbits, turtles, fish and salmon paddies. I don't remember if this was during World War II or not, but there was a lot of belt tightening going on during this period of time.

* * * *

Daddy was the most distrustful person in the world when it came to having to deal with folks who did not agree with his way of thinking, especially when it came to dealing with girls. Daddy felt any man who didn't rule their daughters with an iron fist was weak. Until he was forced to give us some freedom, the only place we were allowed to go was to church with momma. We weren't allowed to go to visit friends because daddy felt all the young girls we knew on the plantation were too fast for us to hang around. Being fast meant the girls liked flirting with boys. The church was about three miles from where we lived, but we didn't mind the walk because it gave us the opportunity to meet other children our age that we could play with. We attended church every Sunday morning and in the evening. It would be dark by the time the evening services were over, but we didn't mind because there were other people walking with us. I loved church, and it wasn't just because I got a chance to interact with other children. I truly believed God was going to show me better days when I got old enough to be on my own. Although daddy made sure we went to church every Sunday with momma, he never attended church himself. So not only did we interact with girls at church, but with the boys as well. If daddy had known this he probably would have attended every service.

* * * *

Attending school in Corinth, Mississippi was an unforgettable period in my life because of the distance we had to walk to get there, and the food we took to school for lunch. The school was about two miles away and located on the other side of the bottom. The bottom was deep in the woods where no one went unless they were hunting or doing something illegal and didn't want to get caught. It was always damp and swarming with biting insects in the summer. In the winter, because of the moister, the ground would be frozen and there would be big icicles hanging from the trees and bushes. There was an old wagon trail that ran through the bottom that was once used by woodcutters. However, it was overgrown from a lack of use over the years. Our nearest neighbor was the family living by the church in the opposite direction of the schoolhouse. Every morning we got up around 5 a. m. to eat breakfast before taking that long walk through the bottom to the school, on the other side of the woods.

Along with the biting insects, there were animals that we had to be very much afraid of, like black bears, wildcats, and wild boars. We were told that the scent of our lunches we took to school would draw the attention of the animals. As we walked through the woods, we were very conscious of the molasses bucket we carried to keep our food in because we knew the lid was not airtight, therefore, the animals could smell our goodies. Luckily for us, we never had a lunch that appealed to any of the animals in those woods. Some of them probably smelled their kinfolks in those buckets. We pretended that we had bologna sandwiches or wiener sandwiches in our bucket like the well to do kids had in theirs. Unfortunately, we didn't know what bologna and wieners tasted like. We had hogs and cows, so our school lunches consisted mostly of big slices of pork or ground up salty meat like hamburgers in a biscuit. On more occasions than I care to mention, we also had our share of wild game pack into our lunch buckets.

* * * *

We lived so deep in the woods when we lived in Corinth, we didn't have a water pump. We had to go quarter of a mile to a well to get water for the house. I got so tired of having to tote that water bucket day after day, especially on washdays. On a normal day we only needed a couple of buckets of water for drinking and cooking, but on washday we needed between eight and ten. My arms and legs would get so tired carrying those buckets. I didn't really mind helping momma wash the clothes, but I hated carrying the water from the well. Again, Lenora was too sickly to carry her fair share of the load.

* * * *

Keeping our moves in the order they occurred while growing up is hard to do because we moved so much. We moved from the Mississippi Delta to Corinth, Mississippi, to Tiptonville, Tennessee, back to the Mississippi Delta, to Haiti, Missouri, and back to Tiptonville, Tennessee. The last move to Tiptonville was my last move. It was there I got married and settled down.

One house we lived in while we were living in Mississippi was a real piece of work. This particular house had two holes in the floor when we moved into it big enough for us to put our hands through. Instead of fixing the holes right away daddy told momma to cover them with something, which ended up being she stuffed rags into the holes. We would pull the rags out of the holes and hide things underneath the house through the holes. However, we knew when it started to rain, whatever was under the house we had better move it in a hurry; otherwise it would get washed away. When it rained hard we laid on our stomach on the floor, remove the rags, and watch the water running underneath the house. We threw pieces of paper through the holes in the floor and watch as they were whisked away with the flow. On those days when the rain was extremely heavy the water rose up to the holes and threatened to come into the house. When this occurred momma or daddy would shoo us away from the holes and stuff the rags back into the holes to keep the water out. We kids thought it was cool to be able to watch the water running underneath the house. After several hard rains daddy fixed the holes and spoiled our fun. Again, we saw the silver lining in an unfortunate situation.

The best time of the year for me, regardless of where we lived was Christmas time. We would get up in the morning all excited because we knew Lenora and me, would be getting baby dolls, and it didn't matter that the dolls were always white. The dolls we got for Christmas were torn up within six months because every time daddy and momma complained about the unfair treatment of white folks I would beat the crap out of that white doll. I didn't care that my childish tirade meant nothing in the grand scheme of things. After the dolls were gone we would cut pictures of little white girls from the Sears & Roebuck catalogue, tie the picture to a broken piece of stick, use corn silk for hair, and pretend they were dolls. The other reason I liked Christmas was momma would cook a big meal and lots of cakes. She would cook a whole ham, turkey and dressing, yams, collar greens, biscuits, and cornbread. On New Year's Day she would add black-eyed peas to the meal for good luck for the coming year. We were allowed one slice of cake from several different cakes momma cooked per day, which was usually about six or seven. Those cakes lasted from Christmas until the New Year.

* * * *

When I was 12 years old I used to go hunting with daddy, sometimes at night, because he needed someone to watch his back because there were men in the surrounding counties who wanted to hurt him because he made the best moonshine whiskey, and had the best hunting dogs in Mississippi, I thought. To add to the reasons they disliked daddy was he was sleeping with half their wives. Not knowing the whole story, I thought the men were just being mean to him. Every chance they got they would steal his dogs or kill them one by one. At first I got mad when those mean old men would kill one of daddy's dogs, until I realized the dogs were being treated and eating better than we were. Although I felt guilty about it, there were times when I would be glad when someone stole, or killed one of his dogs because he spent more money on them than he spent on me. Of course I never told him that because he would have beaten the crap out of me. Even with all his faults, I stuck by him and did whatever he asked me to do for him until I got married and left home.

* * * *

Zelma Wade is my momma because she is the woman who raised me. My biological momma name was Donnie. She died from TB at the age of 33 years old. I remember going to the hospital to see her and feeling so sad for her. When she went into a fit of coughing she would spit up blood. It did not stop her from combing Lenora's and my hair. She always tried to assure us that everything was going be all right. As her condition worsened, she could no longer comb our hair and she would cry because she could no longer take care of us. Daddy would tell her he wasn't going to bring us back to the hospital to see her if she was going to carry on like that, because she was only making it harder for the children. That we were already scared to come to the hospital because we didn't know if she would be dead or not when we got to the hospital. Of course that wasn't true, but we weren't going to tell momma that because it would mean we were calling daddy a liar. We valued our behinds so we kept quiet. She was dark skinned and had long black pretty hair.

Daddy said my biological momma was a mean woman. What he didn't tell us was she was mean because he was a womanizer and a gambler, and she wanted him to stop doing both. He said one night while he was visiting her in the hospital he fell asleep. When he woke up, she was standing over him with a straight razor trying to decide whether to kill him or not because one of her friends had visited her earlier that day and told momma she had seen him with another woman that very day. He said being afraid, he didn't move. He pretended to remain asleep. He said she just stood there for a while and then said he wasn't worth it. Sometimes I wondered just how much daddy really loved my biological momma.

After our biological momma passed, daddy met momma (Zelma) and she took care of us while he worked, drank, gambled, and womanized. She never mistreated us, and she treated us the same as she did her own children. It didn't take long for daddy to fall head over heels in love with her. Everyone on the farm said daddy was crazy about Zelma because she was a high yellow woman and pretty as heck. It didn't take daddy long to make his move and ask her to marry him. I was happy about the marriage, but Lenora was still emotionally attached to our biological momma so she wasn't happy at all about daddy marrying Miss Zelma.

One of the reasons she felt daddy had betrayed our biological momma was because our biological momma had to work right along beside daddy in the fields, but when he married Miss Zelma, he told her he didn't want her working for no one. All he wanted her to do was stay at home and raise the children. Lenora never got over feeling daddy and Miss Zelma had betrayed her momma memory and looked for every reason not to like her. I can say with certainty that momma (Zelma) loved us and treated us as her own.

* * * *

I got married at age fourteen while we were living in Tiptonville, Tennessee in 1949. Like Joe Nathan, I could no longer stand living under daddy's roof because of his dominance and indifference to how we felt about what we thought our lives should be like. When daddy moved to Mobile, Alabama, I stayed in Tiptonville with my husband. It was after they moved from Mobile I lost contact with them. In 1961, I saw an ad a lady had put in the local newspaper that said she could help anyone find their long lost family members. I forget where she was located, or how much I paid her, but it wasn't in Tiptonville. It only took her about a month to find out they were in Arkansas and gave me a telephone number where I could get in contact with them. I was so excited when momma answered the telephone. Momma was so happy to hear from me, but she was going through a crisis at the time. Daddy and my brother Charles were in jail in Forrest City, Arkansas, but I can't remember what for. I was working and had money so I sent momma the money to get them out.

I kept in contact with my family, but didn't get a chance to visit them until several years later when they lived around the lake on Highway 20 down below Ernest Toney's store in Arkansas. The first time I met my brother Robert he was in the military and was home on leave. We were hugging and carrying on so much that daddy acted like we were trying to cote each other. He actually asked us what was going on between us. We laughed and told him that we were just glad to see each other for the first time. I was glad to meet all my brothers and sisters I was meeting for the first time. I have never lost contact with my family again, and never will.

*   *   *   *

Summary

Although growing up in the cotton fields in the south was hard, I thank God I had a family that loved me and protected me while I was growing up. The family bond we shared was strong, although we didn't always agree with daddy's strict disciplinary measures. I am also thankful that the strong family bond momma and daddy instilled in us children are as strong today as it ever was, because even though I wasn't around to see most of my younger brothers and sisters grow up, their love for me has never waned. I praise the almighty every day for allowing me to be a member of the Wade family.

Annie Ruth Wilson
Born: December 24, 1939
Place of Birth: Corinth, Mississippi

CHAPTER #4
ANNIE RUTH

I was born December 24, 1939 in Corinth, Mississippi to James Davis and Zelma Holmes. Two years later, my mother gave birth to my baby sister Myrtle Christine in 1941. I don't know what happened between them, but they ended up going their separate ways. Me, and Christine were split up. My daddy never said whether he and my mother were ever married or not, but he is the one who raised me along with his wife Annie Lee (Jones) Davis. They were married in 1941 when I was two years old, and my sister still an infant. I don't know how I ended up with my father, but everything worked out fine. Everything also turned out ok with my sister, so the way I see it, it was all a part of God's plan for us.

* * * *

My first childhood recollections happened during WWII. My daddy was in the military, so we did a lot of traveling. I can't remember all of the different army bases where my daddy was stationed, but I remember Virginia and Massachusetts very well. I remember these two states because we traveled by train between the bases in the two states. As far as the bases themselves, I don't remember the names.

It was an exciting time for a little "Colored Girl," as we were called back then, to be riding on that big old train along with a whole bunch of soldiers headed all over the country to different military bases. The "colored only" railcar was always so crowded that we were only able to get up the steps far enough to set the suitcases down. Since there were no seats, we had to sit on our suitcases. I would love to describe what the colored car looked like, but I never got to see the inside of it because of the overcrowding. Still, it was quite a ride.

Another thing that made the rides on the train so exciting was my mother made me a little Women Army Corp uniform that made me look like a little female soldier. The real soldiers really got a kick out that. They said the uniform made me fit right in with them. Along with the uniform, my mother made a little brown matching soldiers' bag, and sometimes it got quite heavy because the soldiers were very generous with their change. This went on for about two years. I was about three years old when the war started, around 1941.

After daddy's stint in the army was over, we moved back to Corinth, Mississippi right in time for me to start school. Corinth was divided into three sections; white, colored middle class, and the black ghetto. The white side of town was where the rich white people lived and blacks were not allowed. We lived in the colored middle class part of the city where the teachers, preachers, undertakers and other black professionals with nice paying jobs lived. Across the railroad tracks was where the black dregs of society lived. Black people in the ghetto were disliked by the colored middle class the same as the white people. Being I was young, it never occurred to me we were enforcing the lifelong teaching of the white slave masters throughout history who pit one class of blacks against the other. As it was during slavery we believed because we were well off, it made us better than them. In our determination to prove we were as good as white people, we mentally suppressed the truth that we were still black. Regardless of how much money we had, white folks still called us niggers the same as they did our fellow blacks across the railroad tracks. Of course the storeowners in every neighborhood in Corinth were white.

I missed the adventures of mingling with the soldiers and riding the trains, but with time, it was only a distant memory. I was five at the time. We lived right across the street from the big brick elementary school. I was one of the rare kids in the neighborhood. I enjoyed school, especially reading and spelling. However, everyone had that one subject they would rather lose an arm than have to take. My dreaded subject was math. No matter how hard I tried, I just couldn't get it as I did my other subjects. The only thing I can say good about math is a "D" is passing. I thank God there were other subjects to take in school; otherwise I would have gone insane. Another thing I enjoyed about the elementary school was the lunches. I swear the meals tasted so good and home cooked; it was as if our parents took turns cooking lunch for us.

My third grade teacher was our next-door neighbor and my mother's friend, so you know I didn't get away with anything. Sometimes I felt school never let out because in the evening, my teacher would come over to visit mama and would continue the lessons of the day. I didn't realize it at the time, but she just wanted to ensure that I was successful in school and in life. She wasn't the only one concerned about me. The church members where we worshipped were just as hard on me as my parents were. The community was close-knit, and every parent did their parts to help protect the children from harm. They also encouraged every child in the community to succeed. We lived by that old African proverb "It takes a village to raise a child." Therefore, every grown-up in the community was my mother, father, and grandparent.

The grown-ups who pushed us the hardest were the elderly. And because they didn't work, they were the nosiest. When us kids would get into some mischief, and thought we had gotten away with it, one of those old guardians of the neighborhood would report exactly what we had done to our parents. They didn't accept excuses for not doing a good job in school, or giving our parents a hard time. No matter how mad you got at the elderly for getting on your case about something or for getting you in trouble because they told on you, there was no such thing as disrespecting them, not if you wanted to live. I didn't appreciate it at the time, but they helped me to become a pretty good human being. Boy, we sure could use that today.

One thing that never bothered me while I was in school was the fact my school was segregated from the white schools. I couldn't have gotten a better education in another school in Mississippi, black or white. We were able to belong to or participate in whatever organization, club, or sport we chose. I would hear mother and her friends talk about how hard it would be on black kids if the schools were integrated. They said the black parents would have to be on their toes to make sure their kids got the classes they needed to be able to get into college. The guidance counselors would steer the black girls toward home economics and the black boys toward the cotton fields, or toward becoming greasy auto mechanics. The clubs, organizations, plays, etc. would be strictly for the white kids. Sports would be a different story, simply because black kids are better in sports, which would make the school look good.

One of my favorite things to do in school was to act in school plays. I was good at memorizing lines, like Gretel in the fairy tale Hansel & Gretel, or Snow White, etc. One play I was in during my senior year, I had to say a line that was both funny and embarrassing. Here I was a 16 year-old virgin on stage holding my two dolls I got for Christmas saying, "Oh happy day I'm the mother of twins." I said it so awkwardly that everyone cracked up because they knew I was uncomfortable saying it. Still, I enjoyed acting!! Other than being in plays, I was a member of the 4-H club, worked on the school newspaper and was the historian for our senior class.

One thing I was not good at was sewing. In home economic once, we had to make a dress and model it in a fashion show at school. After I finished with the dress, it was the worst looking thing I had ever seen in my life. The hem was crooked and uneven, making one side of the dress shorter than the other side. The zipper was off center and didn't work very well. I was so embarrassed having to wear that screwed up dress, but I didn't let anyone on the stage, or in the audience know it. As far as they could tell, I modeled the dress with great pride. If it had been cooking, I would have rocked the stage because cooking was my thing.

One teacher I will never forget was named Mrs. Emma Lathon. She taught the 5th grade. She was a stickler when it came to us speaking English correctly. She would have none of that ignorant, slave way of talking in her classroom. If you came into her classroom saying things like, "I's po, nome, nuthin, y'all, yo'n, ougther, 'fore, heah, hebben, prob'ly, or leven," to list a few words, she would go completely bonkers. She would make the kids write and practice these words the correct way until she was satisfied the kids could say the words properly. Although she would let the word "mama" slip occasionally, she preferred we use the term "mother." I really appreciated her teaching me to speak English correctly because I knew when I became an adult it would come in handy.

When I was young, I wanted to be a teacher or a nurse. I wanted to be a teacher because I was influenced by my teachers. I thought they were some of the greatest people in the world. They knew everything. What our bodies were made of, how the earth was formed, knew about all the countries in the world, how to speak correct English, how to write about anything they wanted to, and they even knew how to solve those dreaded math problems. I wanted to be a nurse because I was told how important nurses were to doctors and hospitals, and how they helped sick people to get well. I wanted to be in the helping business.

*   *   *   *

Holidays were wonderful, especially July 4th. The whole neighborhood would bring a dish to the community picnic bash. The tables would be spread out with anything you wanted to eat and you just helped yourself. There would be fried chicken, country ham, fish, greens, cornbread, biscuits, cakes, and pies. Of course, there would be big bowls of kool-aid. The platters, plates, glasses, and bowls were real glass from someone's house. The silverware also was from someone's house. With all that food outside waiting for us, it would seem like the preacher's sermon was going to last forever. We kids may have been the first ones to reach the picnic area, but we didn't dare touch anything until after the grown-ups had fixed their plates. The men's plates were fixed first, then the children, and lastly the women. After the formality of serving dinner was over, it was a free for all. We would stuff ourselves until we could hardly move. Celebrating holidays like that doesn't happen today.

*   *   *   *

There was one very frightening experience that I went through. We were living on Scale Street in Corinth, Mississippi when a white man came and took my mother's cousin out of the house. My mother's cousin lived on a plantation in some other part of Mississippi. She and her family were being held in slavery and were not allowed to leave, so my parents went down in the dead of night and snuck them off the place. My mother's cousin was staying at our house and the other members of the family were staying with other people in the community. Somehow the plantation (slave) owner found out that she was staying with us and came to get her.

I had just gotten home from school for lunch when the plantation owner showed up. I was about eight or nine at this time, so I didn't know what to do. When he knocked on the door, my mother's cousin told me to answer the door and say she wasn't there; but as soon as I opened the door, he forced his way in and found her and started beating her over the head with a stick. I ran to the Buick dealership where my mother worked and told her what had happened. The dealership owner notified the state police and they caught him before he could get too far with her.

When the state police found out that the white plantation owner was holding my mother's cousin and her family in slavery, the FBI were called in. They charged him with whatever they charge those kinds of people with, and put him on trial. When the trial started, my mother and father testified against the white plantation owner for barging into our home and kidnapping her cousin. The white people in the plantation owners' town got mad and threatened to kill us. The whole community got involved after we were threatened. The men in the community stood guard outside our house at night in case the Klu Klux Klan decided to try anything. Thank God they didn't.

Being I was only nine years old, no one told me what happened to the Plantation owner. I did over hear my mother and father talking about it and said the white plantation owner lost everything he owned. I didn't realize until later how much danger my folks were in going down there in klan territory to testify, or that we were in jeopardy at home. It was quite scary.

* * * *

I graduated from high school in May of 1956 and we moved to Jamestown, NY in December. I hated Jamestown initially, especially the weather. It took a couple of years to adjust, but I finally accepted my faith and joined my fellow New York State neighbors in making our city the best it could be. I graduated from the business college in Jamestown, only to be informed that no black secretaries were hired in Jamestown (New York State)? It took four years after I graduated from college to get a job as a secretary at the Boys Club. A very nice man took a chance on me and I did not disappoint him.

When people talk about racism back in the 50s, it is always about the police dogs and Billy club welding police officers in the south. They don't associate racism with New York State, but I'm here to tell you racism was alive and well. However, it was subtle. There were no colored or white only signs. Therefore, you could sit in a restaurant and be ignored, or stand in a checkout line and be looked through. Once on an outing with my white college classmates, we were at a restaurant with a swimming pool. My classmates thought it was a good idea to go swimming while we were there. After my instructor talked to the owner of the restaurant, I guess it was the owner of the restaurant, she had a strange look on her face. In an apologetic tone she informed me that I was not allowed in the pool. I may have been upset at being discriminated against if not for the fact I couldn't swim anyway.

So I had no intentions of getting in the pool. We left the restaurant immediately. At least in the south there were posted signs that let black people know where they stood. Give me straight honesty in your racism any day.

* * * *

Although Christine and I were reared by separated parents, our love for each other has never been stronger. An attempt to keep us in touch with each other, and my biological mother, was made early in our childhood, but it didn't work out. When we moved back to Corinth, Mississippi in 1943, my daddy looked up my biological mother and sister because he felt it was important that I stay connected with them. In the end, our different economic situations and my family's move to New York killed that well-intentioned idea. I talked with my mother a couple of times, and Christine came and stayed with us once for a few days and that was it. Because we lived on the affluent side of town and them on the other side of the railroad tracks, the relationship with my biological mother and sister didn't continue the remainder of the time I stayed in Corinth. After moving to Jamestown, I lost all contact with them because they never stayed in one place for very long. We may have been separated, but I never lost the love I felt for my biological mother and sister. As far as the mother who helped my daddy raise me, I loved her dearly because she was the mother who wiped away my tears when I fell, wiped my nose when I had a cold, calmed my fears when I was going through the stresses of high school and college, and was there to nurse me back to health when I got sick.

* * * *

Summary

I didn't grow up with my brothers and sisters, but they invited me into their mist with love and open arms. I can see in their action that God played a major role in their upbringing, so

I have nothing but praise for mama and their daddy. They raised them well.

Myrtle Christine Blakeley
Born: March 28, 1941
Place of Birth: Corinth, Mississippi

CHAPTER #5
TEENIE

I was born March 28, 1941, weighing 8lbs, 7oz, in Corinth, Mississippi to the proud parents of James Davis and Zelma Holmes. I was the second, and last, child that the couple produced, my older sibling being Annie Ruth. While I was still an arm baby, my momma and daddy separated because they no longer loved each other. I don't know who decided to split my sister and me up, but I ended up staying with momma and Annie moved away with our daddy. I guess I stayed with momma because I was still being breast-fed. After the split, momma struggled to survive, being she was a single woman with a young child. God saw how hard of a time momma was having supporting herself and me, so he sent Joseph Harrison Wade into our lives to help out when I turned 8 months old.

Mister Wade was a widower who had lost his wife to TB several months before meeting my momma. She left him with three young children, Lenora, Vera Magdalene and Joe Nathan. He needed a permanent baby sitter and momma needed help supporting us. It was a perfect match. As it turned out, the match was so perfect they decided to get married and make the family complete after several months of courtship. Later there were more siblings added, which ended up being 7 sisters and 7 brothers for a total of 14 children.

* * * *

Growing up in a big family in the 1940s and 50s on a farm

was hard. The $1.50 to $2.00 a day for chopping cotton didn't go very far. It wasn't enough to keep everyone fed and in new clothes, especially during the winter months when there was not much farm work for the farmers to do. Daddy stayed busy during the winter months repairing the farm planting and harvesting equipment, mule harnesses, wagons, cow pasture fences, and anything else that needed repairing. Daddy hunted and fished to supplement the food he was able to buy. And to supplement the meager income the family brought in he sold bootleg whiskey and gambled a lot. Daddy had the reputation of being one of the luckiest men alive. The only reason I believe they called him lucky was because he managed to stay alive, because he was not the most loved individual in the community. There were quite a few men who wanted to do him harm.

    The lack of funds to buy new clothes for everyone assisted momma in becoming very proficient at clothes making. It wouldn't have traumatized us having to wear momma's hand sewn clothes if the clothes hadn't been made from flour sacks, including our underwear. You can imagine the embarrassment we felt when we would go to school and the girls whose parents had a little money wore pretty store bought underwear and we were wearing flour sack drawers. Whenever they got a glimpse of our underwear, they teased us unmercifully.

    Momma and daddy worked long hard hours, and still there were plenty of days we didn't know what we were going to have to eat from day to day, or whether we were going to eat at all. Somehow daddy and momma would always find some way to put food on the table, which more often than not was the dreaded potato or salmon paddies. I know we had more to eat than potatoes and salmon paddies, but it seemed that was all we had because we ate so much of it. We welcomed the rabbits, squirrels, fish, coons, and possums to supplement the diet, anything but potatoes and salmon paddies. Everyone in the family old enough to work did so to help momma and daddy provide for the family, it was a team effort.

*　　*　　*　　*

Not wanting to face the harsh reality of everyday life on the farm, I would sit and daydream for hours. The man I would meet and fall in love with would be light skinned with pretty straight, black hair. He would wear suits to work like the white men I saw who worked at the bank, but he wouldn't be stealing black folks money like they did. He would have a black shiny new car that would be the envy of the community. We would have a maid to cook for us, and every morning at breakfast we would have eggs, bacon, sausage, grits, oatmeal, pancakes, and toast. For lunch we would have whole hams, cornbread, collard greens, with ham hocks, green beans, and rolls. For dessert we would have different kinds of pies, cakes, and candy yams.

Momma and daddy wouldn't have to work, just sit around all day on the screened-in porch of their big white house my husband would buy for them. My brothers and sisters, well, they would still live with momma and daddy. When my husband and me, had children, they would have straight black hair just like white folks. There would be no kinky haired kids in my house, no siree. Me myself, I would go to one those fancy, white folk hair salons and get rid of my nappy hair. I would walk out of the place with long black hair flowing down my back. When the daydreams ended and I found myself still po', hungry, nappy headed, and living with broke parents; despair would return to swamp my yearning young heart. Until the next day when the dreams took a hold of my mind again and showed me what it was like on the other side of the fence. Mr. Right would give me all the luxuries life had to offer.

*   *   *   *

Being I was the oldest child after Magaline left home, and female, there was tremendous pressure put on me because I had to deal with school, help with the cooking, washing and ironing, work in the cotton fields, help take care of my brothers and sisters, and help keep the house as clean as we possibly could. More often than not, it was a losing battle with all the dirt that was tracked into the house on a daily basis. On rainy days, I wanted to scream because those darn boys would never wipe the mud off their shoes or feet if they were running around outside barefoot, including daddy.

When I did attend school my concentration suffered. The stress of being forced to grow up at such a young age at home, combined with the stress of everyday life at school, I was an angry, mean, anti-social young child. The slightest comment, or the wrong stare from a classmate would set me off. So I consistently got suspended for fighting. If not for fighting, it would be for being disobedient toward my teachers. I felt my teachers didn't really care if I learned or not. They wanted everyone to think they were big stuff because they had enough education to be teachers. I told them I bet most of them hadn't even been to no college. They just wanted to show everyone that they were the bosses and we had to do whatever they said. Dealing with the stress of school and the daily activities I had to perform at home, also made me a troubled child. Unfortunately, there was another stressor that helped shape my destructive behavior.

I never felt that my step-daddy really accepted me as one of his own because every time Sue and I would argue, or fight about something, he always said it was my fault. We would bring water in for the night to drink, and for momma to use for cooking the following morning. The other children would go in the kitchen and either drink it all or waste it playing. When daddy got up the following morning he would blame me for there not being water in the house. When I tried to tell him why there was no water in the house, he never wanted to hear it. This struggle I waged to be accepted on an equal basis with my brothers and sisters caused a lot of irritation and frustration between us, which made him say rude and brutal things to me. And because my momma never defended me against those brutal, degrading comments daddy made, it caused me to wonder if she loved me as much as she should have.

As I got older and more independent, and more knowledgeable about what went on in the world, I started looking at things in a different light. Friends, the same age as I was, were experiencing some of the same frustrations in their homes with their biological fathers, so I felt a little better knowing it was the weak mind of a man taking his frustrations out on a child because of his own oppression by white men. I still rebelled against rude behavior and comments, but I understood why he was the way he was. I also came to realize that the lack of money and the constant struggle to put food on the table for such a fast growing family was a big contributor to the tension that was almost always present in our house. Momma wasn't a loud woman, and very seldom did she argue, but she had a way of getting her point across.

In the light of this realization, I didn't want to put any more burdens on my parents than I had to, so I made a promise to myself that I would never have any children in their house. I never got over the feeling that I was on the outside looking in as far as my daddy was concerned, so the psychological warfare between us continued unabated. I kept my head up and my pride intact.

When I reached the age of fifteen, daddy decided that he had had enough of my disrespect and insolence, so he made me leave. It didn't bother me to be from under daddy's rule, but it really broke my heart that my momma didn't say anything in my defense. She didn't say a word while I packed my things, or when I left. Deep down in my heart, I knew she really didn't want to see her child thrown out of the house, but there was nothing she could do. In those days, whatever decision the man of the house made that was the end of it. My having been ask to leave from under daddy's roof may have been traumatizing if not for my friend Tommy T. who had made arrangements with an older couple he knew for me to live with them until he returned home from working on a Mississippi river boat. They welcomed me into their home, and was very nice to me. I think that was sometime in August. I stayed with them until Tommy T. returned home in December and I moved in with him and started a new phase in my life.

* * * *

While my brothers and sisters have fond memories of living on Cow Bayou, for me it was the turning point in my life.

Another reason I was happy about leaving Cow Bayou was the house we were living in was haunted. As for my siblings who were old enough to remember that house will tell you about the footsteps we heard every night; but for me the bump, bump, bump, in the night materialized in the form of a woman. One night, once again ignoring the footsteps and things that went bump in the night, I went to sleep.

Later that night I awoke in a deep state of fear. I had a feeling that someone was standing over me. My hair was standing on end and my nerves felt raw. Trembling in fear of the unknown, I opened my eyes to face whatever the night had to offer, and sure enough there was a very tall woman leaning over me with a flour sack. She was dressed in white, and said nothing to me. Although I could see her face clearly, I don't have the faintest idea of what she looked like. For several seconds I stared at her to see if she was going to do anything to me, she didn't. She continued to hold the flour sack open for me to look into for some reason or other, but I didn't bother looking to see what was in the sack, or why the woman was holding it out to me. I closed my eyes for a few seconds and still trembling, opened them again. To my surprise and relief, she was gone. For the next few nights I slept with my pillows over my head. The woman never materialized again. Later in life, I wondered what it was the woman was trying to show me. Momma always says it was probably my guardian angel that was trying to give me something special. Oh well, I'll never know.

*   *   *   *

I'll never forget how hard it was for our family to survive on those cotton plantations in Mississippi and Arkansas. It was hard for me to understand how we could work so hard year round and still have nothing to show for it. All we could do was put our hopes and dreams in the hands of God and hope for the best. The only thing that kept me going during the cotton chopping and cotton-picking seasons was the quarter daddy gave me every weekend to spend as I pleased. A quarter in the 40s and 50s went a long ways. It would buy enough candy to last the whole week if I budget it right.

* * * *

Summary

Growing up on the farm chopping and picking cotton was hard work, but it was the emotional stress of having to take on more responsibilities around the house than a child should have to bear at such an young age that affected me the most. Adding to that stressful time, in my life, was dealing with an authoritarian daddy who I questioned whether he loved me. The bond between my momma and my siblings were always strong, and remain so today. Thank God. I also thank God for His guidance and love during the trials and tribulations I experienced during my childhood.

Charles T. Wade
Born: November 30, 1942
Place of Birth: Corinth, Mississippi

CHAPTER #6
BUBBA

I was born November 30, 1942, in Corinth, Mississippi. Being I was the oldest boy of the clan, I had to set the example daddy wanted my younger brothers to follow. So I had to take on a lot of responsibilities around the farm and the house at an early age. I also had to start work early because I had to help keep the family fed, which meant not only was an education not a priority, it was discouraged because eating was more important than going to school. We didn't know at the time it was a lack of an education that kept us in our state of poverty. The understanding on the farms throughout the south in the 1930s, 1940s and 1950s was when black children reached field hand age, around 6 years old, half a day of school during cotton picking season September – November was enough for us during those months. It was more important to get the cotton crops in. If we were lucky enough to reach the eighth grade, it was determined by the white farmers that black children had enough education for what we were going to do for the rest of our lives; which was work their cotton fields to make them rich while we remained in poverty and suffered the racist indignities of the white populace.

Of course some parents who could afford it made sure their children graduated high school and then sent them up North to attend college. Most of them chose to stay up north to work after graduating. They came home to visit occasionally, but the south for them was soon a distant memory. Unfortunately, those parents could not make their children un-black, although they tried. As a result of this self-hatred thinking, some black families ended up with two different mindsets. The black family members who stayed in the south knew they were black, poor and despised by most white people in the world; whereas the northern educated blacks who fled the south deluded themselves into thinking they were no longer as black as their fellow southerners, and that white people liked them.

Anyway, us black children and our parents were made to believe there was nothing in those schoolbooks that would help us be anything other than farmers; therefore it was a waste of time to send black children to school to get an education they were never going to use. Many times I heard daddy's white foreman say black kids didn't need an education beyond knowing how to farm; which meant chopping and picking cotton, plowing with mules, and working at the cotton gin. True to the tradition in most black families on the farm back then, I dropped out of school after the third grade to work full time in the fields. I didn't give it a second thought because most of my male classmates was working right alone beside me. That was the way it was on the farms in the south. So like a good farm hand, I did what was expected of me without questions. I don't even remember ever having a problem with white people because all I did was work, work, and work some more.

* * * *

We were living on Cow Bayou when I started working. The wages were $2.50 a day for chopping cotton, and two cents a pound when we were picking cotton. Both jobs required us to be in the field from sun-up to sundown. When I got home from the fields, the day did not end there. I would have to chop wood for the stoves and pump water for the mules daddy used to plow the fields. We didn't own the mules. The white farm/plantation owner rented them out to daddy to use to plow the fields for planting cotton crops during the spring, and other chores during the summer and winter. Therefore, he was obligated to take care of them. I don't remember how many mules daddy had to take care of, but it was quite a few. Although I had the most responsibilities of all the children in my family, we all worked really hard while growing up.

I remember thinking we kids were going to have a lot of fun when we moved to Cow Bayou, in Arkansas, from Mobile, Alabama, because there was a lake close by the house where we could go fishing and swimming whenever we wanted to. It probably would have been fun if I weren't scared half to death every morning when I got up to make fires in the stoves, or my friends didn't live on the other side of an old rundown haunted gambling house.

We hadn't been in the house long before we started hearing noises in the attic. A short time later the noises moved back and forth from the attic to the kitchen. Being I was the oldest boy, one of my morning chores were getting up in the morning to make fires in the kitchen stove and in the living room stove during the winter months.

I would lie awake most every night in that house listening to the sound of someone, or something, in what sounded like brogan shoes going up and down the stairs or walking around in the attic before dozing off to sleep. When daddy would wake me up in the morning to make the morning fires, whatever was walking around in the attic would now be walking around in the kitchen, rattling the pots and pans. The rattling wasn't loud enough to wake anyone in the house up, but plenty loud enough for me to plainly hear. I was terrified each and every morning I got up to make those fires. The thump, thump, thump, rattle, rattle, rattle would cease when I stepped through the doorway into the kitchen, but I could feel the icy stare of the haint (ghost) that inhabited the house. The fear would start at the base of my spine and make its way upward until my hair would stand on end. Sometimes I would catch myself tiptoeing into the kitchen in hope that whoever, or whatever was in there, wouldn't hear me coming into the kitchen because I didn't want to make it mad. I don't know what I would've done if I had actually snuck up on the haint, but I never thought about that. The amazing thing about the whole ordeal was I never saw what or who it was that made the noise. I would have thought I was nuts if I was the only one who heard the footsteps and other noises. My sanity was saved because my brothers and sisters heard our unwanted guest also. I could have written the ghostly incident I experienced in the house off as an isolated incident and convinced myself that there were no such thing as haints, but my ghostly encounters did not end there in the house. The old juke jaint [gambling house] just down the road from where we lived had a history of its own.

*   *   *   *

At age 8, I was never afraid to walk alone at night, so every weekend I would go to visit different friends whose families had a television. Regardless of what family it was, they usually lived at least a mile away from our house. Some nights it would be so dark you could hold your hand in front of your face and couldn't see it. Anyway, as I said, there was this old juke jaint [gambling house] that was between where we lived and the people's houses I used to visit. Rumor had it that some really mean dudes had been hung in the trees in front of the building for committing awful crimes, such as murder, rape, and bank robbery. And other men had been killed in fights inside the building over gambling bets, debts, and women. The place was so run down it was obvious that the place hadn't been used in a long time. The grass had grown up level to the windows, and the honeysuckle vines almost covered the whole building. However, for some reason nothing covered the windows; as if someone made sure they would always be able to see what was going on in the world around them.

I believed the stories that were told about that old juke jaint being haunted were true. On several occasions at night when I approached it on my way home from visiting friends, it look like someone had lit a candle in the building and I could hear music playing. It would be the type of music that momma called the "devil music." I could see the shadows of the men and women dancing and having a good time, but they had no recognizable features. One of the stories told often by our parents, to keep us in the house, was that one night one of the shadows had actually came out of the house and carried a seven year old boy into the house, and he was never seen again. So on these occasions when the house was lit up and the people were dancing, I always stopped short of the house to calculate my chances of being grabbed by one of the haints from the house as I ran by it. I would be so scared, but going by the house was my only way home. I would fill my lungs with air, say a quick prayer for God's protection, and run by the building as fast as my legs could take me. Once I got past the house and insured no one was following me, I was okay.

When I told daddy about the candlelight coming on and the music coming from the juke jaint after the first incident, he said he already knew about the place and assured me that it had to be candlelight because electricity hadn't been available in that building for years. He finished by saying, as he always did when talking about the dead, "Son the dead can't hurt you, it's those lying dirty bastards who are still living that you have to be concerned about." As crazy as it may sound, although I was scared to death every night I had to pass that building, whether it was lit up or not, it didn't keep me at home, because once I got past the house, the fear would leave me. The same thing applied to getting up in the morning to make the fires. Once the lights were on and everyone was up and milling around, I forgot about the rattling pots and pans until the following morning when it was time to get up and go through it again. I guess I was afraid to face the haints alone. I enjoyed living on Cow Bayou and had a lot of fun playing, fishing, and hunting while we lived there; but I was one happy camper when daddy decided to move. I never had to deal with haints in our house again.

* * * *

Prior to us moving to Cow Bayou, we lived in Mobile, Alabama. It wasn't a proud time in my life because we didn't have a lot of anything, and on occasions we went hungry. During those lean times it seemed all we had to eat day in and day out was Irish potatoes and salmon paddies. I was envious of the white kids because they had candy and good food to eat, good clothes to wear, and Santa Claus brought them all the good toys to play with. I knew there was no way I could get new clothes and toys like the white kids, but I figured I could get my hands on some of the candy to curb my hunger and satisfy my sweet tooth. How? I started stealing candy from the local grocery stores. It wasn't always because I wanted to eat as the white kids did. Sometimes it was because I was hungry, or tired of the pitiful food momma was putting on the table. Later my philosophy about why I was stealing from white people changed.

When me, Sue and Christine would go to one of the local grocery stores for momma or daddy, we would be given the exact amount of money for what momma or daddy wanted. We never had enough money left over for a penny piece of candy. I knew stealing was wrong because daddy and momma told me it was, but I listened to my daddy and momma complain every day about how the white people were stealing from them every day of their lives. So, I figured if it was okay for white people to steal from my momma and daddy, it was okay for me to steal from them. Usually Sue or Christine would get me to distract the store owner while they filled their pockets with whatever they thought they could get away with. And while they were paying the storeowner for the items momma or daddy sent us to get I would lift whatever I could and make my get away before the storeowner knew what happened. On several occasions I got caught stealing, but it never deterred me because the next time I went to the store, I would take up where I left off from the previous errand.

I remember at one particular store I didn't really have to steal anything, because the white lady who worked there thought I was real cute and would give me candy anytime I asked for it. But she didn't extend that courtesy to my sisters. So in my mind, she had to be punished for not being as generous to my sisters as she was to me. One day while my older sister, Christine, was paying for the items momma had sent us to get, I had taken something. I don't remember what it was, but it was quite large for a kid my size and I was headed for the door. Seeing I had something in my hand that I hadn't paid for, the lady asked me if I was going pay for the item. I put on the most innocent face I could muster, and I asked her what she was talking about. She pointed to the item in my hand and said, "That item you have in your hand." I looked down as if totally surprised to see that I actually had something in my hand and said, "I didn't even know I had that." The lady laughed and told me I had better put that stuff back before she had to spank my butt. I said, "Yes ma'am," and put it back. Unfazed about being caught stealing that day, I continued to appropriate things from the store without paying for them. I vowed I would continue stealing from them as long as they were stealing from my momma and daddy.

When I reached approximately 12 years of age, my sister Christine was 14, we had to get up at 4:00 a.m. in the morning to cook breakfast for the family before going to work in the cotton fields when momma was sick. That meant getting up before the rooster crowed at the dawning of a new day. Think about that; we got up too early even for the roosters. They were supposed to be the first things up in the morning, if you believe in that folklore crap, and we would beat them up. I learned to cook oatmeal, grits, bacon, sausage, salmon paddies, to cut up Irish potatoes [hash browns today], and to cook biscuits from scratch. Daddy and momma bragged to the neighbors about how well I could cook. I didn't realize it was considered a sign of being feminine, if you know what I mean. The word "cooking" and "man" was very seldom used in the same sentence on the farm if there were women and/or girls in the house. Daddy said he wanted all of his boys to learn to cook, wash clothes, and sew the holes in their clothes in case they had to live on their own without a woman, or if their wives up and left them. However, any feminine thoughts in anyone's mind about me went out the window when it came time for work, because I could hold my own with the best workers in the fields. Everyone said a funny boy wouldn't work as hard as I did.

*   *   *   *

It got cold as a witch's tit or a well digger's ass during the winter months in Arkansas. I never knew what those phrases meant. Because I never felt a witch's tit, and there was no way I was going to feel a well digger's ass. It was phrases the men used, so I figured there had to be something to it. If I used those colorful phases in front of momma she would ask me, what I know about titties and people's asses. Black kids did not look an adult in the face when being questioned. I would lower my eyes, say "nuthin", and get the hell out of her presence as quickly as possible.

A standard piece of clothing that was mandatory for every boy in the family in every household in Arkansas was long johns. Long johns were a body suit with a buttoned down fly in front to allow us to take a whiz, and buttoned down flaps in the caboose so we didn't have to take them off when we had to take a dump. The long johns came in handy on those cold winter mornings when I had to crawl out of bed, and when worn as an undergarment. They added protection against the outside elements. Unfortunately the long johns didn't provide too much protection when we had to visit the outhouse on those cold windy nights. It was one of the coldest trips in my life when I had to get up and go to the outhouse in the dead of winter. The wind would whip through the cracks in the outhouse right up the open flap of the long johns. We prayed to God at night during the winter to give us the strength to control our bowels until morning.

Sometimes the weather would get so cold at night, the pump would freeze. On those cold mornings when the pump froze, my brothers and I would build a fire around the pump to un-thaw it so we could pump water for momma to use to cook breakfast with, because normally we drank all the water we brought in the house for the night. The long drawers were a blessing on cold mornings like these.

*   *   *   *

Graduating from the hoe chopping cotton, I started plowing in the fields with mules at the age of 13. Plowing cotton with mules was referred to as one row cultivating. I referred to it as hard work. The leather strap would cut into my shoulders sometimes and they would be sore for a long time. Daddy had momma sew some cotton padding on to the straps, but my shoulders still got sore. Sometime those old mules would get so hardheaded and ornery. I wouldn't be able to do anything with them. Knowing that I wasn't as strong and mean as my daddy, they would jerk me all over the field. But when daddy took a hold of the reins, they would straighten up because they knew daddy had a habit of hitting them right between the eyes with whatever he got his hands on whenever they acted that way. It was amazing how well those old mules would follow instructions after being hit between the eyes. I felt their pain because daddy would whip my butt with whatever he got his hands on that he figured wouldn't kill me. On days off from plowing in the fields, I would take those same mules and go to the woods, cut down trees, attach them with chains, and drag the logs to the house by myself. Once I got the trees to the house, my younger brothers would help me saw or chop the trees up for the cook-stove and the stove used for heating the house. My hands would get so cold while cutting down and hauling those big trees, I would lose all feeling in them. But I couldn't stop cutting wood until daddy said we had enough to last for a while.

* * * *

As I said earlier, an education was not stressed as a way to get ahead for black kids in Arkansas, so I only went to school for a few years. I had to quit school to go to work in the fields to help support the family. I had plenty of company because my friends Sam, Jimmy, and Herschel Lee all dropped out of school to help their daddies support their families. Being the majority of the families were sharecroppers, each family was responsible for getting their crops in on time. Because of the size of our family, we didn't have any problems in reaching that goal. Therefore, we never needed help from our neighbors to bring in our crops. Unfortunately, there was one neighbor who never got their crop in on time. So after we finished getting our crops in, daddy would make us, along with him, help Ms. Bean them with their crops. Us kids would be so mad because while we were in the field working our behinds off, Ms. Bean's boys would be hunting, fishing, playing, or plain goofing off. If they would have been working instead of doing other things, they could have gotten their crops in on time like everyone else. Instead, Ms. Bean would wait for us to finish our crops because she knew daddy was going to make us help them. Teenie did some really low down cussing because we had to help Ms. Bean and her boys bring in the crop, but she didn't let daddy hear her because he would have whupped her butt. Even the adult neighbors would beat the living daylights out of us kids if we cussed in their presence.

* * * *

During the fall and winter months, we boys would hunt rabbits and squirrels a lot. Sometimes we killed some and at other times we didn't. Daddy was the true hunter in the family, because along with hunting rabbits and squirrels, he used to go coon and possum hunting alone at night. We would sit around watching him prepare his carbide headlight so he would be able to see the coons when the dog treed them. The carbide stunk to high heaven. He would make us go to bed at 8 o'clock, and he would leave the house around ten o'clock at night and wouldn't return until daylight sometimes. Usually he would return with a couple of big fat coons or possums that were good for a couple meals. We would watch as he dipped the possums in scalding hot water and pulled the majority of the hair from the possum's body. The hair he couldn't remove by hand, he burnt off. He would throw it into the hot coals in the stove, or into the ash of a fire he made outside, to remove any hair that may have been missed. When the possum was pulled from the ash, it would be an ashy gray. The whole time the possum's hair was being removed, by burning it off in the ash, and daddy gutting and cleaning it, we would be joking about how the possum never stopped grinning. The coons he skinned. To skin the coon, he would cut the skin around the feet and then cut slits down the sides and the center of its back, and we would help skin it.

In the spring and summer when daddy wasn't hunting, he was sink net fishing with neighbors. He would bring #3 tubs full of fish home all the time and we would have to clean them. Christine and Sue would cuss and fuss the whole time we were cleaning the fish, but no one complained when momma fried up a bunch of them and put them on the table. The coons, possums, and fish were the filler when we didn't have hogs or money to buy meat.

*   *   *   *

I remember one time daddy's pant leg caught on fire while he was fixing a flat tire. He ran and jumped into a ditch that had water in it to put his pant leg out. Back then when daddy fixed a flat, he would take the inner tube out of the tire, blow it up to find the hole, stick a piece of stick in it so he wouldn't lose the hole, let the air out of the tube and prepare it for repair. The flat tire repair kits contained a can of glue with a brush in it. The top of the can was coarse and used for scraping away dirt and grime off the inner tube, and patches of different sizes to seal the hole. You would clean the area around the hole by using the scraper, then you would brush on some glue and set it on fire, let it burn for a short period of time and then blow it out. The heat helped seal the patch. Then the patch was placed over the hole in the inner tube; let it cool and the tube would be fixed. On this particular day we watched as daddy brushed too much glue on the inner tube and some ran onto his pants leg. When he lit the glue, it went up in flames, including the glue on his pants leg. We risked getting whipped because we laughed our heads off. Daddy pretended to be mad at us for laughing at him, but he laughed also because it was really funny, watching him jumping around trying to beat the flames out before jumping in the water.

Another incident that happened when we were living in Mobile, Alabama involved daddy making and selling bootleg whiskey. Someone in the community, who was mad at daddy, told the police about his bootlegging operation. Late one night around midnight, the police conducted a raid at our house trying to catch daddy with the booze. They searched the house from top to bottom, but couldn't find where daddy had hidden the whiskey.

When they shined their flashlights on the bed where we were sleeping, they couldn't believe the number of children sleeping in the same bed. One policeman called the others over to see the bed full of children. They just shook their heads, finished their search and left. What they didn't know was the whiskey they were looking for was underneath the mattress we were lying on. There were about 10 of us in the bed. Daddy loved to tell that tale to anyone who would listen.

* * * *

Momma never worked in the cotton fields because her health was too fragile to allow her to be exposed to the unbearable heat and cold that was life in the cotton fields. So she ended up working as a maid for white families. The white families she worked for lived in town. She had no transportation to get to and from work so she had to catch the bus, which were 3 or 4 miles from where we lived. The bus couldn't run on the dirt road because of its condition, and it would get stuck when it rained, so I would walk her to the bus stop about 5:00 a.m. every morning and meet her in the evening about 6:00 p.m. and walk home with her. It never got too hot or too cold, and I never got too busy, to walk momma to and from that bus stop every day. Momma was never late getting to work and I was never late insuring she got home when she got off. My older sister, Teenie, called me a momma's boy. That was fine with me because I made it a point to always be there for my momma. I even hung around the kitchen and helped Momma cook on numerous occasions, and I helped wash the dishes. I even helped her wash our dirty clothes on the weekends, and God knows there were a lot of dirty clothes to be washed.

* * * *

I remember when daddy and a bunch of men used to shoot dice out in a clearance they had cleared in the cotton field across from our house. When the policemen would try to catch them, we would see them running and jumping over fences to get away. It was amazing that he always got away, because Daddy would already be drunk before he left the house. He didn't drink during the workweek, but come Friday, Saturday, and Sunday, he would make up for lost time. But he was always sober enough to go to work come Monday morning.

* * * *

I've already mentioned when I used to cut and haul wood with the mules by myself when the woodpile was depleted. Usually that was during the fall when the most important priority was to get the cotton crops in. But after the crops were in, daddy, me, and my brothers would go and cut wood weeks at a time so we wouldn't have to go back during the colder months of the year; but sometimes we had no choice. Although cutting wood was not our favorite chore we didn't really mind it that much. We just didn't like the cold. During long cold spells it was depressing to watch how fast the woodpile would shrink right before our eyes, because it meant we would have to go cut more wood.

* * * *

When we moved from Alabama to Arkansas, nothing changed. We still worked hard chopping and picking cotton and I continued doing a lot of cooking. My sisters say I had lots of girlfriends while we were living there, but I don't remember any girlfriends. I remember playing baseball with my brothers and sisters. I remember picking cotton by the moonlight, but only one sack containing 50 to 70 pounds of cotton. I did this every night except on Saturday and Sunday, to get a head start on everyone else the following day.

* * * *

As I said earlier, we never lived in another haunted house. However, I did have a ghostly experience while living in Wabash,

Arkansas. One night me, and a couple of friends, Sam and Herschel Lee, were on our way home after attending a party at one of our friend's house. We were laughing, joking, and horse playing when we saw three men in glowing white shirts and dark pants approaching us. The closer they got, we could see there was something strange about them that didn't look right. We knew all the guys our age, and the older men in the community, but not these guys. We thought maybe they were from out of town visiting someone out in the country. Sam, being the most aggressive of us three said we should jump them when they got even with us. Herschel Lee told Sam he was crazy, that those guys might be escaped lunatics, or murderers that escaped from a chain gang or something. I wasn't about to fight nobody. When the guys got even with us, we spoke to them, but they didn't respond to our greetings. They didn't even look in our direction, nor did the expressions on their faces change. Where ever it was they were going, they were transfixed on getting there as quickly as possible. They were walking so smoothly, it looked like they were gliding and their feet weren't even touching the ground. Those guys must have been wearing black shoes because we couldn't tell if they even had feet. Their faces were indistinguishable, although it wasn't that dark. They had no distinguishable features at all. After gliding by us, we felt a cold chill run up and down our spines, and it wasn't because of the weather because it was summer. We turned and watched them disappear into the darkness. Not one of us admitted that those guys had scared us. We were trying to figure out what it was about those guys that scared us, when they didn't even acknowledge our presence.

  We were still standing around talking about them when a girl named Becky, who walked the dirt roads at night as much as the boys in the community did, appeared from the direction the guys was going. When we asked her what she thought of the three weirdoes she just passed, she said she hadn't met anyone. She said we were the only guys she had seen on the road. We told her that was not possible because the guys had just passed us a few moments ago and there was no way she would have missed seeing them. She laughed and told us we had best lay off the moonshine whiskey because we had started seeing things. We put on brave faces while we walked home, but we kept looking back over our shoulders just in case the faceless guys decided to come back our way. Although those guys scared us that night, it didn't stop us from going to visiting each other at night or going to parties. Beside, we never saw them again.

*   *   *   *

Summary

Looking back at my childhood there is only one thing I would change if I could, and that would be daddy drinking and gambling habits. Other than that, I would leave everything else as it was. The child hood fear of ghosts and goblins was a part of growing up. We had such strong family ties, and love for each other, that we overcame all situations we faced as a family. I thank the almighty for us having such a strong family bond, which is alive and well even today.

Glenda Sue Wade
Born: January 31, 1945
Place of Birth: Corinth, Mississippi

CHAPTER #7
SUE

I was born January 31, 1945 in Corinth, Mississippi. Every family has a black sheep of the family. I guess in our family, that black sheep was me. I was a real rebel without a cause. I felt life owed me something and I was going to get it by hook or by crook. So I found myself doing things that I knew wasn't right, but I did them anyway.

* * * *

It's been such a long time since I was a child. My memories of those days are blurry. However, I do remember living in a lot of different places while growing up because we moved all the time. We were living in Hughes, Arkansas when I started working at an early age. I would say when I was around six years old. It was back breaking work because daddy was sharecropping, and we had to ensure we made a profit at the end of the year. Unfortunately, we made very little money after everything was settled at the end of each year. I do remember one year we were picking our cotton crop daddy said the crop was good and we should make a nice little profit. He said if it was as good as he thought it was going to be, he would buy us whatever we wanted once the dues were settled.

Well, what we wanted more than anything in the world was a television. We had to go to a neighbor's house to watch TV. It wasn't really all that bad listening to the shows and soap operas on the radio, but we wanted to keep up with the Joneses. So you can imagine the excitement we felt when we told daddy what we wanted, and he said he would get it for us. Knowing we would be getting a television after all the cotton was in, we worked double hard with very little complaining. As the cotton bolls disappeared from the field into our sacks, the more excited we became. When that last boll of cotton was picked and sold, we kids celebrated because it was only a matter of time before we would be able to sit in our own living room and watch our own brand new television. But it wasn't meant to be. As always, when daddy started drinking and gambling, he was subject to doing foolish things with our money. I say our money, but he always reminded us it was his money since he was the head of the household.

    We waited several days after daddy had settled the account with the white farm/plantation owner before asking him why he hadn't brought the TV home yet. He told us not to worry he was going to get it. A couple of weeks passed and still there was no television. Momma told us we could forget the television because daddy had blown all the money drinking and gambling. Needless to say, we were as mad as children could get at that time, which meant we pouted whenever he was around. We didn't dare say anything out of line to him because the results would have been a good beating. I knew it wouldn't do any good, but I wanted to know where the money had gone. As it turned out, I didn't really want to know.

    One weekend several weeks later, daddy took Teenie and me to town with him. We were walking down the street headed for the only department store in the town when a woman we knew daddy was messing with came out of one of the bars wearing a pretty, shiny black mink coat. We thought it was mink; it could have been rabbit hair dyed black, but it was still pretty. What we overheard her say made the coat look ugly and expensive. She told the lady she was walking with to take a look at the new mink coat Joe Wade had bought her after settling his cotton crop. I was fit to be tied. After hearing her say daddy bought the coat, I knew why we didn't get a television. I got as mad as a child could get in those days. I gave that wench the dirtiest look I could muster. I thought I was as mad as I could be until the conversation continued between the two women.

The other woman who was walking with that jezebel looked over her shoulder and told her to keep her voice down, because Joe Wades' daughters were walking right behind them. That old wench gave us a sarcastic look over her shoulder and said she didn't give a damn about us knowing about her coat, and walked on down the street admiring her-self in the new coat. If I had been grown, I would've scratched her eyes out, even though I knew it was not her fault we didn't get the television. I hated daddy for a long time for putting that woman before his own children. But all was forgiven later when he finally did bring a TV home several weeks after we overheard that old wench talking about the coat daddy bought her. Where he got the money for the television, I didn't care.

Momma never said anything to daddy about his women chasing, but us kids knew what he was doing. That hussy daddy bought the coat for wasn't the only girlfriend daddy had. When I was about seven, he had a girlfriend and we would stop by her house almost every day on our way home from school. She would feed us and then tell us to go home and see if our momma needed us to do anything for her at the house. We wanted to ask her why she always said that, knowing momma didn't get off work until 6 pm. That same woman even had the gall to come to our house while momma was home and eat with us. On more than one occasion, she sat on daddy's lap and fed him, all the time joking that she was just messing around with him. To our amazement momma never said a word to either one of them. She told us there was nothing going on between daddy and the woman because the woman was one of her best friends in the neighborhood. I thought with a friend like that, you didn't have to look far if you needed someone to kill and not feel badly about it.

*   *   *   *

When we lived in Mobile, Alabama the house we lived in was unbelievably small. It had only two bedrooms in which twelve people had to live, so it took some creative ideas on the part of momma to make sleeping arrangement for us kids. Daddy and momma occupied one bedroom, of course. To make enough sleeping space for the kids, she put two beds in the other bedroom and one bed in the kitchen, which daddy had to drag in at night and back out in the morning before she started cooking breakfast. The good thing about sleeping in the same bed with so many kids was in the winter, our body heat kept each other warm. The down side was there was a lot of kicking because we were practically stacked on top of each other, and in summer there was the opposite effect. It would be so hot it was almost unbearable. Since our situation was not unique, we kids took everything we encountered with a grain of salt.

* * * *

    To offset the lack of money he was able to earn chopping and picking cotton daddy ventured into the art of making bootleg whiskey. He had a long list of satisfied customers who came to him every weekend, and on days when rain forced them from the fields during the week. He got such a good reputation for having the best moonshine in the county the white moon shiners became jealous. That jealousy turned to treachery when the white moon shiners went to the local police station and paid the sheriff to put him out of business. On a tip from a black informant one weekend that daddy had a fresh batch of moonshine at his house, the police made their move around 10pm or so. It didn't matter what time of the week it was we were in bed by 8 pm. That Saturday night was no different. It didn't mean we were asleep, just that we were in bed.
    We didn't know what to make of the fact daddy came home so early on a Saturday night. Normally he was out drinking, gambling, or delivering his whiskey until late at night. As it turned out, he got home in time to hide his new batch of moonshine before the arrival of the police. He had been tipped off by one of his most loyal customers that a black piece of rat filth had ratted him out and the police were on their way to his house to catch him with the goods. Daddy made us get out of one of the beds and put the

whiskey in between the two mattresses and then told all ten of us to get in bed and pretend we were asleep. He said if anyone made a sound, he would beat him or her to within an inch of his or her life after the police left.

Daddy and momma was sitting at the breakfast table pretending to be carrying on a conversation when they saw police officers going to the back door to prevent his escape in the event he decided to make a run for it. The sheriff knocked on the door and daddy let him in. He told daddy that it had been reported he was dealing in moonshine whiskey and they were there to search for it, unless he wanted to give it up. If he cooperated with them, they would go easy on him. When daddy said he had no idea what they were talking about, the search began. They turned the house upside down, but found nothing. Becoming frustrated, one officer said maybe the whiskey was in the bed with the children. They looked through the bedroom door and couldn't believe their eyes. Upon seeing all of us in the bed, one officer said there was no way in hell he was going to wake all us kids up. The officer who had suggested searching the bed where we were pretending to be asleep said he didn't give a damn how many little niggers were in the bed, he wanted to search under the mattress. The reluctant officer said there were no way he was going to dump all those damn kids out of bed to look for moonshine; beside there were too many of them in the bed for there to be anything else. We snickered under our breaths as they walked out of the room, with those whiskey bottles sticking us in the ribs and in the behind. After the raid was over and the policemen had left, daddy got his tote sack and filled it with the moonshine and made his deliveries. This incident became one of his favorite stories to tell.

* * * *

Me, Teenie, and Bubba were a posse of three. Where one went, you could find the others. Since Teenie was the oldest and I was the boldest, Bubba copied what we did, whether it was good or bad. On most occasions, it was bad. Me, and Teenie rebelled against the establishment because we didn't feel it was fair for the white kids to have everything they wanted and we had nothing. So to even things out in our minds, we started stealing whatever we got our hands on from the local grocery store. We would take turns distracting the sales clerk while the other one and Bubba would take whatever they thought they could get away with. When we got down the road, we would share the stolen loot.

When we weren't striking back at an unfair society by stealing from the local grocery store, we were taking apples or pears from people yards or some white man's apple orchard. In most cases, it wasn't even necessary because there were numerous abandoned houses with apple or pear trees in the yard which anyone could take whenever they wanted to. It was a personal thing for me. For some reason, everything tasted better when I took it without permission. We got caught occasionally, but it only made us more determined the next time we went to the store or took apples and pears. I got so good at taking stuff, I would steal stuff off the counter while the sale clerk was ringing up whatever momma or daddy had sent us to get.

Not everything we did was illegal. The cotton and soybean fields all had irrigation ditches that would leave puddles of water and mud holes everywhere. When the puddles started drying up during the summer, we would find craw daddies (Crawfish) waiting to be taken. One of our favorite past times, was going to those mud holes and puddles and catching those craw daddies for an afternoon snack. The only part of the craw daddy we would eat was the tail. Teenie was the better cook of the two of us, so we would pull off the tails and she would fry them. They really tasted good. The only problem was it took so many of them to make any kind of a meal, but we didn't complain.

*   *   *   *

I don't remember where, or what farm we were living on, but I remember getting ready to move into a new house across the street from the one we were living in. I don't know for the life of me why we were excited about the move. The only possible reason had to be because the house we were living in was more of a dump than the one we were moving in to. The excitement lasted about two days because the house was just another run down shack of many. To top it off, we were still dirt poor and worked like dogs. One thing I can say, we may have lived in run down shacks and we were dirt poor, but we never went hungry. I just got tired of eating the same thing all the time which was usually potatoes or salmon paddies. Because of this lack of a variety of food stuffs to choose from me, and Teenie turned into scavengers. We would eat grapes, bananas, and anything else edible from people's garbage cans. If momma or daddy had caught us eating from the garbage cans they would have tan our hides good. However, a whupping was the farthest thing from my mind when I found perfectly good bananas thrown away. Bananas in any condition were my favorite. I knew momma and daddy would have brought fruit for us if they could afford to, but they couldn't so we helped ourselves as best we could. I thank God we had cast iron stomachs, and never got sick from eating out of the neighborhood garbage cans.

*   *   *   *

One of the hardest times we faced as a family was when daddy left home one year and went to New York for several months to work. A city slicker daddy met at a crap game convinced him that work was plentiful in New York and he would be able to send for his family in no time. So daddy sold the idea to momma that he was going to work in New York to make a better future for her and the children. He told her he would be able to send for us in no time. Momma wasn't completely sold on the idea but figured if he could get a job in New York it would be better than scratching and clawing to make a living on the farm. However, she let daddy know she would not be holding her breath waiting for him to get that wonderful job that would solve their money woes. It was a good thing she didn't because she would have been a dead duck. Daddy borrowed enough money for a train ticket and a roadhouse room for a couple weeks when he got to New York. He was then off to seek greener pastures in the big apple. While he was gone, he sent money home to momma to take care of us; but it was not on a consistent basis, so there were times when all we had to eat was potatoes and salmon paddies. If not for a male neighbor who felt sorry for us, I don't know if we would have ever had anything to eat beside potatoes and salmon paddies. Every other week, he would bring big bags of groceries with bacon, sausage, beans, rice, salt pork, meal, and flour. I don't know if daddy ever paid the man back for helping us while he was gone, but we really appreciated the man. Momma never complained the whole time daddy was gone. And if she was ever angry because of the length of time he was gone, or the fact he never found the job he had promised her he would, she never took it out on any of us.

When daddy came home, he didn't have any money. He said he spent the last few dollars he had, to buy his ticket home. He told of what it was like walking the street day after day looking for work. The man had told him he would have no problem finding work at the docks unloading the cargo ships that arrived in port on a daily basis, but the ship captains only hired those workers they already knew, or had worked for someone they knew. A few hands got their friends hired, but not many. Daddy said he didn't have any friends on the inside, so no one would hire him. He found himself hanging out with the dregs of society in a homeless shelter because he couldn't afford a place to live. After two weeks of pounding the pavement he got a job washing dishes in a restaurant, but it didn't pay enough for him to even think about moving us there. After finding a place to stay and paying his rent on a weekly basis, he barely made enough money to send home to us. Although he looked and looked for a better job, he couldn't find one. So being fed up with his living conditions and lack of ability to get a better job, he came back home. It was back to eating Irish potatoes and salmon paddies twice a day, once in the morning and again that evening. After daddy got back home, the man never bought us food again. Daddy didn't accuse momma directly, at least not in front of us children, but we all knew he was jealous that the man had helped us while he was gone. He even hinted that momma was messing around with the man, and that was why he was helping her. All momma said to daddy when he made these subtle accusations was God was going to strike him dead for having such evil thoughts. He didn't want to, still thinking the man had messed with momma, but daddy eventually thanked him for looking out for his family while he was away.

*   *   *   *

Me, and a friend of mine were always doing crazy things. One crazy stunt me, and my girlfriend pulled had to be one of stupidest stunts we pulled the whole time we were growing up. We knew this woman who was one of the best cooks in the neighborhood, and she fed any child who asked her for a meal. Well, that was too easy for me, and my friend. How were we supposed to enjoy the food if it was given to us freely? We watched the woman cooking through her kitchen window trying to figure out how we could raid the kitchen with her still in the house without getting caught. We decided the next time she went to watch television we would make our move. As luck would have it, we watched as she grabbed her hat and left the house. I guess she needed something from the store, which was a short distance from her house. As soon as she turned the corner we went through the woman's window and stole some of the food she had simmering on the stove. To show how comfortable we were with what we had done, instead of going somewhere to eat the food where we wouldn't get caught, we sat right outside the kitchen window of the woman's house. Believe it or not, we were totally surprise when the woman came back home because she had forgotten something and caught us eating her food. We lied and said we had gotten the food from someplace else. Of course she knew we were lying, so she told daddy what we had done and he beat the crap out of me. All the time he was whupping my butt, he said all we had to do was ask the woman for the food and she would have given it to us. I wanted to say I knew that, but I didn't want any extra licks on my behind. As I said before, it sounds crazy, but stolen food tasted better, especially when you got away with it. My friend suffered the same fate as I did when she got home, but it didn't stop us from doing stupid stuff.

* * * *

Daddy and momma made us go to Sunday school and church every Sunday. Being the best the devil had to offer, I would cuss all the way to church and all the way back home. The church ladies demeanor and fancy hats provided nonstop jokes, as well as the baldheaded preachers and deacons. The kids would bust a gut laughing. The more they laughed, the more I cussed. One Sunday the preacher made an announcement that the police was looking for some kids who had broken into a neighbor's house and stolen their money. If anyone knew who those little hoodlums were they should let the police know. On our way home with me cussing up a storm as usual, we saw the local sheriff patrol car in the distant headed in our direction. Although we had done nothing wrong, we took off through the blackberry patch looking over our shoulders for the cops pursuing us. Luckily for us, there were no cops chasing us. If there had been we would have gotten caught because Deedie was so clumsy, he got hung on the blackberry vines and we had to get him untangled. I told him if the police had been after us, they sure would have caught us because of him. He pouted all the way home but I didn't care. He shouldn't have been so clumsy. He was always trouble to us, but we let him hang around us anyway.

* * * *

When we moved to Yazoo, Mississippi, we moved into a flood zone. We didn't know how bad the flood problem in the area was at the time we moved in, but after the first major rain, we found out in a hurry. We went to bed that night listening to the rain beating down on the tin roof of the house. When we awoke the following morning, the water was rising so fast we knew it was only a matter of time before it would come into the house, even though the house stood on the four-foot high stilts. The owner of the farm/plantation knew the area was pronged to flooding, so he came out to the house on a tractor, towing a trailer, too check on us. Sure enough, we had to get the hell out of there before we got washed away.

The farm/plantation owner backed his tractor and trailer up to the porch, which was even with the porch, so we could get on the trailer without getting wet. Along with us kids, daddy put seven dogs on the trailer with us. He and momma sat on the tractor with the driver. By the time we were all loaded, the water was real high, and almost came onto the trailer. It was touch and go for a while because the road was so muddy, but we made it out safely. Daddy had gotten up that morning, along with my brothers, and bagged the meager clothing we had and the bedding and placed them in the attic to keep them dry. The farm/plantation owner let us stay in his basement until it was safe to go back home, which was two or three days. A couple months later, the house flooded again, so daddy said to hell with that place it was time to move again. We had only been in the house about six months and we were flooded out twice.

While we were staying in the farm/plantation owner's basement in Mississippi during the second flooding, daddy went and offered his services to a farm/plantation owner in Arkansas. When he got back to Yazoo, Mississippi in the middle of the night, he was driving a borrowed truck from that farm/plantation owner. Daddy loaded one mattress, all of our blankets and sheets, a wood heater, the children and the dogs and we moved to Arkansas. When we got to the new house in Arkansas, momma and daddy slept on the mattress. Momma made pallets for us kids to sleep on until daddy got a loan from the boss man to get beds for us.

* * * *

We all had our own little quirks while growing up. Teenie got whuppings for standing around looking at airplanes flying overhead. Bubba was a momma's boy. He did just as much cooking, and cleaning, that we girls did. Deedie was clumsy and followed us around like a little lost puppy. Biddy was a pretty boy that all the girls liked, but he was so shy and scared of them, I thought he was retarded or was a sissy boy. Bobo was so accident prone that no newborn animal we caught to play with was safe. No matter how hard he tried to prevent it, he always ended up killing it somehow. Oyce was daddy's favorite, so she was always getting us in trouble whenever we messed with her. Even though I knew I would get in trouble, I whupped her butt every chance I got. Mag and Lenora, my older sisters, left home before I could form an opinion of them. And I had left home before forming an opinion of Pon'k, Will, Margaret, and Gene but I'm sure they had their little quirks also.

* * * *

At a very young age momma would take me with her every evening to find and milk the cows. Not only did I not know how to milk the cows, I was scared to death of them. To me, they were giant creatures just waiting to either step on me or fall over on me. Therefore, every time I sat on the stool beside momma to milk those cows, I knew it was going to be my last day on earth because one of them was going to crush my skull in somehow. The fact that momma had been milking cows since she was five and was still alive, gave me no solace. Because of the fear of the cows, I never did learn to milk them very well, but it didn't stop me from being first in line when it came time to drink the milk or eat the butter with my biscuits.

* * * *

As bad as we kids were, sometimes you would think daddy and momma would ensure they left nothing within our reach when they left the house that would cause us to hurt ourselves. Well, that didn't always happen. As was the custom with all the farm hands, food was bought on a weekly basis. So every weekend, momma and daddy would go grocery shopping. We didn't have a car, so momma and daddy would ride to town with one of the neighbors. Whomever that neighbor was, they would in turn leave their children at our house for us older kids to look after while they were gone. Well, on more than one occasion when they left for their weekend grocery shopping spree daddy would leave a bucket of bootleg whiskey sitting on the kitchen table for his customers to sample while he was gone. I thought if you gave black folks a chance to drink free, they would never leave until all the whiskey was gone. To my surprise, men and women would stop by, sample the booze, and put in their order and leave. The people momma and daddy caught a ride with this particular Saturday had one of the biggest families in our part of the world. He had to get a pick-up truck in order to haul them around. We were used to daddy leaving whiskey on the table for his customers to stop by and taste before putting in an order, but not our guests. Unfortunately for us, we were influenced by our older guests to have a grown-up party. So while momma and daddy were in town, we older kids got drunk. It only took a couple of drinks of the 100 proof of whiskey. When momma them got back from grocery shopping, we were a sight for sore eyes. Daddy and the other children's daddy thought it was the funniest thing in the world, as they watched us staggering around the house. The neighbor piled his kids into the bed of the truck, on top of each other like loaves of bread, and off they went for home. The next day, our heads felt like they had exploded. Daddy laughed and said he didn't need to whip us because the hang over was punishment enough. There were approximately thirteen drunk kids staggering around the house; what a sight. Oddly enough, daddy kept right on leaving the bucket of moonshine on the table as usual. I was about thirteen at the time. Because of that drunken weekend I didn't touch it again until I was almost grown.

*   *   *   *

When we moved to Cow Bayou, Arkansas, we were still sharecropping, and daddy added to our workload. While living there, we had what seemed like one of the biggest gardens in the nation. We would go to the cotton fields and work hard all day, and when we got home, we had to work in the garden. It wasn't too bad during the summer because all we had to do was keep the garden free of weeds and morning glory vines. However, come harvesting time, we would have to pick peas, tomatoes, butter beans, corn, squash, snap beans, and okra to be canned. Along with the main garden, we would have to work in the truck patch. That's where the watermelons, dew melons, peanuts, sweet potatoes, cantaloupes, Irish potatoes, and sweet potatoes were grown. We worked in the gardens from summer through the fall. We also picked blackberries, mulberries, and muska dimes for momma to make jellies and jams out of. We weren't happy at the time the work was being done, but on those cold winter days, that canned food tasted awfully good.

*   *   *   *

Before the younger boys got old enough to cut wood for the stoves me, and Teenie had to help Bubba cut wood and saw wood for the stoves. When we went to the woods with daddy to cut down trees for firewood, our feet would get so cold that daddy had to make a fire for us to warm them. Sometimes our feet would be so cold, we would hold them too close to the open flames and our socks would catch on fire and we wouldn't realize it until someone told us. Our feet would be just that cold.

The house we lived in on Cow Bayou was haunted. Every night we would hear something, or someone, walking around up in the attic or in the kitchen. I never saw anything but I know someone, or something, was in that house. No one was ever brave enough to go up into the attic at night to find out what was up there. We thought daddy wasn't afraid of anything, and even he never ventured upstairs into the attic at night. I'm sure he heard the same noises that we did. It sounded like the attic ladder had been pulled down and the footsteps was coming down and going back up the stairs. He told us it was our imaginations because nothing in its' right mind wanted a house full of chilluns they had to raise. I didn't believe him for one second, but since I never saw anything, I blew the noises off as something I had to deal with until I was old enough to move out on my own, if we stayed there that long. Like my siblings, I was a happy child when we moved from that house.

* * * *

Daddy used to complain all the time about momma chewing tobacco and dipping snuff. She told him when he stopped gambling, drinking wine and whiskey she would stop with the tobacco and snuff. I couldn't understand what the fuss was about because 99% of every adult on the farms, male and female, black and white, chewed tobacco and dipped snuff. Daddy was in the minority when it came to tobacco. He didn't smoke, dip snuff or chew tobacco. He didn't even chew tobacco while playing baseball, which was truly odd because the two went hand in hand. He always said if it were up to him, none of us would pick up that nasty habit. While we were young, he attempted to instill in us what a nasty habit it was in hopes we wouldn't be tempted to try it at too early an age, because he knew it would be our decision to make in the end.

Yours truly couldn't wait to start doing the things grown-ups were doing. So at age twelve, I took a big bite out of momma's plug of Red Mule chewing tobacco and was chewing away when daddy walked into the house. I stopped chewing and attempted to leave the room when my loving sibling Tennie told daddy I had a chaw of tobacco in my mouth. He gave me a menacing look and said if I did have tobacco in my mouth, I had better swallow it, and it I did. I stayed in the room long enough to give daddy the impression that I never had any tobacco in my mouth in the first place. I stayed in the room as long as I possibly could before calmly leaving the room. As soon as I was out of his sight, I ran outside and puked my guts out. I got sick as a dog, but daddy never knew it. If he had known, he would have beaten me half to death because he didn't want us chewing tobacco. When I got old enough, I chewed tobacco; which prompted the same remarks from daddy he made to momma about the evils of chewing tobacco. However, he never said anything about the evils of drinking alcohol. I took full advantage of his accepting nature toward booze when I got old enough to drink. And boy did I drank, I drank like a fish.

* * * *

January, February, and March were the months between cotton planting, cotton chopping and cotton picking seasons. We only had three outfits each to wear to school. When we got home, the first thing we did was take off our good clothes and change into work clothes. Besides school, the only other time we could wear our good clothes was when we went to church. Notice I said good clothes, not new clothes. Our good clothes were usually hand-me-downs from a neighbor or bought from a second hand store. Momma made us girls' underwear out of flour sacks, and we greased our legs with the cooking grease momma used to cook with, so our legs wouldn't be ashy. We went to school smelling like a slab of bacon or a piece of fatback.

Our shoes were also hand-me-downs or second hand. And to make them last as long as possible, when the sole of the shoes would start coming loose, daddy would use baling wire to tie the sole back to the upper part of the shoe. Sometimes our shoes would be wired from heel to toe. We were embarrassed to wear those shoes to school, but it didn't do any good to complain because momma and daddy weren't able to afford new ones. Sometimes we would walk down the halls at school dragging our feet on the concrete floor, and the wire in our shoes would make sparks fly as it came into contact with the concrete. On those occasions, our classmates would laugh, and make fun of us, which made it doubly embarrassing, but we had to wear them anyway. Our motto was, the shoes were better than having to go barefoot, at least during the winter months.

* * * *

When we moved to Wabash, still in Arkansas, things started getting better on the food side. Every year, the Mississippi River flooded its banks. When the water receded, it left tons of fish in water holes where the ground had depressions in it. The holes would be filled with every kind of fish in the region, i.e. carp, buffalo, gar, catfish, trout, brim perches, bluegill perches, drum, crappie, etc. Daddy and other neighbors would take their sink nets and catch the fish by the tubs full. I got so sick of cleaning fish, I would gripe and grumble the whole time I was cleaning them. The griping and grumbling didn't cease until the fish were on the table. Our deep freezer stayed full with frozen fish. Hunting in this part of the country was good also. So along with the fish, daddy and my brothers would kill plenty of rabbits, squirrels, opossums and coons for us to eat. I didn't have to worry about cleaning the game daddy them killed because that was considered a man's job.

* * * *

Daddy expected us girls to pull our load in the cotton fields, so at age thirteen I was picking 300 to 315 lbs of cotton every day. At four o'clock every evening, I would be finished picking my quota for the day. Then daddy would tell me I could take it easy. My siblings disagree with me about how much cotton I could pick, but I know how much it was.

Daddy was hard on us girls because he didn't want us to end up pregnant. Until we were teenagers, he wouldn't let us go anywhere but to work and church. We couldn't even visit the neighborhood girls because he felt they would be a bad influence on us. He didn't know it, but I was the most negative influence of all the girls in our neighborhood because I flirted with every boy I encountered and cussed like a salty marine.

* * * *

Summary

Being the black sheep of the family, I was always on center stage. Be it good or bad. It took the love and strong discipline of my parents to set me straight and prepare me for life. And believe me. I push the patience of my parents to the limit. I can also look back and see the love my siblings had for me. Growing up in this large family was a blessing in disguise, because I had a support system that helped me along the way. I am thankful that God has guided us over the years and has kept our love for each other strong.

Sammy Wade
Born: February 4, 1947
Place of Birth: Corinth, Mississippi

CHAPTER #8
DEEDIE

I was born February 4, 1947 in Corinth, Mississippi. I started working when I was about 6 years old. I had to help my sister Sue chop her row of cotton because she couldn't keep up with everyone else in the field. Because I was helping my sister and not chopping a row of cotton myself, I didn't get paid. My sister got paid because she was the oldest. At first it was exciting being in the field with the grown-ups and the older kids. It made me feel more grown-up. However, as the summer dragged on and the temperature heated up, the hours seemed longer and longer. I found myself longing for those carefree days when I was at home beating up my younger brothers and sisters. I guess daddy was impressed with how well I handled chopping cotton because my year of free labor continued when cotton-picking time rolled around. Sue and I doubled up on one row of cotton and put our cotton in the same sack. I don't remember how many pounds we averaged per day, but it seemed like a lot to me because we were in the field a very long time every day.

The following year, at age 7, I started working on my own. I worked from sun-up to sundown for $2.00 per day chopping cotton. It was so hot working those fields, we would be thankful every time a cloud appeared in the sky to block the sunrays beaming down on our weather beaten heads. If the clouds became dark and widespread enough, we would pray for rain. It was a real treat for us when we were fortunate enough to have a day off in the middle of the week. With the sweat running down my sides from my armpits to my waist, and me leaning on my hoe staring at the burning sun, I wondered if farming was my destiny in life. Or would some unseen force come into my life and lead me down a different path than that of my daddy. The question itself was never a pressing one for me as a child because I didn't mind farming. It was out of curiosity more than anything else. I had no real yearning to leave the farm, nor did I ever hear the call of the wild. It doesn't mean I didn't complain about the long hours and the poor wages because I did, but I was content with being a farm hand.

However, I did question being a farmer on occasions because after working in the field chopping cotton for twelve hours a day we had to do chores: i.e. sawing wood, picking up chips, chopping in the garden, and watering the mules. I would even go with Momma to help milk the cows. That first full year of working in the field set the stage for a lifetime of working on the farm.

*   *   *   *

We were one of the most cotton pickiness' families on any farm. The family as a whole picked approximately a bale of cotton a day during the peak of the cotton harvesting season. At the age of 13, I was picking 300 pounds of cotton a day. Although daddy believed in all of us putting in a hard day's work in the field, he was not heartless. If you were sick, he wouldn't force you to work. He would simply say for us to go home and tell momma what was wrong so she could doctor on us, which usually meant a big spoon full of castor oil. Daddy treated us all the same in regard to sickness. So naturally after realizing daddy's standard policy under these circumstances, my stomach began to hurt at least once a week. These stomachaches usually occurred when I got tired of picking cotton during the middle of the week, and we were picking close to home. I don't know why but I never played sick when we were chopping cotton.

Unfortunately, I abused this being sick privilege because I would go home and beat the crap out of my younger brothers and sisters. I was too young and naïve to realize my stomachache ploy wasn't going to work forever. The only reason I got with it as long as I did was because no one believed a kid in his right mind would want to take castor oil weekly. Sure enough, because of my constant compliant of being sick daddy came to the house one day after I had complained of a stomachache to make sure I was sick. When he walked in the house he caught me beating up on one of the younger children. He grabbed me by the arm and said he thought I was sick. I tried to explain to daddy that after momma gave me the castor oil, I started feeling much better. He said if I was feeling well enough to be beating up on my brothers and sisters, I was well enough to come back to the field. I said I was still too sick to go back to the field. To show how much he believed my story about still being too sick to go back to work he whupped my butt pretty good and took me back to the field with him. I don't remember ever being sick again after that whupping.

* * * *

I remember going to the woods when there was snow on the ground. We would cut down trees and haul the logs back to the house where we cut them into firewood size pieces for the stoves. If we didn't cut enough wood to satisfy daddy on any particular day, we had to go back the following day and cut some more. The last chore of the day, winter and summer, was we had to saw firewood for the night when we got home and take it into the house, along with chips and kindling wood to start a fire the following morning. During the summer months we didn't need as much wood because the only fire we needed was in the kitchen stove for momma to cook. Bubba was the oldest of us boys, so he had to get up every morning and make the fires. Every morning while we were living on Cow Bayou, he would complain that he heard something in the attic, or someone walking around in the kitchen when he got up in the morning to make the fires. I heard the noises at night too, and was thankful I didn't have to get up to make the fires.

* * * *

Me, Bobo, Biddy, and our friend Patterson, who we called Pat, used to go up to this abandoned house and help ourselves to the juicy red apples that grew there. When we weren't taking apples and pears from other people's trees, we were taking watermelons from daddy's watermelon patch. We would bust them open on the ground until we found one that was ripe. The watermelons that we busted that weren't ripe, we threw them in the ditch. Whenever Daddy found the thrown away watermelons, he always blamed Pat and we would laugh at him. Pat would tell daddy it was all of us who took the watermelons, but daddy never believed him.

It wasn't our fault Pat got caught taking stuff from other people's gardens and watermelon patches and was branded as the neighborhood thief. His reputation made it easy for us to point the finger at Pat whenever the neighbors complained too loudly that they believed it might be us who were stealing from their gardens. Pat's family was one of the few families who never had a garden or grew watermelons. They had to buy their vegetables and watermelons from their neighbors. Pat was our perfect out every year when we decided to raid someone's watermelon patch.

*   *   *   *

Once when we were supposed to be picking the last of the late blooming cotton, Biddy, Bobo, and me went rabbit hunting instead. I don't remember why daddy didn't go to the field with us that day, but we took advantage of it to do something we wanted to do. We killed a lot of rabbits that day, so daddy let us off with a job well done. However, he made it known to us he wasn't happy with us missing work. We knew he meant that if we missed work and didn't have anything to show for it, we would be in trouble. We figured if we went back to the same area we hunted the previous day, we would kill just as many rabbits. After all, we had missed almost as many rabbits as we got, but it didn't work out that way. We only killed a fraction of the number of rabbits we had killed the previous day. Knowing that we were in deep doo-doo because of the number of rabbits we killed, we hesitated in going home. When daddy got home and saw the puny amount of rabbits we had bagged, he was true to his word. He beat the crap out of us for skipping another day of work and coming home with little to show for it. We never skipped another day of work, regardless of how many rabbits we thought we might be able to bag.

* * * *

I remember one day daddy had beaten the crap out of several of my brothers and sisters for some reason, I don't remember what for. I had hidden in a closet while the butt whupping was being handed out. I laughed as each one swore whatever it was they had done they would never do it again between each lick of the strap on their behind. After whupping everyone in the room and swearing the next time he would beat them half to death, he turned to leave. For an unknown reason, I felt it wasn't right that everyone in the room had gotten a whupping and I hadn't. My subconscious mind was telling me not to be stupid as I felt myself stand and reach for the doorknob of the closet door. I took a deep breath and stepped out of the closet from where I had been hiding and told daddy he hadn't whupped me yet. At first there was a look of surprise when I stepped from my hiding place. The surprise look changed quickly to unbelief. I could see the "you ask for it and I'm going to give it to you" look on his face. I think he whupped me more for being stupid enough to volunteer for a butt whupping than for whatever it was we had done. Afterward, I chastised myself for being stupid enough to reveal myself. I swore I would never be that stupid again, but unfortunately, I never got another chance to hide from daddy while he was whupping butt.

* * * *

An embarrassing moment in my life occurred one night while I was sleepwalking. One of my sisters and her boyfriend, Sue or Teenie, I don't remember which one it was, was sitting in the kitchen talking to her boyfriend. According to her, I walked into the kitchen where they were talking and got up on the kitchen table, got under the tablecloth and went back to sleep. While my sister and her boyfriend were laughing at me lying there on the table asleep, they saw yellow liquid oozing onto the table where I laid curled in a ball. I had peed on myself. My sister said her laugher turned to embarrassment when she realized what had happened. She said she gave me a change of clothes and put me back in bed while her boyfriend laughed himself silly. When she told me what had happened the following morning, I didn't believe her because I never woke up during the whole episode. She said if I didn't believe her, she would have her boyfriend come over and confirm her story. I told her I didn't believe her, and I wouldn't believe her stupid old boyfriend either. I told her they had made everything up because they both knew daddy didn't like boys being at the house late at night, and they thought I was going to tell on them. In the country, ten o'clock at night was unacceptable for a girl to have company. I said they were both silly, therefore I doubted if it even happened. Sue and Teenie's lack of memory concerning this incident further convinces me it never happened, but I was teased unmercifully for a long time because of what they said I had done.

* * * *

I was a really good baseball player. I could hit the ball better and farther than my brothers and the other boys we played with, or against. I was also a better outfielder than the other boys. I believe I could have made it to the Major League if I had stuck with it. But like so many other talented black kids who were raised on a farm, I seen no future in baseball. Our school was so small we couldn't even afford to field a baseball team because we didn't have money for equipment and uniforms. Therefore, no major league baseball scouts ever came to watch us play in the cow pastures. We didn't even have a Negro semiprofessional team in any of the places we lived. Daddy was proud that I could play baseball so well but when it came to work, baseball was a weekend thing. I spent a lot of time trying to figure out how to get away from the farm long enough to see if I was good enough to play with the big boys, but never had the funds to go and try out with any teams in the cities like Little Rock, Arkansas, or St. Louis, Missouri. At least that is what daddy always told me when I brought up the subject up. I think daddy figured I was needed on the farm more than chasing a fleeting dream.

This doesn't mean we weren't serious about our baseball playing when we were growing up, we were, especially the intramural games between the kids who lived in town and us country kids. When we played the city kids on their real baseball diamonds, it was serious business. Our baseball diamond was a cow pasture. We marked off the infield, cut the grass and used pieces of cardboard boxes or pieces of wood for bases. Many times while sliding into second, third or home plate, you were assisted by a hidden or missed cow paddy. Or when you were chasing down a long fly ball, you would hear the squish as you stepped on a pile of cow dung. Sometimes the cow paddies were discreetly placed on the field when we played the city teams. It was a joy to watch their clean uniforms change colors when they slid into a pile of cow dukey.

* * * *

On more than one occasion while playing baseball with friends, we would play beyond the time limit set by daddy, usually because the game had gone into extra innings. He didn't mind us playing, but when it was time do our chores he expected us to be home on time to do them, which was a couple of hours before sundown. Therefore, on these occasions, we met daddy coming down the road with half a tree in his hand. He would whup our butts all the way home.

* * * *

Bobo, Biddy and me, had a bad habit of jumping on the neighborhood kids and beating them up for no reason whatsoever. We also found ways to get out of going to church on Sundays. One Sunday we told momma we weren't feeling well so we could skip church and go fishing in the lake. While we were sitting there laughing and carrying on, not caring if we caught any fish or not, from somewhere on the lake or in the woods, someone with a commanding voice told us we should be ashamed for skipping church and being out there fishing on the Lord's day.

The voice suggested that we go to church or go home. We looked around but didn't see anybody, so we grabbed our fishing poles and ran home as if the devil himself was after us. I had never been so scared in my life. We thought, eventually, one of our neighbors would confess to scaring the daylight out of us but no one ever did. We never went fishing on a Sunday again.

* * * *

One of the houses we stayed in when we lived around the lake was located in a flood zone, and whenever we got a lot of rain, our house would flood. We would have to go and stay in the boss man's basement until the water receded. This normally was for about three days, but the stay wasn't free. While staying in the basement, the boss always found something for us to do. I remember shucking a lot of corn. After the floodwaters receded, we went back home until the next flood. Luckily, we only stayed in that house for a short period of time, but during that time we got flooded out more than once. After each flood when we got back home, we had to take shots once a week for 3 weeks because the mosquitoes were known to carry malaria.

Daddy used to say our hides were too tough for the mosquitoes to penetrate, therefore, he didn't have to worry about us getting sick. He made sure we got the malaria shots anyway. He said the only reason he made sure we got the shots was to spend as much of the white folks money as possible.

* * * *

Summary

Life growing up on the farm was hard but with daddy and

momma's guidance we did okay. As I said, working on the farm did not bother me. I was comfortable with the hard work, and with my brothers and sisters to play and fight with my childhood was a good one. I wouldn't trade my childhood for any other.

Musa Akil Saeed (Roosevelt wade)
Born: January 16, 1949
Place of Birth: Ruleville, Mississippi

CHAPTER #9
BIDDY

I was born January 16, 1949 in Ruleville, Mississippi. Growing up on various farms as children, we were exposed to hard work; sometimes under extreme conditions to keep the family housed and fed. The average age of the children on the farm when they started work was around six years old, but I started at an even younger age. Although there is disagreement between me and my older siblings, I distinctly remember starting to pick cotton at the tender age of 4 years old. Most of the time the cotton was taller than I was but there I was with my little flour sack picking along-side of daddy. I don't know how much I picked, but I do remember picking cotton when I was 4 years old.

When I was around six, I got into the habit of standing around watching birds when I was supposed to be picking cotton. I would pick a while, then stop to watch the birds flying overhead, or from one location to another in the field. I was fascinated with the flight of the birds. It was as if they were defying the laws of nature by being able to soar through the air at will. I daydreamed of being able to fly like the birds did. I could see myself looking down on my daddy and my brothers and sisters as they toiled away in the fields. I could see myself flying over the muddy Mississippi River, dive bombing the riverboats and crapping on anyone who happened to be on deck. Most of all, I dreamt of being free to do whatever my heart desired, without a care in the world. When I was in this dream world for an extended period of time, it always brought a stern warning from daddy that if I didn't keep my mind on what I was doing, I'd better. So intense was my interest in the birds, and the desire to be able to fly, like them, I ignored daddy's warnings.

One day while in one of my trance like states, watching the birds flying overhead, daddy pulled up several stalks of cotton and commenced to whipping my butt good. I heard him warn me that if I didn't get back to work, he was going to whip my behind, but it was as if his voice came from far away and it wasn't really me that he was talking to. However, any doubt of who daddy was talking to became very clear as the blows of the cotton stalks rained down on my back, behind and legs. I was not intentionally ignoring daddy, but he beat my butt as if I was. After that whipping, my day dreams of being able to fly like the birds came to an abrupt end. And in a very short time, I lost all interest in bird watching. To show how effective that whipping was, I don't bird watch to this day.

My early start in the cotton fields gave me an advantage over the other kids who didn't start picking cotton until age 6 or 7 years old, because when I was around 11 or 12 years old, I was picking 300 lbs of cotton a day while other kids my age could hardly pick one 150 lbs. Not many grown-ups could pick as much as I could. I took pride in being able to pick more cotton than most of the older children and grown-ups. It gave me great pleasure to see the looks of astonishment as I toted [carried] my stuffed cotton sack that was so full it was as stiff as an ironing board, to the scales to be weighed. Along the route to the scales I would hear people whispering, "dem Wade boys sho kin pick some cotton. Old Joe must be mighty proud of dem." I would smile to myself, but my feeling of superiority would vanish because right behind me would be Deedie with a sack even heavier than mine.

Deedie was the one person who always burst my bubble. No matter how much cotton I picked, he would always beat me. I wouldn't tell him that I was competing with him, but I was. I would be picking at a frantic pace trying to match him bow for bow, but I would soon be discouraged as I watched his sack fill up faster than my own. His movements from stalk to sack were so smooth and fluid, I would swear that he wasn't even trying to pick as much as he did, which made it all the more frustrating for me.

I tried for years, but I never beat him.

When I first started picking cotton, the longest sack in the field was a six footer, which was used by the men. By the time I left the farm, the sacks were anywhere from 9 to 12 feet long. The straps to the sacks had to have cotton padding sewn into them to prevent the straps from cutting into your shoulders as you dragged the sack along the ground. To anyone who has never picked cotton, they don't realize that there was a technique to it. When we first started picking cotton as kids we pulled the cotton from the bow one at a time and threw it in the sack. Daddy showed us we would be more productive if we picked until our hands were full and then threw the cotton in the sack. The first year picking cotton, daddy would pretty much call that a training year and didn't expect too much from us, although he showed us how to be more productive. However, from our second year on, he demanded that we use the technique he had shown us to reach our potential. He taught us that the constant bending and straightening would cause undue strain on the back, and it slowed you down. You stood up to stretch your back whenever you needed to, not because you could or wanted to see what was going on around you. And he taught us never to carry two rows because the excess switching from row to row wasted time and slowed you down. I figured out for myself that if the cotton row was low, I was able to pick faster when I straddled it because that eliminated unnecessary movement, which allowed me maximum productivity.

I remember when we arrived at the cotton fields in the early morning during cotton chopping time the cotton leaves would be wet with dew. After piling out of the car, or off of the back of a truck or bus, we always hesitated slightly before getting started because we knew the wet dew was going to soak our clothes. It was always unpleasant because the dew would be cold as it seeped through the fabric of our pants and shirts, and the girl's blouses. When the sun rose it would cause the dew to glisten giving the impression that it had rained overnight, but missed the earth underneath the leaves. We were happy when the sun rose and its' warm rays dried us out, which usually took half the morning. The shorter kids would get wet from head to toe and wouldn't dry out completely until around lunchtime, which was at 12 o'clock. These dewy mornings were horrible times to be chopping in the cotton fields if you were a little kid or short in stature.

*　　*　　*　　*

When we were living in Tiptonville, Tennessee I lost a part of my body there. I was about 2 ½ or 3 years old. My brother Deedie and I were playing a stupid game where I dared him to cut off my fingers. At that age, I don't know what possessed me to play such a stupid and dangerous game. I would put my hand on the chopping block and move it when he attempted to cut my fingers off with a double blade ax. The game lasted for only a short period of time, because after each unsuccessful attempt by Deedie to hit my hand, I got a little bolder and let the ax get a little closer each time. Finally, on one occasion I was too slow in drawing my hand back, and whack, he cut off two of my fingers. I'm sure Deedie got a whipping for cutting off my fingers, but the pain I felt at the time prevents me from remembering if he did or not. Every time I look at my missing fingers, I wonder what possessed me to play such a stupid game.

*　　*　　*　　*

Cow Bayou was my favorite place to live, but there was sadness there also. It was on Cow Bayou that I lost my first love. His name was Spot. To me he was the greatest hunter and the fastest in the pack. He was my sidekick everywhere I went. Spot was my loyal and trusted friend. I got into many fights about that dog. Spot liked to come into the house and my sisters would hit him with a broom, and I would jump on them for hitting him.

Back then it was common for dogs to get bit by rapid bats, coons, foxes, other rapid dogs, and other wild animals. One of our other dogs, named Queen, were bitten by one of those rapid animals and several days later showed all the classic signs of being infected by rabies. She was slobbering, foaming at the mouth, snapping at anything that touched her, and walking around dizzily.

When Queen came near the house growling and snapping at everything that moved, including the other dogs and Spot, they jumped on Queen and fought with her. Since it had to be assumed that all the dogs that fought with Queen had been bitten in the fight, daddy was forced to poison them to prevent the possibility of them becoming rapid and biting us children.

Daddy got up early the following morning after the poisoning and threw the dead dogs into a big ditch in the woods. All of the dogs that fought with Queen died the night they were poisoned, except Spot. We found him a short distance down the road. His breathing was shallow, his eyes were glazed over, and we could tell he was in bad shape. We ran to the house and told daddy we had found Spot and he looked and sounded really bad. I don't know if it was to appease us kids to make it look as if he was concerned about Spot, but he picked Spot up and carried him to the house. Daddy looked as if he was really sad because of what he had done. If he did feel bad, it was because he knew how much I loved that dog. I was blinded with grief at the loss of my best friend. Daddy gave Spot some grease to try and counter the poison he had ingested. However, the poison had eaten away Spot's insides and he died a short time later. To my brothers and sisters, it was just another dead dog because daddy had a habit of getting rid of dogs that would not hunt. Most of the time he would lose his temper while they were in the woods and would shoot the non-hunting dog on the spot. It was truly a sad day for me when Spot died because I had lost a true companion.

There were two other sad memories I experienced when we were living on Cow Bayou. The first was when our sister Betty Ann passed away. I knew she had been taken to the hospital earlier in the day, but didn't know the seriousness of her illness. I remember clearly when they brought her home because a white doctor came to the house to treat her. That was the first time I had ever seen a white man in our home. That night, Betty Ann passed away because of a severe case of pneumonia. It was a sad time in the Wade household for a long time after she died.

The other sad memory was when momma received a letter from family members informing her that her only sister had died.

What made the notification of her sister's death even sadder was my momma didn't receive the letter until several weeks after her sister was buried. So my momma didn't get a chance to say goodbye to her only sister. The pained expression on momma's face made me feel real sad for her. All I could do was take hold of her hand and tell her I was sorry auntie had died. For reasons unknown, the post office didn't get the letter to her on time. I know we moved a lot, but I don't think the letter was late because of a change in our address, but she never found out why it was so late in getting to her. I don't think she fully got over not getting the chance to give her sister a final goodbye.

*   *   *   *

While living on Cow Bayou, my brothers and sisters and I came to the conclusion that the house we lived in was haunted. Every night we heard noises as if a man was walking up and down the attic stairs, or up in the attic. During one hot summer night my fears that the house was haunted were confirmed. It was during one hot summer night when I got tired of sleeping in the bed with a large number of my siblings, so I made a pallet on the floor where it was cooler. On this particular night I could feel the hair on the nape of my neck stand up. I thought it was going to be another one of those incidences where I imagined an invisible haint [ghost] sweeping across me and would keep going; but when I looked up there was a short little man in a suit and hat standing over me. I did not recognize him, and he didn't say anything to me or make any attempt to touch me. I pulled the covers over my head and prayed that the man would go away. I don't know what time of night it was when the man appeared, but I do know it was morning before I peeked from under the blanket to see if he was gone. For the next week, I slept in the bed with my siblings with the covers over my head. I was happy that I never saw the man again. When I told daddy about the man standing over me, he said it wasn't the dead I had to worry about, because they can't hurt you. I took his word for it, but thanked the almighty I was never bothered again.

* * * *

Another sticking point my siblings and I have is the term of stealing. I remember taking apples that did not belong to us, but the trees were located in the yards of abandon houses. The question was, if the apples were not yours and you took them without permission, was it stealing? Or, in the process of taking the apples, if you concealed yourself from being seen by other people, wasn't that an indication that you were doing something wrong? I say if the house was abandoned, that meant the apples were community property. As far as concealing myself while taking apples, I can explain one occasion. On that occasion when we crawled to the location to take the apples, there were white people at the house cleaning up the place. I still didn't call it stealing, because we didn't know if they owned the place or not. I just didn't want them labeling us as thieves. I'm sure that's what the white people cleaning up the place would have called us. However, I'm not saying we never stole anything because we did, but it was not apples.

What we did steal were ice-cold coca colas from the ice barrels the fishermen left on their chartered buses. Townspeople would charter a bus to come to the country to fish in the lake because it was a popular fishing location. We would wait in the bushes until the people would get off the bus, go down the embankment, and throw their hooks into the water. We would then sneak on the bus and help ourselves to the ice cold coca colas that would be covered with ice in a big wooden barrel. We did this for a couple summers and never got caught. The only thing we got in trouble for was getting caught throwing rocks at the people fishing. And of course we got a beating for it.

* * * *

When we were living around the lake, Deedie, Bobo, and myself were on our way hunting over the levee. Daddy always told us to wait until we got over the levee before loading our guns; but since we had to walk through a cotton field to get to the levee, we never knew when we might jump a rabbit. So I never paid any attention to those instructions. This particular morning as we were on our way, I looked up and there was a deer walking adjacent to a fence that separated the cotton and soybean fields. I unloaded on the deer, "boom", knocking it over. When the deer got to its feet, in its desperate attempt to get away it got hung on the fence. I was thinking how proud daddy was going to be when we showed up at the house with a deer in tow instead of the usual two or three rabbits. As I waited to hear the roar of Deedie and Bobo's guns, I thought how we would be the talk of the town for a long time. Not hearing the boom I thought was coming, I started yelling for them to shoot it. Needless to say, I was disappointed as I watched the deer get out of the wire, regain its footing, and run over the levee to freedom before I could reload to shoot it again. I kept telling myself that maybe if I had been using a heavier shotgun shell, the one shot would have brought it down. When I asked Deedie and Bobo why they didn't shoot the deer they said their guns weren't loaded because daddy had told them not to load their guns until they reached the levee. I didn't believe them because they normally loaded their guns the same as I did when we left the house. Whether they listened to daddy this particular day no longer mattered, but I still wonder what it would have felt like to walk into the house with a deer in tow.

* * * *

My favorite time of the year was wintertime, because that was hog killing time. We knew the following morning we were going to have fresh liver for breakfast. As kids, it was fascinating to watch daddy and a couple other men from the community get up before dawn and make a fire under the big black steel pots in the front yard. While sitting around in the crisp morning air smelling the smoke from the burning logs, they would be laughing and telling jokes until the water started to boil. Neighbors always helped each other when it was hog killing time. While us kids played, we would have one ear cocked listening for daddy to say "okay its time." The anticipation of what was about to happen was not lost on the hogs either. They would be snorting and grunting as if talking to each other about what was going to happen to at least one of them. They would then move to the back of the pen and avoid human contact as much as possible.

When the water started to boil, daddy could be heard saying, "okay boys, let get this over with." Upon seeing the men headed for the pen the grunts and snorting of the hogs would get louder and they would try to close rank so as not to be separated. Like humans, they felt safer in numbers. Unfortunately for the hog that had been chose to be sacrificed for the good of mankind, their numbers didn't matter. Daddy had chosen weeks in advance which hog was to meet his maker. Along with the men, us young boys would separate the doomed animal from the rest of the hogs and herd it into a chute to be slaughtered. After all, when we became men, it would be our job to carry on the tradition. Once it was in the chute, either daddy or one of the other men would hit it in head with a sledgehammer, right between the eyes "smack!" The impact of the sledgehammer would scatter their brains and they would fall over, nerves switching involuntarily. On some occasions it would be a 22 cal bullet between the eyes that did the job. One of the other men would quickly cut the hog's throat and then plunge the long black butcher's knife into its heart to quickly end it's suffering, but not before the wounded heart spurted its life blood into a waiting pan to be eaten later. Although this was not standard procedure, daddy had been known to throw the hog into the boiling water while it was still kicking when the pot was near to where the hog had been knocked down. The hog would remain submerged in the boiling water until the hair on the hog was scalded enough that it could be pull off easily by hand. It would then be taken out of the water, and everyone who could reach the hog would pull the hair from its body as quickly as possible before the carcass cooled because if it did, it would be harder to remove the hair. Once the hair was removed, it would be hoisted up to be gutted, steam rising from the still hot body when it came in to contact with the cold morning air. The fine hair not pulled by hand would be shaved off with a big butcher knife.

We watched fascinated as daddy with the expert precision

of a skilled butcher make a slit the length of the hog's underside, but not all the way through in fear of cutting the intestines. It was believed if the intestines were cut the feces from them would taint the meat. He would then go back to where he started the incision at the anus, cut around it and tie it off with a string to prevent any of the content from spilling out. Next he followed the incision he made earlier, but this time he would carefully cut the cavity completely open. There would be two pans sitting near the head of the hoisted hog; one for the liver, lungs, heart, and kidneys, and another one for the intestines, affectionately referred to as chit'lings [chitterlings]. Momma would quickly whisk away the pans to clean the liver, lungs, heart, and kidneys. The intestines were set aside for the time being because it took a while longer to clean them, so they would be taken care of later.

After the insides of the hog had been emptied and thoroughly washed out, it was taken down and cut up. The fatty sides of the hog would be cut into squares which would give us cracklings and the lard that momma would use to cook with during the winter. Cooking the crackling was the last part of the hog-killing job. Momma would use the same big iron pot daddy used to scald the hog in to cook the crackling in. We would take time from playing every so often and sit and watch the crackling cooking. Usually before the crackling was completely done, momma would give us some to eat right out of the pot. We would ooh, ooh, ooh, blow, blow, blow, the meat until it was cool enough for us to pop it into our mouths. The chewy skin was our favorite part of the crackling. We then returned for a repeat until momma gave that final "no more." Daddy sugar cured the hams, shoulders, tenderloin, and slabs of bacon and stored them in the smoke house. The feet, pork chops, ears, and hog head would be placed in salts to keep it from spoiling. Daddy would then cut pieces from almost every part of the meat to be used to make sausages. We had our own sausage grinder. We children took great delight in grinding the meat up to make our own sausage, because it gave us pride not having to depend on the white people at the store for our bacon and sausage. After the sausage was grinded momma would season it and pack it in small burlap casings.

The only part of the hog no one enjoyed cleaning was the chit'lings [chitterlings]. Momma would cut the intestines into short lengths and we would squeeze the feces out of them before dunking them into the big tubs of water and washing them out. First we washed them in the warm water and then the cold. The only fun part of washing the chit'lings was filling the casings with water and sloshing it around in them before dumping the water back into the tub. Then we would turn the intestines inside out and wash them again. The stench was awful. Momma usually had to rewash them because we kids cleaned them just well enough to get away from there. However, later during the winter the stench was all but forgotten when momma served up big pots of steaming hot chit'lings with potatoes and crackling cornbread. The hog's head would be boiled until the meat fell off the bones. From this momma made hog's head souse, snout and all. Hence, the saying that black people ate everything of the hog except the oink rang true.

Another reason we enjoyed hog killing time, along with the reasons mentioned above, was because we knew we would be eating those big thick slices of bacon and sausages to go along with momma's big flaky biscuits and bier rabbit syrup. The food would be so good we would take the grease from the bacon or sausage and add it to the syrup before sopping it up with a biscuit. I believe the reason we were able to eat that greasy food and not suffer serious side effects from it was because as soon as we ate it, daddy made sure he worked it out of us. And when we weren't working, we were either hunting, fishing, or running around playing five or six hours a day. The fat we ingested as children wasn't given a chance to accumulate in our system. Yes sir, just thinking about those cold winter mornings I can still smell and see one of the joys of my childhood.

*   *   *   *

When I was about seven years old, I would be playing and my side would start to hurt. At first the pain was mild, so I ignored it and continued playing. Several days later, I could no longer ignore the pain so I told momma about it. She pressed my left side with her index finger where I said it hurt. Every time she pressed the sore spot I would holler and tears would come into my eyes. The look on her face told me that whatever was going on in my side it was serious. She told daddy that she didn't think I should have to go to work that day. One thing about the old man, as everyone will attest to, when you were sick he didn't force you to go to work. So I had counted myself lucky because if I could stand the pain, it meant that I would spend the day playing with my siblings who were to young too work, if beating up your little brothers and sisters can be described as playing.

As the day wore on, my side started to hurt more and more until I could no longer stand without being in excruciating pain. Momma made me lie down and wait for daddy to get off work. When he finally got home that evening, I was burning up with fever and was sure I was going to die before they got me to a doctor's office. Seeing the pain I was in, and considering the high fever, daddy decided to take me straight to the hospital. The ride to the hospital was the most uncomfortable ride in my life because the only way to get to the hospital was down this long dirt road, and it was dry and full of holes from the last rain we had gotten. It seemed daddy hit every pothole he could find on the way before reaching the paved highway that took us to the hospital in Memphis, Tennessee. The county very seldom graded the road to make it easily passable. However, once we made it to the paved highway it was smooth sailing all the way.

Upon arrival, daddy went into the hospital and came back out with a wheelchair for me because I was in too much pain to walk. After being examined, the doctor told daddy and momma that they had gotten to the hospital just in time because my appendix was about to bust, which could have killed me. I was immediately taken to the operating room and my appendix was removed. When I regained consciousness I was sharing a room with a little white girl who had had her appendix removed earlier that day. We talked like we were old friends who hadn't seen each other in a long time.

The best thing about my stay at the hospital was it made

me feel special. Daddy, Momma, and our neighbors all brought me stuff and gave me money. When I asked momma and daddy why they didn't bring my sisters and brothers to the hospital to see me, daddy said they would be seeing me soon enough when I got home. The day nurse was nice to me and I liked her a lot. I stayed at the hospital for three days. The morning I was discharged from the hospital I discovered all the money I had been given during my stay was gone. I don't know who took it, but I believe it was the night nurse because she was always fussing with herself about not being paid enough money for the job she was doing. When I told daddy and momma that I suspected the night nurse of taking my money, they all laughed and said I had either lost it or had given it to that little white girl who had gone home the day before I did. I liked her, and her momma who was nice to me, but not enough to give her my money.

It didn't matter how much I denied giving the white girl my money, no one believe me. Even my brothers and sisters teased me for giving my money to that little white girl for months. I wished that white girl hadn't left before I did, then they may have believed me about the nurse probably taking my money. I think they kept teasing me about that little white girl because they were jealous. And because when I got home, I got special attention from momma and daddy, and they gave me almost anything I asked for within reason.

It gave me great pleasure when the girls in the neighborhood would ooh and ahh as they examined my battle scar. Of course I lied and said it didn't hurt a bit, and when my siblings would tell them I was crying like a baby when they took me to the hospital, I denied it. I wouldn't allow anything to spoil my time in the spotlight. But, as the old saying goes, nothing lasts forever. I was back in the cotton field two weeks after the surgery, and the fields treated no one special.

* * * *

In 1935 daddy was living on a plantation in Mississippi with his first wife Donnie. According to daddy, the plantation owner where he lived accused him of being a liar and a cheat because he had demanded his equal share of the profits from that sharecropping year. The plantation owner told him if he didn't stop bothering him he would have his black butt hung for disrespecting a white man, so daddy decided to move. The black families living on the plantation told him no one could move off of the plantation unless the white owner allowed them to. Daddy told his neighbors he didn't give a damn what that white man said, he was moving, because after cheating him once that white man would always cheat him. Of course he didn't go and tell the plantation owner he was leaving, and he didn't tell any of his black neighbors when he was leaving because he figured if he told the wrong person he/she would squeal on him.

    The plantation owner got wind of daddy's desire to leave. He stopped by the house and asked daddy if the rumor he heard about him trying to leave the plantation without his permission was true. Daddy assured the plantation owner it was nothing more than a rumor because he was perfectly happy working for him. Several days later daddy loaded a wagon with all their belonging in the middle of the night to leave the plantation. The white plantation owner hadn't believed daddy when he said he wasn't going to attempt to leave so he had several white men watch the house, and they were supposed to stop daddy if he did try to leave. Daddy had told Donnie, after making the decision to leave the plantation that they would probably run into some white men before they got off the farm and there would probably be trouble. She said she was with him whatever he decided to do, so it was with that understanding they loaded the wagon and proceeded to leave the plantation. Daddy drove the borrowed wagon with a double barrel shotgun in one hand and the reins controlling the mules in his other hand. Donnie had a level action Winchester rifle lying across her lap, and she knew how to use it.

    The white men hired by the plantation owner had watched as daddy and Donnie loaded the wagon and kids and took off. I believe the children were Joe Nathan and Mag. Anyway, the white men waited a short distance down the road to confront them. When daddy reached their location the white men rode out onto the road and asked him where he was going. Daddy said he told them that were none of their business, so if they didn't mind he wanted to be on his way. The leader of the group told daddy they couldn't allow that to happen, not until he settled his account with the plantation owner. Daddy told them he had no idea what they were talking about, and since he had did nothing wrong the only way he was going back was after they killed him and his family. He cocked both hammers on the shotgun and Donnie chambered a round into the Winchester and moved it to a position that would allow her to engage the men quickly. Seeing daddy and Donnie were serious, the men backed down and said they were going to tell the plantation owner what had happened. Daddy told them to go ahead and do that, but in the mean time they would be moving on. The white men galloped off, and daddy and Donnie went on their way. They didn't run into any other white men from the plantation while leaving Mississippi.

It is amazing the reaction you get from white people when a black man or woman is not afraid to die for what they believe in. Even back in the 1930s if a black man or black woman was carrying a gun and was willing to use it, they left them alone. White people weren't stupid, they knew when to back off and live to fight another day. According to daddy this was not the only time he would have to stand up to a white boss attempting to cheat him out of his hard earned pay.

* * * *

Joe Wade was a very brave man. He was not afraid to die for what he believed was right. He told me about a time when white people used to cheat black people out of their wages all the time, and the black men wouldn't say anything about being cheated out of their pay. They were afraid their white bosses would either fire them for being called a cheat or have the klan pay them a visit one night.

One Saturday on payday, he didn't say what the job was, daddy went to the boss man's office to pick up his pay for the week. When the boss man gave him his money he counted it right in front of him before leaving the office because of the man's reputation for cheating his workers, and sure enough he was being cheated. When daddy demanded the rest of his money, he and his boss got into a heated argument. After seeing the white man had no intentions of paying him, daddy told his boss they were going to pay him now or later. When daddy turned to walk out of the office the boss man came from behind his desk and kicked him on his leg as he walked away. Daddy said he turned around and decked that bastard.

The boss man's two brothers were outside the office and came running into the office after being told a darky was beating the hell out of their brother. Upon entering the office and seeing their brother on the floor, they jump daddy. Daddy said he knew if he stayed in the middle of the floor to fight them they would surround him and over power him, so he backed into a corner so they couldn't get behind him. Every time one of the men came within punching distance he'd knocked him down. Finally they got smart and all three of them rushed him at the same time. They got him down to the floor intending to beat him to death.

During the whole ordeal there were five black men watching as daddy fought with the three white men. Not one of them helped him fight the white men, but one young black man did say, "Oh no. I ain't gonna let y'all kill him. If y'all don't stop I'm gonna hav'ta help him fight y'all." Upon hearing another black man willing to fight if they didn't stop beating him, they let daddy up. The boss man told daddy he respected a man who stood up for himself. He told daddy to come on over here and get his pay. The white boss then announced he was paying everyone the wages they were owed. Daddy said he had known some white men who enjoyed a good fight and didn't hold grudges whether the men they fought were black or white. This white boss seemed to be one of those white men. On the other hand his brothers wanted daddy strung up from the highest tree. The boss told his brothers to leave him alone, but daddy said he knew they wouldn't and his white boss would eventually take his brothers side. Knowing the feel good attitude on the part of his white boss wasn't going to last, daddy never went back to that job. Black men were hung for less than hitting a white man. Daddy said he walked away from that job feeling pretty good because no one got cheated out of any of their pay that day.

* * * *

I loved my daddy very much, even though I never told him. It wasn't masculine during the 1940s and 1950s for boys to tell their daddy that they loved them, and vice-se-versa. I cannot remember my daddy ever telling me that he loved me, although I knew he did. Daddy showed he loved me by always providing for me.

* * * *

Summary

It was two of the greatest parents in the world that raised us. They loved us, guided us, and prepared us for the world. When we kids had our conflicts they reminded us that no matter our disagreements we only had each other to depend on in the end. The hard times I experience were made easier because daddy and momma taught me that trouble doesn't last always. Because of them our love for each other is as strong today as it has always been.

Robert Madison Wade
Born: December 28, 1950
Place of Birth: Pritchard, Alabama

CHAPTER #10
BOBO

I was born December 28, 1950 in Pritchard, Alabama. I am the 10th child of the clan. I have always considered my birth date a curse because momma and daddy always combined my birthday and Christmas gifts. While my siblings anxiously waited for their birthdays to come because momma and daddy always tried to do something special for them, I would know what my birthday gift was three days before it actually arrived. Therefore, I felt cheated out of a birthday gift because I would get it on Christmas day.

* * * *

I don't remember how old I was when my younger sister, Betty Ann, died. I do remember Momma and Daddy being sad, and a lot of neighbors visiting the house to give their condolences for their loss. What stands out in my mind about Betty Ann's death is momma telling a moving story about an incident that occurred not long after she died. The story went as follows.

Not long after Betty Ann passed a neighbor of ours, Miss Lily, came to visit Momma to comfort her because of her loss. She often comforted people in the neighborhood because it was rumored that she could confer with the dearly departed and let the families know whether their loved ones were in a better place, or if they had questions as to why they had to leave this earthly life. Momma said Miss Lily kept tilting her head sideways and looking around the room as if she was hearing things. She didn't pay too much attention to her until Miss Lily pointed in the direction of where the television was sitting and told momma that an angel was standing there holding Betty Ann and she was happy. When Momma asked why was the angel there? Miss Lily said the angel said she knew momma didn't understand why God took Betty Ann at such a young age. She was there to put her heart at ease. Tears welled up in Momma's eyes and she asked Miss Lily where was the angel, holding Betty Ann, was standing. Miss Lily said she was standing beside the television. Momma said she went over by the television where Miss Lily had indicated and sat down. She told Betty Ann how much she and her daddy loved her and missed her. Momma told her she knew the reason she had died was because God wanted her to be with Him in heaven. After momma said this, Miss Lily said both Betty Ann and the angel was smiling. Miss Lily told momma the angel said they had to leave. She just wanted her to know that Betty Ann was being cared for in the house of the Lord. Momma said, "Bye, bye, baby. Mommy loves you so much." Momma said after this incident the heaviness she felt in her heart left her because she knew her baby was in God's hands, and she was happy. True or not, the story always pulled at my heart strings when momma told it because of the happiness that shone on her face.

* * * *

We grew up without indoor plumbing so going to the outhouse was sometimes an adventure in itself. I remember one summer there was a report of a black bear eating out of people's garbage cans and attacking them if they happened across it. One night during this heightened period of fear and alertness, daddy had to go use the outhouse. To my dismay he chose me to go with him to stand guard while he took a dump. He got a flashlight, handed me the shotgun he kept propped in a corner by the kitchen door and it was off to the outhouse we went. Here I was, standing watch while my daddy used the toilet. It wouldn't have been a problem if he only had to take a whiz because we had what we called night pots to relieve ourselves at night. The pots we owned were not some glamorized item like the so called chamber pots that rich folks led the poor to believe they possessed. Our night pots were usually empty one-gallon molasses cans. With as many kids as there were in the house, it was a guarantee that all the cans would be filled by daybreak. Sometimes in the winter we boys would feel our oats and would go take our whiz off the porch, and watch the steam rising from the stream of hot pee by the light of the moon. I am happy to report that I never had to shoot a bear, and no one else in the community did either. And no one in the community ever got attacked by a bear.

Most of the time during the winter it would be so cold in the house we didn't even want to get out of bed to use the night pot, let alone go outside. We would do our best to hold off on any bodily functions until daybreak because daddy or Bubba would have made a fire by then, and the house would be nice and warm. So as you can imagine, there were numerous accidents while waiting until the last second to get up to use the pot. Well, not numerous but one major incident on my part.

One cold winter night when I was about five years old I had to use the potty, but it was so cold I couldn't tear myself from the confines of the warm winter blankets. I lay wide-awake trying to figure out a way to relieve myself without having to get out of bed. Instead of doing the right thing and getting up to use the pot, I held the pee until I couldn't hold it any longer. The laws of nature took over, but instead of getting up and trying to make it to the can to pee in, I soaked my sister Oyce. I knew before I even finished peeing on my sister, momma or daddy was going to come in the bedroom, see what I was doing, and whup me silly. Since Oyce was younger and more of a baby than I was I didn't think momma would whup her for wetting the bad. Unfortunately, upon finding the wet bed momma wore her butt out. I never told anyone what I had done because I knew they would've told on me, and momma or daddy would have whupped my butt good.

*   *   *   *

Before I was old enough to work in the field, me, Oyce, Pon'k, and our friends would play in the front yard and throw clods of dirt at the passing cars, buses, and trucks that transported the cotton choppers and pickers to and from the various fields they were working in. One day a cotton choppers bus was passing by and we threw clods of dirt at it as we usually did. This day the bus came to a screeching halt a short distance past the house and the people came piling out of it and running toward our house. We knew we were going to get our behinds beat for throwing at the bus when the people told on us. We ran into the house and were looking for a good hiding place when the people started knocking loudly on the door. Momma opened the door to see who was banging on the door like that.

Everyone who had gotten off the bus tried to talk at the same time. Momma told the people to calm down and tell her what was wrong. She was informed by the cotton chopper whose voice overrode everyone else's that they had seen a snake going through one of the side windows of the house. Momma told them to come on in and help her search for the snake. Knowing we were not in trouble, we came from the back room to join in the search for the snake. A couple of the men found the snake under the woodpile in the kitchen and killed it. Momma thanked them and they were on their way. We didn't relax until the bus disappeared in a cloud of dust down the road. Since momma didn't say anything to us about us throwing clods of dirt at the bus, we figured the folks hadn't told on us. Emboldened by this knowledge we went back outside and waited for the next bus to pass.

That evening momma told daddy what had happened regarding the snake incident, including that a couple of the choppers told her we were throwing clods of dirt at the bus. Daddy put homemade stripping around the windows and forgot about it. Our punishment was silence, because we didn't know if we would be punished or not. So we jumped every time daddy came near us, because he was known to start whupping butt without warning when momma told him we had misbehaved during the course of the day. It was bedtime before we relaxed because one of the older children told us daddy had told momma she should have whipped our butts for throwing the clods of dirt at the bus when it happened, but since she didn't, it was too late for him to do it.

I don't remember momma ever saying what type of snake it was. As far as the snake was concerned, it was insignificant because it was dead.

Another incident concerning a snake was while momma was watching her favorite soap opera, "Dark Shadows." Momma said she thought she saw something moving in one of the cracks in the wall behind the television. The movement had been so subtle she wasn't completely sure if she had seen it at all. Although we lived in the country and snakes were plentiful, they very seldom ventured into anyone's house, the preceding incident being one of the exceptions. The snakes were more afraid of us than we were of them. Statistics showed that 99.9% of all snakebites occurred as a result of humans invading the snake's territory. So momma cast aside any thoughts that it might be a snake in her house, again, and chalked the movement up to being either a figment of her imagination or a rat. With some reservations momma continued to watch T.V.

When momma saw the movement again she knew she wasn't crazy. That she had seen something move in one of the cracks behind the television. Brushing aside any doubts whether she had actually seen any movement in the cracks or not, momma decided to take a closer look. As she approached the wall she kept telling herself she wasn't crazy and she wasn't seeing things. Momma felt no fear, just an overwhelming desire to find out what was moving around in her wall. She approached the wall cautiously, prepared to evade whatever was crawling around in the crack if it attempted to attack her. Once she got close enough to see in the cracks, she saw what it was she had seen moving in the crack. There, in one of the larger cracks in the wall, was a three-foot long black and yellow snake lying there not moving. Momma knew from the snake's markings it was a nonpoisonous king snake, but a snake just the same. She knew the snake was probably hunting for the rats that lived behind the walls, but the snake had to be killed anyway, or it would build a nest in the house and produce off springs that might end up biting one of them. Momma went outside and got the Kaiser blade so that she could kill it. The Kaiser blade was a 12inch long, 4 inch wide, flattened piece of metal sharpened on both the top and bottom of the blade, and curved upward at the tip. The blade was attached to a four-foot long wooden handle. It was used to cut brush when clearing a field or around the house.

When she again approached the wall momma realized she wouldn't be able to whack it because the crack was too deep for the blade to reach the snake without cutting the wall, and the last thing she wanted to do was cut another hole into that weathered wood. The only way she was going to be able to kill it was to get it to come out of the crack. Momma moved the television and the table out of the way so when the snake came out of the wall, she would have enough clearance to complete the job without breaking anything. Throughout all the commotion the snake did not move a muscle. After the television and the table had been moved out of the vicinity, momma took the Kaiser blade and turned it on the flat side and started poking the snake to make it come out of the crack.

Sensing it's life was in danger the snake wiggled and squirmed trying to get away from the insistence poking of its body, but it only had one way out. Having no alternative, the snake squeezed itself from the crack and hit the floor heading for what it thought might be safety under the couch. As she had used the Kaiser blade so often to cut small bushes and tall weeds, the blade made a loud thud as it sliced through the snake's neck imbedding itself in the floor. Momma picked up the headless body of the snake and threw it into the ditch adjacent the house and came back and got the head and threw it into the ditch also.

When she told daddy and the rest of us children what had happened, we the boys thought it was funny. We considered the invasion of the snake as part of living in the country. There was no fear that our house would be overrun by snakes. Daddy said the cats weren't worth a damn at catching the rats running crazy through the house maybe the snakes could do a better job at catching them. We never had another snake venture into our house, as far as I remember.

* * * *

My first personal experience with overt racism occurred when I was six years old. Momma baked a cake for the foreman's wife and told me to take it to her. I walked along the road occasionally kicking the tall weeds that grew beside the road to see what kind of insects would be disturbed. The boss lady's house was about a mile away from where we lived. The closer I got to her house, the more I wondered why momma them was so nice to them white folks when all they did was boss them around and treat them like they was dirt. Momma said when I got older I would understand that God didn't see color, and to be a good Christian we weren't supposed to see it either. And as far as the white folks being mean, God would deal with them in time. I was only six years old, but I didn't buy into the let God fix it. I heard daddy say over and over again if black folks had to wait on God to stop white folks from being mean to black folks, we would be waiting forever. I knew everything done on the farm was based on color.

The mile walk was a short distance compared to how far we had to walk to see several of our friends who lived as far as five miles away. When I arrived at the lady's house I was eager to give her the cake and be on my way home. I didn't know why I felt so uncomfortable about delivering the cake. The foreman's wife cleared everything up for me when I knocked on her door.

The lady came to the door and looked down at me as if I had stolen her favorite piece of silverware. She asked me if I was stupid or what, that all darkies knew they had to make their deliveries at the back door of the house. When I told her I was sorry, that I didn't know that, it seemed to make her madder. She said any nigger with half a brain would have known that, regardless of his age. She said she was going to tell my momma to teach me how things were when it came to white folks and black folks. To put the icing on the cake and make sure I never forgot my place, she told me to go back out to the road and approached the house again, but this time I was to go to the back door.

Getting as mad as a black six year old in the south could get, I went back out to the road and kept going. I swore momma would have to kill me to get me to take anything else to that old mean white lady. When I got back home with the cake still in hand, I just knew momma was going to whup me, but when I told her what had happened she took me into her arms and told me that was the way things were in the south, but assured me that things were slowly changing. However, she did give me a warning that if she ever told me to take something to someone else again and I brought it back, it would be at my own risk. I thank God momma never asked me to take that old mean witch anything else. True to her word the lady showed up at our house that afternoon and told momma she had better teach me how things worked in the south before I ended up hurt or dead.

* * * *

One day I stayed home from school because of illness. I was around 7 years old. After the noontime meal, momma took a nap and I was bored. I told Oyce to watch as I set the peeling wallpaper on fire with a match and then beat it out with a pair of daddy's old work pants. Each time I let the flames get a little bigger before putting it out. Oyce kept saying, "I bet'cha you won't let it get real big." Being gullible as all get out, I accepted the challenge. I lit the paper and watched as the flames rose up the wall. When it got almost to the ceiling, I tried to put it out, but the flame was out of control. While I was fighting the flames, Oyce ran into momma's bedroom and told her the house was on fire. Momma jumped up, ran into the bedroom and beat the fire out with a wet bath towel she had been using to wipe her forehead because it was a hot day and we didn't have a fan.

After putting the fire out, she was ready to whup some butt. In the most pitiful voice I could muster, I said I was sorry. For good measure I threw in a couple of sickly coughs. She told me if I wasn't sick she would have tanned my hide real good. Sister Oyce kept telling momma if she didn't whup my butt, I would probably end up burning the house down. While Oyce was putting in her two cents I was thinking to myself, "You wait until momma goes back to sleep, I'm going to beat your behind." Momma didn't go back to sleep so I didn't get a chance to get back at Oyce until we were at school the following day. I told the ugliest boy on the farm that she liked him, Harold or something like that. Anyway, I had accepted a dare and won, although I almost burned the house down.

*   *   *   *

Although I hated farm work, I would get caught up in the moment at each of the different seasons of farming. There is something magical about spring. It is that time of year when the ground thaws and it is time to turn the soil and start life a-new. The smell of the freshly turned earth waiting for the new seeds to be planted was comforting. It gave me hope that someday like the soil, I too would start life anew somewhere far away from the farm. Someplace where white people would not control my life and that of my family and other black folks. I don't remember my parents supporting any civil rights movements, but my daddy always told us if a white person put his hands on us, we had the right to defend ourselves. Chopping, or nursing the cotton to help it grow tall, strong, and productive gave us a false sense that the land was good to us. The land may have been, but the owners of the land were not. It was fascinating to me to see how the cotton grew from a little seed, to a strong green plant full of cotton boles, and finally developing into a sea of white texture that was demanded worldwide. When we were not chopping or picking in the fields, we could be found playing in them.

When the fields turned into big white fluffy clouds, I would involuntarily yearn to get started with that year of picking. However, that first day in the fields when I would hear the grown-ups complaining about how we would be cheated out of our fair wages again this year, it reminded me why I had to get away from the farm when I grew up. One particular scale used a bell weight that was moved along a long thin piece of metal with numbers on it. When the bell weight was placed on the number that balanced the scale, that would let you know how much cotton was in the sack. Rumor had it that the center of the bell weight had some type of metal plugged into it that made the cotton weigh less than what was actually in the sack. After much complaining, by the cotton pickers, because of the scales inaccuracy that type of scale was replaced with a pull spring scale. Again, a cry of being cheated was raised because rumor had it that the springs were wound so tightly that the scales did not give an accurate reading. Once they went to the spring-loaded scales, it stayed as the standard weighing instrument on every farm in Arkansas and Mississippi until king cotton was no longer king. Slowly cotton picking machines replaced us field hands almost completely. However, the complete replacement was not completed until long after I had left the plantation. The first cotton picking machines had small hoppers, so the plantations owners looked for ways to maximize its' capacity. That is where we smaller kids came in. One incident that occurred to me while in one of those hoppers convinced me that my future did not include farming.

When the white plantation owners started using cotton-picking machines they would have us smaller kid get in the hopper and pack the cotton to maximize it capacity. I was around seven when I was given this task of stomping the cotton to compress it in the hopper. I don't remember how long I had been doing it, but one day I almost suffocated in one of the hoppers. Since my brother Bubba was driving the cotton-picker, I didn't have any concerns or thought anything out of the ordinary would occur. He normally kept an eye on the hopper because we could not hear each other over the roar of the machines' engine, so when it was full enough we would go and dump the cotton in the designated trailer. This particular day I packed and packed waiting for Bubba to see if the hopper was full enough to dump, but he didn't. He kept going and going and going, and the space in the hopper got smaller and smaller. When the cotton got to the very top and I was packing it sideways from the back toward me, I ran out of space. I found myself under the chute that was blowing the cotton into the hopper. The cotton covered me. I tried to holler over the roar of the machine engine to let Bubba know that I was smothering in the hopper, but it was useless. I started to cry because I could hardly breathe because of the weight of the cotton pressing down on me. I was sure I was going to die.

I don't know what made Bubba look back to see if the hopper was full enough but I thanked my lucky stars he did. He stopped the cotton-picker and climbed up to the hopper and dug me out. Because he had saved my life I was thankful, but at the same time I was mad because he hadn't checked on me to see if the hopper was full enough as he had in the past. He had always went to dump the load when he saw I had only a very small space left. I felt he got greedy this time. Because of this experience, I was never able to work in the hopper again because I would panic when the cotton got close to the top of the hopper, or the cotton coming through the chute would hit me in the face. My brothers, sisters, and friends called me a sissy because I was scared to get back in the hoppers, but I didn't care because I planned on living long enough to grow old and die in bed. I thank God for saving my life when I was in the hopper.

* * * *

An incident that happened when I was around ten years old cemented the belief in my mind that black men were stone cold crazy to mess with white women. My daddy had an agreement with a plantation owner named, Mr. Baker, where he could borrow money to buy food at the corner store. It wasn't cash money it was more like a food card. It was called a dog pony. The cards came in denominations of $10, $15, and $20 dollars. Usually daddy would send one of the older kids to the boss man's house for the cards, but this particular day he sent me to get it. When I arrived at the house, I knocked on the back door and no one answered the door. Being I never wanted to go back home and tell daddy I didn't accomplish the job he had sent me to do, I peeped through the window to see if anyone was home. I had no interest in girls or women, so my peeping into the boss man's house was totally innocent. Unknown to me, the boss's wife was home, and saw me looking through the window she just didn't answer the door. When her husband got home that evening she told him I was a peeping tom. She told Mr. Baker when she got out of the bathtub and was going to the kitchen, she saw me looking through the window. As

God is my witness, I didn't even see that woman. Like I said, I didn't see anyone so I went back home and told daddy that no one was home.

In the south in 1960 a black male, man or boy, knew it was suicide to even look at a white woman wrong, let alone peeping at one that was supposedly naked. So true to the code of the white dominated south, Mr. Baker came to our house and demanded that daddy whip me for peeping through his window and seeing his wife naked. Mrs. Baker never said I saw her naked. What she said was I was looking through the window when she was going to the kitchen after getting out of the tub. Daddy called me out to where he and Mr. Baker were talking and asked me if I had peeped through Mr. Baker's window and saw his wife naked. I told daddy the truth. I did look through the window but hadn't seen anyone at home and that is why I didn't get the dog pony he sent me after. After hearing this, my daddy told Mr. Baker he had to talk to his wife to see what happened before he would beat me.

Mr. Baker turned redder than a coal of fire at my daddy's refusal to whip me, and called him an uppity nigger. He again demanded that daddy whip me. When my daddy repeated that he wanted to talk to his wife before he would whip me, Mr. Baker reached for me. My daddy pushed me behind him and stood his ground. Seeing my daddy was serious and had no intention of letting him touch me, Mr. Baker said he would be back that night, and my whole family would regret the day I peeped in his window.

I knew the incident was serious because that night daddy sat by the window with all three of his shotguns waiting for the Klu Klux Klan to come for us. You can't imagine the fear of a young black boy waiting for the men in white sheets to come and get him with a rope with a hangman noose at the end of it. I was overcome with the feeling of guilt that I was going to be the cause of my whole family being killed, and I cried. The stories I heard our parents and neighbors tell about what happens to black men who mess with white women swirled around in my head that whole night. Every time I dozed off to sleep, the Klan came to drag me out of the house to hang me. I don't know why, but Mr. Baker and his Klan friends never showed up.

The following day, daddy went to Mr. Baker's house to talk to him and his wife about the accusation and nothing further was ever said about the incident. When I asked my daddy what the boss's wife had said, all he would ever say was for me to never look in the window of another white person's house as long as I lived. Even after the incident was resolved, I lived in fear for a long time. I don't know if it was my imagination or not, but I perceived that Mr. Baker looked at me totally differently after that supposedly peeping tom incident. I thank God daddy never asked me to go to that white man's house for anything ever again.

* * * *

As stated earlier, daddy was a womanizer so I took his word when he talked about what women were like, and what they would do to you if you crossed them. He always said momma was the only woman in the world he loved, the other women were playthings. He said he didn't want me to be like him and screw around when I got married, because when God made momma he broke the mold. There would never be another woman like her, so when I got married I had to treat my wife right or she would leave me. When I asked him why he did what he did, he said it was a man's thing that I would learn when I grew up. Daddy never sat me down and had an official talk with me about the birds and the bees, but his messages about sex came across loud and clear. It was not about how I should be careful that I didn't go around making babies, it was about not having sex at all until I found the right girl. His advice scared me to the point that I thought I would never have sex, even after I got married.

Daddy would tell me I would know when I found the right girl because she would be sent from heaven just for me. If it were not the right one I would know that too because after messing with her my thang would fall off. He told me the way to make sure I didn't get burned by a nasty girl was to take some earwax and rub it around down there. If she was a nasty girl, it would burn her and I was not to touch her. For a young boy who believed his daddy would tell him nothing wrong, I looked at each girl in the community trying to figure out which one would grow up to be a good girl, and which one would grow up to be a nasty woman. This unnatural scrutinizing made me very unpopular with the girls, because it gave the impression that I was a weirdo. The girl did not know it but I had my reasons for feeling the way I did.

Several weeks after one of daddy's sex talks, I was playing in the barn with one of the fastest girls in the neighborhood. Junie Mae Jones. It was said she would drop her drawers for any boy who asked her to. I was around twelve years old and she was at least fourteen. It was rumored she was sleeping with grown men. The other kids we were playing with had gone outside to play hide-go-seek. I knew she was up to something when she took ahold of my hand and pulled me into one of horse stalls. She pulled me down with her, but I only went to my knees. I was shocked when she reached inside the right leg of my shorts and grabbed my private part. I never wore underwear so there was nothing to hinder her groping.

Everything daddy had told me about nasty girls rushed into my mind, and from everything he had told me about loose girls sleeping around, Junie Mae was definitely a nasty girl. I found myself getting excited, but the fear of losing my most prized possession overrode that excitement somewhat, and I tried to devise a way to get out of the situation. I could hear our friends, along with Oyce and Pon'k, outside the barn whooping, hollering, and playing up a storm, but there was no way for me to get their attention without calling out to them. I knew if I did that, Junie Mae would know I was scared of her, and no boy wanted a reputation of being scared of girls.

I moved her hand from me, and layed down on the straw beside her, but I didn't make any move to do anything. When she asked me what was wrong, I said the other kids may come in the barn and catch us, and she would get in trouble with her momma. She laughed and said she wouldn't get in any trouble because she and her momma were sleeping with the same men. Knowing I had to do something to save my pride, I kissed her. The kiss was so sloppy and clumsy Junie Mae laughed and asked me if I was a virgin. I had heard the preacher use the word in church during his sermons about people getting married, but I never paid any attention to it or ever asked anyone what it meant. So, I had to pretend I knew what she was asking me. I wasn't so dumb I didn't realize I would be talked about if she told folks I was what she asked me if I was. I said, "No I ain't that." And to prove to her I was experienced in the ways of seducing a girl, I stuck my hand in her drawers and started feeling her up. She moved my hand and told me I was supposed to kiss her before putting my hand in her drawers.

Following her instruction, I started kissing her on the mouth. For the third time in less than five minutes, she laughed at me and said, "Let's get this over with before someone comes into the barn and catches us." When she removed her drawers, I couldn't believe what was about to happen. She got comfortable on her back and motioned for me to get on top of her.

After pulling my pants down around my ankles, the realization of what was about to happen hit me and I was shaking like a leaf on a tree inside. I had to test daddy's theory about how a nasty girl would react to earwax being rubbed down there before going through with the act. I turned slightly so she wouldn't see me stick a finger in my ear. When I turned back toward her I reached down and rubbed the earwax on her private part and nothing happened. I thought, maybe she wasn't a nasty girl after all. Besides, I had gone beyond the point of no return. I positioned myself to complete the act when I heard "Oh, oh, I'm gon tell momma on y'all." I jumped up from the straw and ran out of the barn with my pants in my hands. Junie Mae got up slowly from the straw, put her drawers on and cussed everyone within hearing distance as she headed off toward her house.

The incident was so dramatic for me, I don't even remember if it was Oyce or Pon'k who caught us and told momma on me. I confessed to momma what had almost happened, and all she did was confirm what daddy had told me earlier, that girls like Junie Mae was nasty. Whenever me, and Junie Mae, happened to meet after that episode, I would keep my distance from her. Realizing I was avoiding her, Junie Mae would stick her tongue out at me every chance she got. She even told all her friends that I was a virgin. Her friends giggled and pointed at me at church and at school, but I didn't care. I convinced myself being a virgin was a good thing. However, I did ask one of my older sisters what a virgin was, because it was a girl who had asked me the question. I don't remember whether it was Sue or Teenie but she said I was so naïve and said everyone knew that a virgin was someone who had never been with anyone sexually. She wanted to know why I asked. I told her one of my friends called me that. After knowing what a virgin was, I felt I had been given a second chance to find the right girl to do the nasty with. And when the preacher said every man and woman should be a virgin when they got married, I knew what he was talking about. I was glad that I hadn't lost my virginity to a nasty girl.

* * * *

I think it is safe to say I was the biggest cluck of all the kids in my family. Two incidents stand out in my mind that shed some light on why I say this. First, my brothers, our friends, and me, used to catch a baby rabbit whenever we found them in a burrow. We would make a circle around it to see how long it would take them to escape. I don't remember eating baby rabbits, just playing with them. One day several of us caught a baby rabbit and had it surrounded. We were whooping and hollering keeping the little rabbit within the circle we had made. The way it worked was when the little rabbit came in your direction you would stomp and holler to make it change direction and try to get by someone else. Well the second time it came my way it was a fatal mistake on its' part. It zigzagged trying to find an opening between where I stood and the kids on either side of me. I guess I looked like the weakest link because it ran straight toward me. At the last second it changed its' mind and tried to change directions. In my haste to keep it from escaping, I mimicked its movements and felt the soft body give as my right foot came down on its head as it tried to get away from me. I looked down at the little rabbit going into convulsions and knew I had killed it. The other kids gathered around and watched as it shook violently one last time and died.

They said I would never be invited to play with any other critters they found because I was always spoiling the fun. They told me I was too clumsy and stupid. It hurt my young pride, but I blew it off as my siblings and friends being cruel and mean because I stepped on the baby rabbit and cut their fun short. Besides, we hunted and killed rabbits all the time. The only difference this time was the rabbit was a baby and I happened to step on it instead of shooting it. This brings me to the next incident of me being a special child.

    I don't remember whether it was after stepping on the rabbit or before, but me, Oyce, and Pon'k was sitting on the back porch throwing rocks at a momma hen and her baby chicks that were following their momma around in the back yard. It seemed to me that the little rocks we were throwing at them weren't working too well because the momma hen never felt the need to move her babies out of our throwing distance. So I figured I needed to get bigger rocks in order to get that old momma hen's attention. Finding the right size rocks, I picked them up and started throwing the bigger rocks at the old hen. To my horror, one of those rocks landed right smack upside the head of one of the baby chicks. As it flopped around on the ground, the only thing I could think was momma is going to kill me. I didn't have time to dispose of it because Pon'k ran into the house and told momma I had killed one of her baby chickens.

    Momma came out of the house, went and picked the baby chick up and asked me if I had hit the chick with a rock. I couldn't lie because Pon'k and Oyce had witnessed me throwing rocks at the chickens and weren't about to let me off the hook. So I had no choice but to fess up. I may have given that confession a second thought had I remembered the pants I was wearing at the time were much too large for my thin waist and I didn't have a belt to hold them up. I was using a rotten piece of string as a belt. In my moment of fear, I also forgot that I wasn't wearing any underwear. I had been running around all day pulling the pants up as they fell from my waist, then tying and retying the string tighter and tighter. Earlier while retying and tightening the string it had broken in half. It's amazing how fear makes you forget simple things like that, because there was no doubt that I was going to be punished for killing the chick.

    Momma got herself a switch from the nearest tree branch and commenced to swale on my behind. In the process of jumping up and down to soften the blows, my pants fell down around my ankles. So, to this day I can feel the sting of the switch on my naked behind. I found out that day that getting a whipping with my clothes on was a blessing. As I jumped around screaming, "oh mama you're hurting my booty." Pon'k and Oyce laughed as if it was the funniest thing they had ever seen in their lives. I never again threw anything at the chickens or their chicks. There were other incidents solidifying my clumsiness, but those two incidents stands out in mind. Whether by accident or on purpose, I took no joy in killing God's creation. I did, however, understand the laws of nature.

*   *   *   *

    Although I hunted and killed rabbits, squirrels, and sometimes birds, I had a spiritual connection to them. I never saw them as animals that had to be killed, but as a part of nature. And as a part of nature they were sacrificing their lives to keep us fed, so life as we knew it would continue. I would feel sorry for the rabbits after I shot it if it didn't die right away. Many times I held a gasping, dying rabbit or squirrel in my hands, stroking their smooth soft fur with tears in my eyes and asking myself why life was so cruel. Why did something have to die so other things could live? I made sure I was alone when expressing these emotions because my brothers and friends would have thought I was weird, along with being clumsy. When I first started hunting, I was too young to figure out how the laws of nature worked, so I podded along day after day asking myself questions I knew I couldn't answer. All I knew was daddy told me God said that was the way it was supposed to be. So I kept my silence, never telling daddy or my brothers and sisters my feelings because I thought they would laugh at me and call me stupid names. However, I did ask momma because I knew if anyone would understand how I felt, she would.

Momma told me I was a very special little boy who God had blessed with the understanding that all things were meant to live in harmony with each other. But I shouldn't feel bad because we had to eat the animals to stay alive because it is all in God's plan, and we were only doing our part to keep nature in balance. If nothing died or was killed, the earth would get so crowded there would be no place for anything to live, or food for anything to eat. She said as long as I didn't abuse my power over the animals and only used them for food I would be alright. Although I sympathized with the animals I killed, I never hesitated to fill my plate when the food was on the table. Being we were hunters meant we always had dogs around the house.

It is said dog is a man's best friend. I attest to that philosophy, as far as animals are concern, because my greatest connection was to dogs. Because of the many scary ghost stories daddy told us, we children were deathly afraid of walking alone at night. As for myself, this remained true until one Saturday night I stayed at a friend's house longer than I had planned. We were having so much fun I lost track of time and before I knew it, it was dark out and time for me to go home alone. My friend's momma told him he could walk me halfway home, which was about half a mile. When we reached the half way point he told me there was nothing to be afraid of, that he walked at night by himself all the time. I put on a brave face, but I was scared half to death. When my friend turned and left he was out of sight in no time flat because of the darkness. Realizing I was now alone it seemed the darkness enveloped me and left me totally blind.

Being we always had a bunch of dogs around our house that followed us everywhere we went, we were never actually alone. At least one was always with us wherever we went. I don't remember which dog was with me that night, but I was thankful that it was. After my friend left us the dog rubbed against my legs as if to assure me that everything was going to be okay. As I reached down to rub his head, the fear I had experienced a moment ago left me. I figured if something or someone tried to hurt me, my dog would fight it and give me a chance to get away. However, that confidence left me temporarily when the dog started barking and ran ahead of me. I was thinking, "What would happen to me if what the dog was barking at killed the dog before I could get past it. Would we both be doomed?" I peered into the darkness trying to see what the dog was barking at to try and determine if it was dangerous. I called the dog but it didn't obey.

In the state of mind I was in at the time I didn't realize that the sky was partially overcast and the clouds were covering the moon, and that was why it was so dark. As I started to get concerned about my wellbeing, the moon came out from behind the clouds and illuminated the landscape as if someone had turned on a light, and not more than twenty feet in front of me was the dog attacking a possum. I laughed and made the dog leave the possum alone because I had never seen a possum fight anything. All it did was ball itself into a ball and play dead, hoping whatever was biting on it would give up and go away because of its lack of aggression. Because of the moonlight I could see almost as clear as if it were day. The dog was happy that it had gotten a chance to bite something, stayed happily at my side the rest of the way home. When I told daddy about the possum the following day, he said I should've brought it home for lunch.

There were other nights, one or more of our trusty dogs and me braved the cold, still darkness of the Arkansas wild and I survived to tell the tale. My putting total confidence in our dogs contrasted with the confidence I felt when walking home with my brothers and sisters at night. I knew when push came to shove it was every man or woman for themselves and God for us all. They would have run off and left me to face the terrors that came out when the sun went down.

I guess my fascination with animals was because I felt their lives were simpler than that of human beings. They didn't discriminate because they came in different colors, shapes, or sizes. The biggest and meanest male of the species took control of the herd, pack, or whatever, and that was the order of things and the rest of the animals went along with it. Man, on the other hand, was always trying to be better than each other based on skin color or who had the most money. The white folks with money thought they were better'n the black folks and the po' white folks.

The po' white folks felt they may not be as good as the white folks with money, but they were damn sure better'n black folks. It came as a real shock to po' white folk's egos and pride when it was revealed to them that there were well-to-do black folks that were better off than they were, and were treated better by the rich white folks who wanted their hands on that black money. Some of the black farm owners felt they were better'n the po white trash who they put in the same category with the black sharecroppers and field hands who didn't have money. It didn't dampen the black well to do farmer's feeling of superiority over the po white trash, even though that po white trash could have them strung up for disrespecting them because they were white. The women, black and white, measured their success by how much money their husband made. The animal's only worry was staying alive, because God had provided them with everything they needed to survive. So I wished my life, and the lives of the people around me were that simple.

* * * *

Having as many brothers and sisters that we had, it is obvious that we were going to get into fights. The fights lasted no longer than it took for whoever got in the hardest lick. One time me and Biddy, got into a fight about something, and I was dumb enough to intentionally let him pop me upside the head with the thought in mind that it wasn't going to hurt too bad. After the fight was over I realized that was the dumbest thing I had ever done, maybe. I could have avoided the blow easily. In my mind I was pretending to be a boxer. I easily slipped the wild punches Biddy was throwing at me. Like a cocky boxer toying with his opponent, I let his punches get a little closer each time he threw one. I could feel the wind from his fists on my face, as the missing blows got closer and closer to connecting. Then the mental retardation clouded my senses and I just stood there so he could give me his best shot. I closed my eyes, held my breath and told myself it was not going hurt, and even if it did, it wouldn't hurt that bad. Besides, all good fighters had to be able to take a punch and fight on, I was thinking. Well needless to say it did hurt and it hurt badly. I went crying to momma. We had other fights, but this one stands out in my mind because I was stupid enough to let Biddy get a clean shot on me.

* * * *

One day Biddy, Deedie, and myself had just left the house on our way to hunt on the other side of the levee. Being we had to walk through a cotton field to get to the levee, we usually loaded our shotguns as soon as we left the house in case we stumbled across a rabbit before reaching the woods across the levee. As we approached the dirt road that ran from the main highway to the levee, there walking down the road without a care in the world was a small deer. We could tell this wasn't the first time the deer had walked the road because it wasn't afraid. Had it known Biddy was in the area, it would have been afraid because he was known to shoot anything that moved. Biddy, always quick on the trigger said, "Look a deer!" He raised his shotgun and unloaded on it. Boom! The deer jumped into the air as the number six shotgun shell pellets hit it in the side. Lucky for the deer, Biddy was using lightweight bird shot shells. Otherwise it would have been lights out for it. In its haste to get away it got hung up in the fence that separated the soybean and cotton fields. Biddy was hollering for Deedie and me to shoot the deer before it got away. Although my mind was telling me to shoot the deer, for some reason I just stood there and watched as the deer untangled itself, regained its footing and ran back over the levee. Either I couldn't bring myself to shoot it, or the gun wasn't loaded. I can't honestly say which it was. I wasn't afraid to shoot the deer because I was used to shooting animals for food, but this day I guess my killer instincts abandoned me. Biddy never did let us forget that hunting incident. When we got home from hunting, Biddy told daddy what had happened. All daddy said was that was okay because our momma's bible said we weren't supposed to eat anything with split hooves anyway, never mind we ate the heck out of hogs and cows.

* * * *

One cold winter day, with the sounds of the crosscut saw and double blade axes taking chunks out of trees still ringing in our ears, we were returning home with a wagon load of firewood we had just finished cutting in the woods over the levee. Bubba was driving the tractor and daddy was on the tractor with him. Deedie, Biddy, and I were huddled in holes we found at the front of the wagon where the logs we had loaded on the wagon were uneven. Braced against the head of the wagon to avoid the bite of the cold north wind, we were trying to keep warm on the ride home. We had no idea what was going to happen because we had made that trip up and down that levee a thousand times. The levee is a steep dam built by the government to keep the Mississippi River from flooding a long string of communities along its bank that ran through Mississippi, Arkansas, and Louisiana. We had taken the same angle we always took when descending the levee with a wagonload of wood. However, this day Bubba made a slight miscalculation of the angle he had taken and the wagon overturned. The three of us huddled down among the cut trees were so concerned about keeping warm, we didn't even react when we felt the wagon starting to turn over onto its side. On numerous occasions the wagon had tilted and almost turned over while we were coming down the levee when daddy or Bubba had miscalculated the angle, so we felt there was no cause for alarm. Before we realized it the wagon was actually turning over and we were rolling out of the wagon along with the logs. It seemed like we, and the logs were rolling out of the wagon in slow motion. We could see the ends of the logs rolling before our faces as we rolled parallel with them. It was a miracle no one got hurt. We didn't even get a scratch. Our only concern was we had to reload the damn wagon. We thought the incident was funny, not realizing that one or all three of us could have been hurt seriously or even killed by those logs we had on that wagon, because over half of the logs were bigger than we were. The tractor didn't overturn because the trailer hitch was not very strong and it twisted where it was attached to the tractor. We teased Bubba for a long time about his inability to drive a tractor down the side of the levee, although we couldn't drive a lick. He never had another accident driving down the side of the levee.

*   *   *   *

One day I was out in the front yard playing when I came across an ant pile with big black ants scrambling all over the place looking for food to take into their mound. I looked around for a caterpillar or some other insect to throw on the ant pile to watch it squirm as the ant attacked it. I found a sacrificial caterpillar on the side of a tree and threw it on the mound and immediately the ants were all over it. The caterpillar twisted in agony as the ants bit into its flesh. Looking at the size of the caterpillar compared to that of the ants, I didn't believe the ant bite that hard. I got this brilliant idea to test my theory by letting one of the ants bite me. I wanted to personally see how hard the ants could bite. I picked out the biggest ant I could find from the mound and let it bite into my left nipple. The pain was unbelievable, but I didn't dare scream out for fear that someone would see what I had done and would tell every kid in the neighborhood how stupid I was. They would have laughed at me for months. The pain was so excruciating I didn't snatch it off immediately out of fear that would make it hurt even more. When I did attempt to pull it off, the body came off leaving the head still attached to my nipple. With silent tears streaming down my face, I removed the ant's head and ran around to the back of house where no one could see I was crying. I chastised myself for being stupid as the pain continued to throb in my aching nipple. From that day forward I felt sympathy for anything that felled prey to those vicious little creatures. The incident with the ant I can blame on the curiosity of a child, but what my brother did to me was cruel.

A bunch of us boys were playing at a spring that ran from a fairly steep hill into the lake. Where the spring met the lake there was a cove where we could always find crawdads to play with. Sometimes, if there were enough of them, we would take the crawdads home to be cooked and eaten. This particular day it was playtime. I could not think of many things more menacing than the big red and black crawdads with the big pinchers always ready to defend themselves. We would back them into a corner and they would spread their pinchers defensively, and we would use a stick for them to pinch. When they latched onto the stick they refused to let go. Getting them to latch onto the stick was how we got them into the bucket without getting pinched, most of the time. Another way to catch them was to scoop them up in a bucket. Having been pinched picking them up by hands in the past, I knew the pinchers hurt; but the pain was bearable because of the thick skin on our hands and fingers. I had no desire to find out how much the pinchers would hurt on other parts of the body. My brother Biddy had an opposite desire, which was to see how much the pinchers would hurt on other parts of my body.

    We had a habit of trying to make the crawdad fight each other by pressing them face to face. On this particular day while we were having a crawdad fight, my brother Biddy took the crawdad fight to another level when he took his crawdad and let it clamp down on my right ear. I jerk my head so hard trying to get away I jerk the crawdad right out of his hand. It swung on my ear like a pendulum. I'm sure the pinch wasn't as bad as it seemed, but the fear of those giant pinchers clamping down and tearing off my ear was very real. I screamed, cried, and cussed to wake the devil. Everybody laughed as I jumped around thinking my ear was about to come off. Biddy realizing the severity of my fear grabbed me by the shoulders and held me still long enough to yank the crawdad from my ear. Although it seem like the crawdad was on my ear for a long time, in real time it was for only a few seconds. I don't know why when Biddy yanked the crawdad from my ear it didn't rip some flesh off, but it didn't. The pinch of the crawdad only caused my ear to swell slightly, but in my imagination my ear was damaged beyond repair. Although we continued to catch crawdads, I never had another crawdad fight with brother Biddy or came within crawdad pinching distance of him. When we got home I told daddy what Biddy had done. He looked at my ear, predicted I would not lose my hearing, and told Biddy not to do it again. I was mad daddy didn't whip his butt, but there were never any thoughts of revenge.

* * * *

One hot summer day we were chopping cotton in one of the many fields that we had to work in, I had to take a dump. Being this was the harvesting season, all the irrigation ditches around the fields were dry. So I entered one of these ditches to do my thing. While squatting there grunting and straining to relieve myself of the built up waste, a big hornet kept buzzing by my face. It didn't bother me because you get used to bugs and insects invading your space while taking a dump in the woods or ditches adjacent to the cotton fields. I guess this hornet felt I was invading his space because on the last fly by he stuck his stinger right between my eyes. The sting was so painful I didn't realize until I was out of the ditch that my pants were still down around my ankles, and I hadn't wiped my butt. Upon seeing a couple of workers in the field looking at me, the embarrassment caused me to squat among the stalks of the field and wipe my behind with cotton and pull up my pants.

I went and told daddy what had happened. It didn't take any convincing on my part because my face had already started to swell. Since it was a Saturday, we only worked half a day. The workday ended at twelve Noon and I was stung around eleven-thirty, so I had to complete the remaining half hour of the workday. When I got home Momma put some kind of salve on the sting that was supposed to keep the swelling from getting too bad, but it didn't worked as well as momma hoped. Sunday morning when I got out of bed, my eyes was almost swollen completely shut. My brothers and sisters called me a black Chinaman because there were slits where my eyes used to be. Momma had to whip up a new home remedy to battle the swelling. Whatever the concoction was it had the swelling down enough for me to be back at work bright and early Monday morning. It turned out the sting ended up being beneficial to me. As a result of the venom the hornet injected into my system, a wasp sting from then on would swell no bigger than a mosquito bite. The hornet's venom built my immune system to the point the toxins from regular insect bites and wasp stings hardly affected me.

* * * *

One of the most painful memories in my life growing up in the south had to do with the lack of respect shown toward black grown-ups. I have never been able to forget, nor to forgive, watching my daddy, momma, and other grown black men and women say, "Yessuh, and nossuh, yes ma'am, and no ma'am," to little white boys and girls no older than me. This was at every age throughout my childhood after I reached the age of about twelve, just because their daddies and mommas were white. I especially remember one incident when I was nine because my momma took me to Mrs. Betty's grocery store with her to get something. I don't remember what it was, but as we were leaving Mrs. Betty's store, her little eight-year old daughter said, "See ya later Zelma." I told her she should call my momma "Miz Zelma." She said she didn't have to because her momma and daddy told her we were Negroes and she didn't have to say Mr. and Mrs. to Negroes. She then stuck her tongue out at me. I was going to pop her, but my momma grabbed me by the collar and told me it was all right. Mrs. Betty told my momma that she had better teach me some manners or I would end up dead before reaching my twenty-first birthday. My momma said, "yes ma'am" and we left the store.

On our way home I asked momma why white folks can talk to us any ole way they want to and we can't say nuthin back to them. She explained to me the white folks had all the money and all the power, so they made the rules. To paraphrase her, she went on to say, "White men were especially hard on black men and black boys because they fear our strength. The same strength their white women love, which drives them insane. You're going to be called some awful names during your lifetime, but don't let it bother you. Remember, words cannot hurt you." I knew she was giving me sound advice, but her words went in one ear and out the other.

I knew in my heart, that when I grew up I would never stand by passively and say nothing while white folks mistreated or disrespected me or my family. Momma knew it also, because I already had a reputation of having a smart mouth by white folks on the farm. Momma chose to ignore that fact, trying instead to get me to be more concerned about my safety. I told her when I grew up I was going to demand the respect I felt I deserved, and would challenge anyone who disrespected me because I'm black. Momma laughed and said if every black man in America felt as I did, black folks wouldn't be treated the way they were being treated. She then tried to get me to make her a promise that I wouldn't do anything intentionally that would make white folks wants to hurt me. Of course I promised, but I knew living up to that promise depended on the severity of my encounters with white folks. The conditions under which we lived as black folks when I was a child growing up in the south didn't make keeping promises of non-violence easy.

Having to go to the back of white owned restaurants to pick up our food irritated me also. I would look through the windows of these restaurants and see white customers sitting at tables covered with white or checkered tablecloths enjoying their meals and I would get angry. When I went around to the back of the restaurant to pick my food up, I would get angry all over again knowing my daddy was paying the same price for the food as the white folks sitting in the restaurant eating. I wanted to know why we weren't allowed to sit down at a table and eat like other human beings. I was told that was how things were in the south. The craziest thing about getting angry at not being allowed to eat in the white owned restaurants was the food wasn't that good. Momma and most of the other black women on the farms could cook rings around the cooks in those restaurants. I only got to eat restaurant food when daddy let me tag along whenever he won some money gambling or sold some moonshine whiskey, which only happened occasionally. Another area that raised my young, hostile ire was the segregated movie theater.

Sitting in the balcony of the theater, I would think of all kinds of nasty things I could dump on the head of those racist, so-and-so's sitting below, snug a bug in a rug. It never crossed my mind that not all of the white kids in Arkansas hated me. I condemned them all because of what Mrs. Betty's daughter said about momma, and the foreman's little red headed eleven year old jerk of a son who acted like he was boss over all black folks because his daddy was the foreman on the farm. It really didn't matter what I fantasized about dumping on the white kids below. I knew I wouldn't because we very seldom had money to go to the movies, so we weren't about to get thrown out for doing something stupid. Besides, if the white ushers found out who did the dumping, that person would be banned from the movie house for life. The only thing we got away with was an occasional spilling of popcorn over the edge of the balcony. Even the spilling of popcorn would bring threats of expulsion of everyone in the balcony from the movie house, or threats of physical harm from the white patrons below.

* * * *

In between the harvesting and planting season on a farm, December-March, there were some lean times financially. To assist the black unemployed families on the farms during this time of year, the government subsidized our diet with blocks of cheese, half-gallon cans of peanut butter, big ten-pound cans of luncheon meat, rice, beans, and cans of salmon called commodities. We didn't view this food as something to be ashamed of receiving because the government was giving white plantation owners thousands of dollars for some reason or another every year. Daddy said it was for not growing too much cotton so the government could control the price. As a matter of fact, we looked forward to daddy coming home with that food because we could super-size our sandwiches by cutting the meat and cheese into big thick slices, and eat something besides those damn salmon paddies. The peanut butter was mostly eaten with a spoon because momma couldn't keep enough bread in the house. I would find the biggest spoon I could and load it up with peanut butter and walk around the house licking it as if it was an ice cream cone. I loved the way it stuck to the roof of my mouth, because I could use the tip of my tongue to push a little bit at a time onto my tongue where I could eat it without swallowing it all at one time. Another reason we appreciated the food was because we had bottomless pits for stomachs. Very seldom did I have the luxury of saying I was full after each meal.

* * * *

While growing up we played a lot of baseball. I was the sorriest of the bunch, compared to my older brothers. We would buy ten-cent rubber balls from the dime store, which were half the size of a regular baseball, and play strikeout. No matter how hard I tried, I couldn't strike Deedie out to save my life. He would have me chasing the ball all over the place. Eventually I would just have to give up and quit. Even when the balls were broken in half and I could throw outside curveballs, dome portion left, inside curveballs, dome portion right, sinkerballs, dome portion bottom, and rising balls, dome portion on top; Deedie still managed to send me in the house mad. Biddy wasn't as good a baseball player as Deedie, but I had problems with him also. Meanwhile, Deedie and Biddy had very little trouble striking me out. I am sure if Deedie had been in the right situation he could have played professionally, because not only could he hit the ball he was an excellent outfielder. They said Bubba, my oldest brother, was also an excellent baseball player, but all I remember him playing was a lot of pretty girls. Whenever we ran out of balls we would tear the heads off our sisters' baby dolls and use them for balls. You can imagine the fights we had because of that.

Since I was lousy at baseball, I took up the game of basketball at the age of thirteen and was determined to be as good as everyone else at something. In addition to playing against my brothers and the neighborhood boys, I would practice alone against imaginary foes in one hundred degree heat in the summer and on frozen ground and snow in the winter. When there was snow on the ground, the basketball wouldn't bounce, so I would just shoot the ball wherever it landed when I missed a shot. Folks thought I was crazy for playing basketball alone in the snow and freezing weather. I just wanted to be as good as everyone else in something. I never got the chance to develop my basketball game in high school because I dropped out of school in the tenth grade and followed my brothers when they joined the Job Corp.

* * * *

The majority of the houses we lived in were run down shacks with roofs that leaked when it rained, and cracks in the walls. Daddy repaired the roofs and walls as best he could. There weren't many complaints in the summer, except when it rained. Momma would use half the pots and pans in the house on occasions to catch the water leaking through the holes in some of those roofs. The cracks in the walls and roof served as a form of ventilation during the hot summer, so there were very few complaints. There were plenty of complaints during the winter because the cold winds cut right through our clothing, while sitting on the couch or floor, watching television. I thank God for the blankets and quilts momma covered us with at night, because they were so thick and warm we could've slept under them at the North Pole without so much as a shiver. The cracks also made it hard to keep the house warm on cold days during the winter, so we went through a lot of firewood to keep the house as warm as possible until bedtime. It helped to keep the wind out when we stuffed paper in the cracks and holes, and nailed blankets over the windows at night to keep the wind out. To help combat the cold, whatever you were wearing at bedtime is what you slept in. As if the run down condition of the houses wasn't enough, we also had to deal with rodents and roaches.

The rats and roaches considered themselves a part of the family. It was a daily occurrence whereby either momma or daddy would complain about the rats eating holes in the flour sacks, the bean sacks, or oatmeal sacks. Daddy would set mousetraps throughout the house at night and would check them every morning. If he caught any rats during the night, he would take a stick and knock them upside their pointy little heads killing them instantly. If he didn't feel like checking the traps he would tell us boys to check for him. We took great pride in being able to crack those little suckers head open with one swing of our sticks. Still, that didn't control the rat population in our house. It was nothing to be watching television at night and look over and in the corner, or on the arm of the couch you're sitting on, and see a rat watching television with you. I remember many a night we would sit in the living room at night shooting at the rats with a BB gun. If you couldn't see the body of the rat, you could see their tiny eyes glowing in the darkness in the cracks in the walls. Not being very good shots with the BB guns, the rats would stop to see what caused the noise when the BB hit close to them and would continue on in their search for food, or where ever they were going.

As for the roaches, when a fire was made the roaches beat us to the heaters in the morning. The counter top in the kitchen would almost be covered with them. The roaches got into the oatmeal, grits, and beans. Momma had to wash everything really good before preparing the daily meals. They would even crawl across the T.V. screen at night when the light was off. Daddy used to kick the cats when he caught them playing with the roaches, and when we asked him why he kicked the cats for playing with the roaches, he would say the cats' job was to catch rats, not roaches.

* * * *

It wasn't all work growing up in the country. We managed to have fun as well. In the summer when we weren't working we went swimming in the lake, although we couldn't swim. Maybe I should call it wading instead of swimming, but we had fun regardless of what it was called. We climbed trees and swung on vines in the woods pretending to be the great white ape, Tarzan. As children, we didn't see the racist incantation that one white man could rule the whole black continent of Africa because he had a catchy yell and a bowie knife. We paid no attention to the fact that in each movie, the natives always killed their fellow Africans that were working for the white safari hunters before they actually killed any white folks. It never crossed my mind to ask my parents why white men in America slept with black women all the time, but Tarzan was never even shown talking to one, when there was nothing but black women in Africa. Or why they led us to believe Tarzan remained a virgin until a white woman happened to show up in the jungle. Did we really believe that Tarzan would rather sleep with female apes than to mess with a black woman? Regardless of the questions never asked, Tarzan was an impressive figure. At other times we played hide-go-seek in the cotton and soybean fields. You would think it was impossible to find anyone considering the size of the fields, but it was not because we would only go a certain distance from where home base had been established.

In the fall we roamed from farm to farm eating watermelons out of the fields, big juicy apples and peaches off of the trees. We ate big red ripe tomatoes out of the gardens, wild purple and green grapes off the vines, and persimmons off the trees. We would gather the fallen pa'cons (pecans) and sell them for extra cash for the family. Sometimes we laid in a meadow of browning grass and watched the clouds passing overhead, pointing out animal shapes.

The winter was spent mostly hunting for game and cutting firewood. If it snowed, we built snowmen and had some serious snowball fights. Whenever we ran across frozen ponds we would pretend to be world famous ice skaters. I enjoyed when it snowed. I would bundle up and go for long walks, sticking out my tongue to catch snowflakes as they fell along the way. I would look at the fresh fallen snow and think, "This must have been what the world was like in the beginning of time before man screwed everything up, pure and unblemished." To me the snow represented purity and as I walked, I wished man could somehow return the earth to its' original form before we lost favor with God.

* * * *

As Sister Pon'k is fond of saying, Sister Sue was just lowdown sometimes. One Saturday we were eating sardines. I don't remember where we got them from, but every kid in the house had their own can. I sat and watched while everyone ate their can of sardines. When their sardines were gone, I opened mine and enjoyed the wanton look on their faces. Sue asked for some of mine. I told her no. She waited until I had eaten about half of my sardines and said, "Ugh Bobo, there was a fly in your sardines and you ate it." Being I had been shooing the nasty black flies away from my sardines since I started eating them, it was highly possible she was telling the truth. Visualizing the flies I had watched eating rotting animal carcasses and human feces, I became nauseous. I ran outside and threw up. Sue laughed at me while she finished off the remainder of my can of sardines. I don't recall how many years passed before I could eat sardines without getting nauseous, because I always associated sardines with nasty black flies. I never told Sue what affect her saying that I had eaten a fly had on me. Again, as Sister Pon'k would say, that was just lowdown. Sister Sue wasn't the only annoying big sister I had.

Sister Teenie wasn't as mean as Sue, but she had an annoying habit that drove us nuts. When she was holding us kids trying to get us to go to sleep, she would pinch our ears and suck her tongue. Once she got into that ear pinching, tongue sucking zone, there was no stopping her. The more we squirmed trying to get away from her, the tighter she held on. We swore when she died and went to heaven she would be pinching on God's ear and sucking her tongue.

Sue and Teenie was just annoying big sisters to us younger kids, but to momma they were her young ladies who she worried about every time they went out and was late coming home on weekends. I remember many Saturdays late at night momma would be sitting at the window staring out into the darkness praying for God to keep them safe because she didn't know where they were. She worried about them because most of the men they messed with were older boozers, womanizers, gamblers, and some of them were as mean as hornets. I would hear her praying to God to protect them from harm. Most of the time when I came into the room and asked her what was the matter, she would tell me to go back to bed. But on other occasions she would let me crawl into her lap. She would stroke my nappy head and hum soothing songs until I went back to sleep. I promised her when I grew up I wouldn't do anything that would keep her up late at night waiting for me to come home because I might be getting into trouble. I didn't know if Sue and Teenie was getting into trouble, but it couldn't be good if momma was sitting up at all times of the night worrying whether they were going to make it home alive almost every time they went out. Again, because I supported momma at times like this, I was called a momma's boy. I wore that momma's boy tag like a badge of honor because she was the most important person in my life.

*   *   *   *

Growing up in the country, most boys were not afraid of things like bugs, frogs, lizards, and snakes. That is why it didn't bother us to run around barefoot. We ran barefoot through the woods playing. We walked barefoot through briar patches picking wild black berries where snakes were known to hide out. We walked barefoot through garbage dumps with broken glass and boards with rusty nails all over the place. Occasionally we would cut our feet on something, but momma or daddy would patch it up and we would be on our way. We even went snake hunting barefoot. Country boys were rare breed when we were growing up.

*   *   *   *

Although Daddy was a good provider and strict disciplinarian, he had a sick sense of humor on occasions. He came home drunk one night after a night on the town of drinking and gambling and started cussing and fussing. He grabbed the shotgun in the living room, woke everyone up and told us to come into the living room and announced he was going to kill everybody in the damn house. Knowing Daddy had a reputation of meaning what he said and kicking butt, we didn't wait around to find out if he was joking or not. We knew for ourselves he wasn't afraid of anything. Growling dogs protecting their puppies or getting their food taking away from them, backed down from him. Setting hens protecting their nests or their baby chicks backed down from him. Large angry men backed down from him. He would go hunting in graveyards in the middle of the night alone. When other people would spend time looking for a stick to kill a snake, he would stump it to death with the heels of his boots. We were told he had spent time in prison for killing some white folks for some reason or another. We figured if he had the guts to kill white folks and they didn't hang him, white folk would probably give him a medal for getting rids of a dozen black kids. So we ran outside and hid until momma came to the door and called for us to come back into the house, where daddy was sitting at the kitchen table laughing with tears running down his face because he thought it was funny he had scared us half to death.

On the flip side, daddy could be very humble. He used to tell about the time Bubba stepped on a rusty nail and the wound got infected and he almost died. As he told the story, his eyes would get moist remembering he almost lost his oldest son. Bubba had been playing barefoot in a junkyard and stepped on a board with a rusty nail in it. As usual, momma cleaned the puncture wound as best she could, put some salve on it, and wrapped the foot with a strip of cloth and life continued. Several days later the wound became infected and Bubba's foot had swollen to almost twice its normal size. Nothing daddy and momma tried made the swelling go down, and he developed a fever they couldn't break. Having no other alternative, they took him to see a doctor. The doctor examined Bubba's foot and his diagnosis was disheartening. He told daddy the nail Bubba had stepped on was rusty and had resulted in Bubba getting tetanus, which in turn, caused the foot to get infected and gangrene to set in. The doctor said because of the seriousness of the infection, not only could he not save Bubba's foot, he doubted if there was anything that he could do to save his life; not even an amputation of the foot would help because the infection was in his blood stream. The doctor said they had waited too long to save their son. He recommended daddy and momma start making funeral arrangements to bury their son.

Weak from fever and unable to stand, daddy took Bubba

home and made the decision to take him to a root doctor, which to some meant a voodoo doctor. He said he had nothing to lose, plus he was tired of hearing momma say they were going to lose their son. Besides, he was very skeptical of anything a doctor had to say, especially white doctors who didn't really care if black folks lived or died. After the first visit to Madame Montaine, the fever was broken and the swelling in his foot started to go down. Daddy said the medicine the voodoo lady used to bathe Bubba' foot in, after making in incision the length of his foot, stunk too high heaven, but he preferred the stink to losing his son. In two weeks, Bubba was up and running around as usual. Other than common colds, it should be noted that Bubba has not been sick since then. However, I thought the poison that was in his foot went to his head when he got older. I say this because Bubba and a couple of his friends got a hair processing kit to straighten their hair. The concoction they used had lye as its base. The stuff was so strong it ate the skin off of their forehead everywhere they had failed to apply enough salve to protect the exposed skin. The stuff worked and straightened his hair, but Bubba would huff and puff while the stuff was burning his scalp. After each usage, he swore the burning of his head to have hair like white folks were not worth it. It took several of those head burning treatment before he got serious, and before we realized it, he was his nappy-headed self again.

* * * *

Although daddy scared the hell out of us when he came home drunk on occasions, as I related earlier, there was one incident where we found the courage to stand our ground. As soon as daddy walked through the door, everyone could tell he was drunk and he was in a foul mood. We tensed immediately because we knew the slightest provocation on anyone's part would set him off. We also knew it was only a matter of time before someone gave him that reason, and no one wanted the honor of having to say it was their fault he went off on us. He stomped around the house huffing and puffing, preparing himself for the reason that would allow him to let off some steam. I don't remember what momma said or did, but she ended up in the crosshairs of daddy's tirade. He lit into her as if possessed by the devil himself. Daddy started yelling and cussing that she wasn't the wife he thought she was. She didn't keep the house clean most of the time, which everyone knew was not true. She was the reason us kids were so bad, that if she would whip our butts sometimes instead of waiting for him to get home we would behave better. If momma whipped us for everything we did wrong it would have taken up most of her day. Momma let him vent until he said she no longer satisfied him in bed. Upon hearing this, she told him he had better watch what he said before he said something he didn't mean. He started to say something further, but momma cut him off in mid-sentence and told him to stop acting like a drunken fool and leave her alone. When she turned to walk away, daddy grabbed her by the arms and said if she attempted to pull away from him, he was going to beat the daylight out of her.

    We kids knew momma wasn't going to stand there and accept anymore of daddy's abusive language or adhere to his threats, which meant he was going to have to beat her if he was to be taken seriously in the future. We kids didn't even think twice about what we were going to do, because we knew we weren't going to stand by while daddy beat on our momma under any circumstances. When daddy grabbed momma by the arms, without thinking, we kids squeezed between them surrounding momma. Daddy said if we didn't get out of the way he would kill us all. We didn't move letting him know we were willing to die to protect her. Daddy watched in amazement as his children stood their ground and maintained the wedge between him and their momma. He broke out laughing like a man who was going insane. When the laughter ended, he said he should get his shotgun and kill us all. Instead of showing any fear, we showed him we were willing to die to protect momma by standing our ground. He said we were all like our momma anyway, and walked out of the house.

    Several hours later he returned home a different man, but we were still on high alert in case he went ballistic again. To our surprise when daddy came back home, he asked us all to gather around, he wanted to talk to us. Reluctantly, we gathered around him in the living room. Daddy became misty eyed as he told us how proud he was of us that we were willing to die to protect our momma. He promised he would never raise his hand against her again, and true to his word, he never did. Still, every time he came home drunk and raised his voice toward momma we were poised to intervene.

* * * *

For a while daddy sold bootleg whiskey, mostly on Sundays when the stores was closed and they couldn't get beer or wine. Whenever someone wanted to buy a bottle or a fruit jar of the stuff and there wasn't any more in the house, daddy would tell one of us where his stash was and we would to go and get it. In the summer time it would be like the twelfth cotton row from the house, fifty paces from the road buried in a burlap sack. In the winter it would be in the hen house in the left corner behind the chicken roost, or under the woodpile out in the backyard. He also provided bootleg whiskey to the folks who came to the house to gamble. When they got drunk, some of them acted a stone fool and daddy would have to throw them out. I don't remember anyone getting killed while daddy held these crap-shooting games at the house, but there were several fights.

Being Daddy provided a place for the men to gamble, he would get a cut of the winners winning and a cut on every pot when the shooter crapped out, (threw three) or snake-eyes (two) on their first roll. We children learned some catchy phases, which are common now, listening to the men rolling the dice. "Come on baby, momma, the children, and my woman, need a new pair shoes, new clothes, a new dress." "If I don't throw a seven, Jesus is a nigger." "Come on baby, white man riding my ass because I'm behind on the rent." "Never shoot craps on a white woman's grave. It's just plain bad luck."

* * * *

As I stated earlier, daddy was a hard worker. I don't remember anyone being able to out work him, at least not anyone we ever met. He could pick as much as four or five hundred pounds of cotton a day, and believe me that was a lot of picking. I was not blessed with the ability to pick as much cotton as he did, or as much as the other boys in the clan. The only boys I could pick more cotton than was Will and my baby brother Gene, who was too young to pick cotton at all.

Daddy berated any man who wouldn't work, or do whatever it took to provide for his family. He used to say we would never starve or go without clothing, even if he had to steal or rob banks. I admired him for that conviction. He always said hard work never hurt anyone. However, because of an incident that occurred one day when we were headed home from the field, I had a saying also, "The work may not kill you but getting to and from the field sure as hell can." I said this because around the age of eight, we were returning home from the cotton field and daddy got in a race with a truck that had passed him on the highway. Being the competitor he was daddy was determined to overtake the truck. While speeding along at a high rate of speed, the hood of the car flew up, cracking the windshield and stayed in place blocking daddy's vision. Bubba, who were riding shotgun, stuck his head out the window on the passenger side of the car and tried to guide daddy to the shoulder of the road. Daddy slowed down and tried to ease off the road. There was a small drop off from the pavement onto the dirt, so when the front tire dropped off the pavement onto the dirt he thought he was running off the road and panic, he over compensated and swerved all the way to the opposite lane into oncoming traffic. We ran head-on into a car coming in the opposite direction. There must have been at least eight people in our car. We were sitting in each other's laps, there so many of us. After the crash, we piled out of the car dazed. While daddy was asking everyone if they were okay, someone yelled, "Bobo is bleeding." In the excitement of the moment, I hadn't realized I had bitten through my bottom lip. At seeing the blood running out of my mouth onto my shirt, it was hard for anyone to convince me I wasn't dying. I don't know how long I bawled, but bawled I did. The ironic part of the wreck was I was the only individual who attained any sort of injury out of both cars involved in the accident. Throughout the rest of my childhood, I used to ask why I was the only one to get hurt in that wreck. The question remains unanswered today because I don't know what lesson I was supposed to learn from it. Unless it was to convince me to get the hell off that farm, which I did at age sixteen. The description of that car is forever etched in my mind. It was a 1955 Chevy Bel-Aire, pink and gray, with chrome moldings.

* * * *

Another incident that stays with me is the morning me, Biddy and Deedie awoke with daddy whipping us with an extension cord. The bad thing about the whipping was, in our hearts, we knew it was probably coming. Daddy required us to fill the chip bucket with chips of wood along with kindling that was use every morning to start a fire for heating the house and the cook stove. For some reason he started making the fires in the stoves instead of continuing to make us do it. The bucket was also used to discard the ashes removed from the wood stoves from the previous day's burning. This particular evening instead of emptying the ash from the chip bucket, as we usually did, which was three quarter full, we all agreed to just finish filling the bucket with chips and hope daddy would let us off with a warning for not emptying the ash. When he got up to make the fires the following morning, everything was ok when he used the chips and kindling to make the fire in the kitchen because he took chips and kindling out of the bucket by hand, but when he dumped the content of the bucket in the stove in the living room to make a fire it was butt whipping time. Talk about being stupid and naïve.

* * * *

While we were living in Wabash, Arkansas, there was a school bully called Little Pinky. Everyone was afraid of him because his dad, Big Pinky, had spent the majority of his life in prison and Little Pinky, they said, would go to the prison and help his daddy work off his time. Rumors had Little Pinky staying as long as six months locked up with his daddy and fighting off grown-ups who tried to whip his butt while he was there.

Little Pinky and his friends had a habit or taking the little kids lunch money. If the kids had no money and brought a bag lunch instead, they would take it and eat it. If memory serves me right, Little Pinky was about thirteen and I was around ten or eleven when our paths crossed the first time. I don't want to give anyone the impression that I was not afraid of Little Pinky. He just happened to mess with something that I was willing to die for, my school lunch. I must have been the hungriest child God ever put on the face of the earth. I was constantly in a state of starvation no matter how much I had eaten for breakfast, and always looked forward to lunchtime to temporarily appease the hunger monster that dwelled in my bottomless pit.

Well this day, Little Pinky walked over to where I was sitting and demanded that I give him my lunch. When I refused, he grabbed the greasy bag out of my hands. Without giving a second thought to the fact that he was going to beat me senseless, I tore into him with everything my ten or eleven year old body possessed. I got in several blows because he was surprised to have a kid fighting him back. During the surprise attack, he dropped the lunch bag. After gathering himself, he popped me upside the head a few times and called me a crazy little Nigga. He told me if I wanted that greasy sandwich bad enough to get my butt whupped for it, to go ahead and eat it. Through my tears I ate my lunch, and dared anyone to try and take it away. I don't for the life of me remember what I had taken to school for lunch that day, but it didn't matter because to me all food was good food.

The second run in with Little Pinky was that following summer while we were picking up stumps clearing a field for the next years planting. He was picking on the little kids in the field. When he got to me, he called me that crazy little Nigga who had fought him at school over a greasy sandwich and asked if I had the guts to fight him again. Since there was no food involved, I was hesitant to fight him, but pride got the best of me when he pushed me and dared me to fight him. All I can say is, the fat lip I received courtesy of Little Pinky was worth the fight because he left me alone after that, physically anyway. Daddy had witnessed the fight and said he was proud of me for standing up for myself against Little Pinky. He assured me that in time I would be able to whip him because I fought just like he did at that age. My bird chest swelled with pride at the confidence my daddy had in me. There was one more unfortunate incident me and two of my brothers had with Little Pinky, but not of a violent nature.

    Little Pinky set Biddy, Deedie and me up, unknowingly to us, that same summer while we were chopping cotton near a house where he went with his daddy to shoot dice. His daddy was on parole for the umpteenth time. Little Pinky broke into the man's house and stole a bunch of silver dollar coins. He knew about the coins because he had been to the man's house with his daddy gambling on several occasions. He put the coins in four separate bags and buried the money on our cotton rows, and his own, where there was grass that had to be cleared to insure we would find it. Little Pinky chopped along beside us and pretended to be surprised when his hoe hit the bag of coins he buried there. Then he pointed out the freshly turned dirt on each of our rows and said he bet there were bags of coins buried on our rows as well. We anxiously dug into the earth to uncover the hidden loot. Sure enough the clink, clink as the hoes hit the bags confirmed Little Pinky's prediction. Pretending to be honest, Little Pinky said the money probably belonged to old man Gilman who lived in the area. He said he knew for a fact the old man buried money in the field all the time. He suggested that he be allowed to return it since he knew who probably buried it there. Being we had been taught to never take anything that didn't belong to us, we were afraid to keep the money because there was no way we would be able to spend that amount of money without daddy and momma finding out about it. The storeowner would be the first to ask daddy and momma where we got all the money we would be spending there. Since Little Pinky told us he knew who the money belonged to, and if we kept it we would get in trouble, we agreed it was a good idea that he returned the money to its rightful owner. He said the old man probably wouldn't miss three dollars, as he gave each of us a silver dollar. Little Pinky reburied the money and said he would return it to the old man after we got off from work that evening.

Several days later a policeman stopped by our house and told momma and daddy that Little Pinky had been locked up for breaking into the man's house and stealing the money, and during questioning said we had helped him break into the house and steal the money. After Deedie explained to the policeman how we came across the money on our cotton rows, the police knew Little Pinky had set us up. We gave the money to the policeman and nothing more was said about the incident, except daddy making sure we had not stash any additional coins in our room. Later in life, at the age of nineteen, Little Pinky was shot and kill in a crap (dice) game over a penny.

According to daddy, straight from the mouth of an eyewitness, Little Pinky was gambling at one of the local gambling houses and talking a lot of noise as usual. An old stranger from out of town was shooting dice for the first time in the great state of Arkansas. He told Little Pinky that he talked too much and gambled too little. Little Pinky, never the one to back down from a confrontation, told the old dude to worry about himself before his mouth made a threat that his behind couldn't back up. Everyone who shot dice at these gambling houses knew there were two things a young gambler didn't do. One, it was never a good idea to threaten an old man with bodily harm if you weren't ready to back it up, because old men didn't take threats lightly. The average old gambler had been in a knife or gunfight at some point in their lives and had an ingrained will to survive. Two, the quickest way to get killed was to try and cheat an old gambler out of his hard earned money. Little Pinky had committed mistake number one early in the game. Later on that evening, Little Pinky covered a two dollar bet of the old stranger with coins. The old man started to count the coins to ensure they amounted to two dollars. Little Pinky got indignant and belittled the old man for doubting his honesty. The old man said, "Okay son, but if you are one cent short I'm going to kill your loud mouth ass." Little Pinky told the old stranger to shut up and shoot the dice. Little Pinky must have had a premonition of what the old man was going to roll because he caught the first two rolls before telling the old dude to go for what he knew. With one roll of the dice Little Pink's fate was sealed. The old stranger rolled a seven. As the old stranger gathered the money, Little Pinky prepared himself for the forthcoming confrontation, because he knew he was a penny short when he covered the bet. The old stranger counted the coins. He looked at Little Pinky shaking his head. Little Pinky wasn't afraid because he had been threatened with death on numerous occasions.

The old stranger simply told Little Pinky he was a penny short, and wanted him to make it right. Little Pinky told the old man he wasn't going to pay him a damn thing. He'd better be happy he got as much as he did, and if he didn't like it, he could either go for what he knew or he could go to hell. After making his bold statement Little Pinky must have sensed the old stranger was serious about killing him because he reached for the gun he had in the waistband of his pants, but he never got it out. While Little Pinky was busy running off at the mouth, the old stranger had taken his 38-caliber pistol from its holster and had it at his side. When Little Pinky reached for his gun, the old stranger simply raised his pistol and blew Little Pinky's brains out.

When the police arrived at the scene of the shooting, and saw it was Little Pinky that had been killed, they didn't even make a report of the incident. They told the old stranger he had done them a favor because they were going to have to kill Little Pinky sooner or later anyway.

* * * *

I used to love listening to the old men in the community tell what it was like when they were growing up because they were mainly the ones that caught true hell in this land of equality. They were the ones who had to figure out how to be respected by their family, and at the same time be humble and subservient to the white man. The alternative was to be a one-day headline, or just another Negro to disappear in this great land of justice for all. They were the ones who were denied the right to vote, or the right to use public facilities their tax dollars helped to build. They were the ones who went off to fight in America's wars to help free people in foreign lands and to help keep America "the land of the free and the home of the brave," only to return home and find that nothing had changed for black America. In many cases in the south, the black soldiers returning home were hung for wearing their military uniforms. They were the ones who did whatever it took to provide for their family, to send their children to school to make life better for the next generation. They passed on the knowledge of how to make the earth work for them, while allowing the white man to believe it was his idea. They were the ones who never stopped smiling no matter what racist obstacles America threw in their paths. They talked about how white men raped their mommas, sisters, daughters, and there was nothing they could do about it. And when it was reported to the justice system, the police laughed at them while they were making the report. They talked about how common it was for white men to come to black men's homes and drag them out and hang them right in their own front yard with the family watching. They survived for kids like me, who they knew would be willing to pick up the torch, add fuel to the flame, and try to make things better for the next generation.

    I found it amazing that they were still alive because I didn't think I could have stood by and let white men abuse me, or my family, without retaliating. I was awed by their strength and pride, knowing no matter what the white man did to them, they were able to keep their families intact and survived because they knew there were better days ahead for black folks in America. They told stories about the drinking, gambling, fighting, and black on black killing. Using grown folks language, I said I wouldn't be a part of the black on black killing stuff when I grew up. I said I wouldn't give them honkies the satisfaction of seeing me act a fool. The old gents took pride in being able to pass on their wisdom of life, and actually see a kid believing in them.

*   *   *   *

On hot summer days leaning on my hoe, straw hat in hand, watching the high flying airplanes with streams of smoke screaming from their tails, I wondered what it would be like to soar through the heavens where there was no more racism and hatred, where everyone treated each other as equal. Usually I would be awakened from my daydreaming by my daddy yelling at me to get back to work. I would tell him about how I wished someday, when I grew up, I would be able to fly a plane. How I would be so important that these old hateful white folks would never bother me again. And I wouldn't have to spend the rest of my life chopping and picking cotton in hundred degrees heat. Daddy would tell me to get those foolish thoughts out of my head because black folks didn't fly airplanes, and even if they could, white folks wouldn't let them. He said white folks wouldn't allow me to do anything other than work on the farm, so I had better get used to it. When I told him about the Tuskegee Airmen, he said those were rich black folks who the white folks let pass because they needed pilots to help fight the war. He assured me no black men were flying the planes I saw flying overhead. I ignored what daddy was saying because usually he was more positive than that. I figured he was having a bad day.

I didn't blame my daddy for not encouraging my brothers, sisters, and me to get an education, or to dream of farm free days in the future. All he ever knew was hard work, and without an education, he didn't know anything about using an education to get ahead. He was the first generation in the history of his family that was not directly tied to slavery in Mississippi, and was the first to go to school. His schooling was interrupted because his labor was needed on the farm. He learned very little and had to quit after the second year of school. The legacy his daddy left to him was to respect the white man, do as you were told, work your butt off, and hope that things would get better someday. The legacy daddy left with me was work your butt off to get what you want, respect those who respect you, and things will get better someday.

You can imagine the dreams I had when it was reported

that man had walked on the moon in 1961. In my imagination, I was the first man on the moon. I had gone there and claimed the moon for black folks. No white folks were allowed unless I gave them permission to come, and then they couldn't be in charge of anything because they didn't know how to share power with anyone. Sometimes I miss those carefree days when my mind took me to anyplace in the world I wanted to go on a whim.

When I wasn't daydreaming about flying airplanes, or going to the moon to get away from the farm, I would find myself watching every cloud in the sky for any sign of rain. It was a child's fantasy come true when it would rain hard enough to keep them out of the cotton fields for a day or two. We didn't care that sometimes we would have to wade through mud when we went back to work. We would spend those days off fishing or just playing. I remember one place we used to go play where there was a sandy bluff we would jump off of. The drop had to be at least twenty feet, but the sand was so loose it was like jumping into a big sandbox. I don't remember who was involved, but one day one boy didn't get out of the way of the jumper behind him in time and got jumped on, resulting in a broken arm. That was the end of that fun because we were forbidden from playing there again, because it was deemed too dangerous. In reality that was one of the safer activities we engaged in. One of the most dangerous activities we engaged in was swimming.

We couldn't swim worth a darn, but at our favorite part of the lake there was a vine that we use to swing out over the water. The brave ones would hang onto the vine low enough so that when they went out over the lake they could drag their feet in the water. The vine provided a lot of fun filled days until one day too many boys got on it at the same time. Biddy, Deedie, Roy, and L.C. pushed off the bank and went sailing into the air over the lake. Their laughing, whooping, and screams of joy were cut short. It took a couple of second before we realized what was happening. The laughter turned to yells of panic when the vine broke and they plummeted downward toward the water. To us on the bank it was holy crap the vine broke, as we watched flailing arms and legs splash into the lake. Those were anxious moments for me because I knew neither one of my brothers could swim very well. I watched horrified as thin arms and legs thrashed and kicked as they made it close enough to the bank of the river to stand up. I was relieved because they lived to tell the tale. I don't know whether it was because they were okay, or if I was being mean because they scared me half to death, but I laughed at them when they stumbled onto the lake bank, soaking wet. The memory of my brothers near drowning in the lake brings me to my near death experience while wading in the waters of the muddy Mississippi river.

  You would be surprised at what washed ashore onto the bank of the river. You would find basketballs, tennis balls, baby dolls, dishes, mattresses, old washing machines and dryers, refrigerators, etc. The major appliances were never useable, but every once in a while we would find tennis balls, rubber balls, and dolls that was in good shape. We had been searching the riverbank for toys we might be able to use. Every now and then we waded in the shallow pools left in the depressions by the receding river water for no particular reason. We came to a pool only I was foolish enough to enter. No one else would enter the pool because they knew although the water looked to be only about chest deep, there was a lot of mud in the bottom of it. I figured my height would compensate for the mud. In I went.

  I took about five steps into the pool, and the water came up to my chest but mostly because of the mud. When I tried to turn around, I found myself stuck in the mud, and sinking fast. After some struggling I managed to turn around, but by this time I had sunk to the point I had to hold my head back to keep my face from going under. I knew I was in a bad situation, but I didn't panic. I remembered daddy telling us if we found ourselves in a dangerous situation don't panic because if you do you can't think your way out of it. I started calling for help, but my brothers and friends thought I was playing because the water wasn't that deep. They laughed and told me to stop messing around and walked off. The mud felt like a vise around my legs. It seemed the more I struggled, the deeper I sank into the mud. Not until the muddy water started entering my mouth, and I was blowing it out of my nose was I able to escape the vise like grip the mud had around my legs. I don't know where the strength came from, but I pulled myself free of the mud and made my way out of the water. I spit out muddy water for what seemed like an hour, before running to catch up with my brothers and friends. I was mad at them because they hadn't believed I was in trouble when I was stuck in the mud. The taste of that muddy water stayed with me for several days. It was probably mental, but the taste of that muddy water stayed with me a long time.

*   *   *   *

    I remember sitting around the kitchen watching while momma cooked. It didn't matter what meal it was, it was just a joy to watch. My older brothers would get up and start the fire before she got up in the mornings. Cooking breakfast she would have bacon, sausage, or salmon paddies going in one skillet, flapjacks in another, oatmeal or grits in a pot big enough to feed an army, and dozens of biscuits baking in the oven. During hard times we would only have salmon paddies, biscuits and molasses for our breakfast meal. It didn't matter, I stilled watched. I can't remember her ever burning the food. She had to learn to multi-task while cooking because she was cooking for an army. And we were always hungry. Sometimes during the day when daddy and the older children were at work in the field momma would make flapjacks and put molasses on them. It was a real treat because I didn't have to battle the older kids, only a couple younger ones, for my fair share. Cooking dinner and supper was no different. The stove would have big pots of either pinto beans with fatback; navy beans with fatback; butterbeans with fatback; green beans with fatback; or black-eyed peas with fatback boiling away sending a mouthwatering aroma throughout the house; and sweet tasting corn bread in the oven.

    It made momma sad when she didn't have the kind, or amount, of foods she wanted to cook for her children. What she did to make us forget we were poor for a little while, was make big flat pans of molasses candy with pecans in it. And occasionally, she would get out her bottle of vanilla extract, the ice cream maker, and whip up a big bucket of homemade ice cream. She would fill the bucket with ice, put in some salt, and we children would take turns cranking the handle, of the ice cream maker. As we turned the handle momma would add additional ice and salt and when the ice cream started to build, we would crank faster in anticipation of the treat to come. Store bought ice cream wasn't as good as the ice cream momma made because she allowed us to help make it, so in our eyes that was what made it better.

* * * *

I used to love Christmas because of the pies and cakes momma cooked. My favorite cake was pineapple with coconut topping. If no one would stop me, I would eat the whole cake at one sitting. This was supposed to be the best Christmas ever because momma had told us Santa Claus was going to bring us the same pistols the cowboys wore that we saw on T.V. You can imagine how excited we were. However, regardless of how excited we were on Christmas Eve we went to bed at the same time we always did. When we got up that Christmas morning, my brothers, and me, ran over each other to get to those wild-west guns. When we opened our Christmas presents there were happiness all around. Biddy got the cowboy pistols of the hired gunman Jack Paladin on the television series "Have Gun Will Travel," along with the calling cards. Excitedly I opened my present and before my eyes was the sawed off rifle and holster of the bounty hunter Josh Randall in the cowboy series "Wanted, Dead or Alive" Deedie got the six shooter of Marshall Matt Dillion, who cleaned up Dodge City. And I ate plenty of pineapple cake to top off a very satisfying Christmas.

* * * *

One thing I never had to worry about was having enough clothes to wear. They were not new, but my butt was covered. Because of the sheer number of us, it was standard policy that when the older kids outgrew their clothes they were passed down to the next child in line. I received the clothes that had been worn by Deedie and Biddy, if they were still wearable. The problem I had with those hand me downs was by the time they became too small for Deedie and Biddy to wear, the pants legs were already too short for me. My growth spurt came early in my life. I was ashamed to wear the pants to school because everyone would ask me when the flood was coming because the cuffs of the pants were ankle high. The shoes never lasted long enough to be handed down because we were hard on shoes. The other thing I hated about the hand me downs was by the time the clothes from Deedie and Biddy reached me they were holy, and I don't mean in a religious sense. It was so embarrassing going to school with holes in the knees of your pants, or big patches covering the hole in the butt of your pants. The kids whose parents could afford to buy them new clothes for school every year were cruel. They would laugh and call us the holy po' chilluns from the farm. This would have bothered me more than it did had it not been for the fact that there were a lot of us po' chilluns at these schools. The soles of our shoes on more than one occasion were repaired with baling wire used to hold hay bales together. And to cover the holes in the bottom of our shoes, we would use cardboard for insoles. Another thing that bothered me while going to school was having a nappy head. But I couldn't really blame anyone but myself because I didn't want my hair combed, it hurt too much. What I wanted was for daddy to keep my head bald, but he said hair would help keep our heads warm. When momma would tell Sue or Teenie to comb our hair, they took great pride in trying pull our brain out through our scalps. It seems the louder we hollered, they more they pulled. The only relief was when they would put lard in our head to soften the curls, but the down size to that was we went to school smelling like bacon grease.

* * * *

I was never really religious as a child because I didn't believe God gave any of the black preachers any power, otherwise, they would have been able to get Him to change how white folks treated us. Listening to the preachers always saying that the bible said we are all brothers and sisters, I couldn't understand how God would allow white folks to treat their black brothers and sisters anyway they wanted to, even kill them and nothing would be done about it. I listened to momma pray to a God who I thought did not hear her, or any other black family suffering the indignities of farm life. I listened to daddy who said momma was praying to a white God who didn't give a damn about black folks that we had to do for ourselves.

Like everyone else in the community I believed God was white, so I never questioned the pictures of the white Jesus that adorned the walls of every black church I attended. Although I wasn't a really bad child, I didn't believe Jesus would care if I was. I remember the yearly revivals at the local churches where kids would drag themselves up to the mourning bench because their mommas and daddies, mostly mommas, had scared them into believing if they died without being baptized they would go to hell.

On Monday morning those same kids who were supposedly saved during revival week, would confess to us that they didn't feel anything. They only did it to make their family happy. I saw no sense in pretending to be something I wasn't. And it didn't help to make me a believer when I would hear momma and daddy talk about preachers sleeping with other men's wives while pretending to be counseling them on religious matters. With all these doubts running through my mind, not once did I not believe that God existed and would guide me in the direction He wanted me to go. I just didn't believe it would be a white God or a flesh and blood man here on earth doing the directing. Momma told me her bible said all men are sinners and fall short of God, so I figured if the preacher fell short there was not much they could tell me. I was thankful momma and daddy never tried to force us to pretend we were Christians. I went to church, but it had nothing to do with belief. I went because they made us. They said going to church would help us to decide if we wanted to be a Christian or not. The beauty of God is He gives you the knowledge and wisdom to eventually make the right decision.

* * * *

I remember some of our neighbor's children and relatives coming back to Arkansas visiting from northern cities and acting as if they were not subject to the same indignities as black folks there in the country. The only thing I was impressed with what they had to say was there were no cotton fields where they lived, and that black and white folks ate at the same cafes and sat in mixed theaters. While I felt being able to sit and eat in restaurants and sit wherever you wanted in public was better than being in Arkansas, I never lost sight that they didn't have it as good as they would have us to believe. They feared the white man's wrath the same as we did. They "yassuh and nossuh" the same as we did while they were home. I watched black folks on television during the Civil Rights Movement in both the north and south getting their head busted open by racist police officers and angry white mobs. So my conclusion was they were deceiving themselves into believing white people in the north liked black folks more than white folks in the south did. It was my belief that white America was white America no matter what part of the country we lived in.

* * * *

Before we got a television I used to sit by the radio and listen to shows like Amos N' Andy, the Lone Ranger, Hop-Along-Cassidy, and the Cisco Kid with my parents and siblings. As the action was described on the radio, I imagined being there. In my mind I saw the Lone Ranger riding high in the saddle as he galloped after the bad guys trying to get away from his frontier justice. I could see Trigger, his white horse, striding easily, smoothly as he overtook the horse the crook was riding on.

I could see Tonto, the Lone Ranger's Indian sidekick, with that big Indian knife in a scabbard and dressed in a buckskin outfit with an Indian headband as they described how he was dressed. I would get jealous that Indians were accepted and black folks weren't. I wanted to be the Lone Ranger's sidekick. It didn't matter I was afraid to ride the mules daddy worked with on the farm from time to time. I'm sure I would have been afraid to ride horses also, but that didn't deter my fantasy. I also wanted a mask, so I could walk around the farm dispensing justice and no one would know who I was.

When the radio described the lone ranger's two pearl handle six-shooters, with the row of bullets on the pistol belt at his waist, I just had to have two six-shooters of my own someday. When a neighbor got a television set and I actually saw the guns on the screen, it only heightened my desire to have them. I ask Santa Claus every Christmas for those six-shooters, but he never delivered. So I figured since he was a fat white guy, he just didn't care about the feelings of a little nappy-headed black kid.

I imagined being present in the saloon during the barroom brawls in every cowboy western. I imagined breaking chairs and bottles over the bad guys head. Or I would meet the bad guy at high noon for a showdown on main-street. My pants pockets were my holsters and my index fingers my six-shooters. I simulated the quick draw as I beat outlaws like Billy the Kid and Jesse James to the draw.

As far as Amos N' Andy was concerned, I didn't want to be either of them because they had no power when they were in the present of white folks. They were portrayed as your typical scary, conniving, jiving, and stupid black men. I felt ashamed whenever I heard the character named Lighting on the radio talk because he sounded stupid and mentally challenged. Television strengthened that shame. I didn't want white folks to think we talked like that, although I had heard some of the field hands I worked along side of talk exactly like Lighting did. My shame didn't stop me from watching the show along with the rest of the family it just made me try harder to learn to talk like white folks. Besides, there were hardly any black faces on television. I never realized the power of television until we got one of our own.

When we got our first television, I viewed it strictly as an instrument of entertainment, not something that could actually influence my belief system. That all changed one night when Sue,

Deedie and me, were watching a murder mystery movie on the late show one Saturday night where a serial killer was killing folks in London and the constables couldn't catch him. After every killing, the murderer would leave a cigarette butt of a particular brand to let the cops know he was the same person killing these people. To make the scenes scary, the murders always occurred under a blanket of thick fog so that the viewer never got a clear view of who the killer was. Our young bodies tensed every time the murderer stalked his victim, caught them and cut their throat, and left his trademark cigarette butt. Like all good mysteries, the bad guy is eventually caught and brought to justice, we thought. When the constables caught up with the killer they shot him full of holes, but when they went to retrieve the body, all that was left where he fell was his trademark pack of cigarettes. The constables searched the foggy area thoroughly but couldn't find the body, only a small puddle of blood where he fell. They scratched their heads at not being able to find the body and went away satisfied with the knowledge that they knew they had killed him. Knowing it was the end of the movie and the constables had killed the bad guy, we waited for the credits to start rolling to signify the end of the movie.

  Instead of ending as we expected, as the fog lifted, the ugliest white man I had ever seen on television, or anywhere else in my life, stood up and pointed at the T.V. screen and said, "Tonight I'm going to get you, and you, and you." Being there were only the three of us watching the movie, it was as if he pointed directly at each one of us. I had never been so scared of a white man in my life. I tossed and turned for several nights afterward, knowing that that murdering white man was going to come and get me in the middle of the night and leave a cigarette butt beside my dead body. It never occurred to me that the only time we had fog was at cotton chopping or cotton picking time, and we watched this movie during the dead of winter.

  My brother and sister said the ending of the movie didn't scare them, but I knew better because the look of terror was on their faces the same as mine when the ugly white man pointed in their direction and said he was going to get them also. When momma and daddy heard about me being scared by a movie they laughed long and hard. In my young mind the fear was real there was nothing to joke about.

*   *   *   *

One hot summer day Biddy, Deedie, and myself were on our way home from playing over the levee when we stumbled upon a yellow jacket wasp nest hanging on a fence post. It was huge, at least six inches in diameter and we could see by the fluttering wings of the wasp. Apparently they were agitated because of our presence. We calculated how far away we would have to be to knock the nest off the post without the wasps knowing where we were. Yellow jacket wasps are very aggressive, so we knew if they knew where we were when we knocked the nest down they would be coming after us. Being we were in a soybean field, it was hard to find clods of dirt big enough to use to knock it down. Where there is a will there is a way. It took a while but we found clods of dirt that would allow us to accomplish our mission. The wasp wings fluttered, and they positioned themselves for takeoff as if they knew what we had planned.

With confidence that the wasps wouldn't know from which direction the clods of dirt were coming from, we started throwing at the nest. It took quite a while before one of us, I don't remember which, hit the nest knocking it to the ground. While we were congratulating each other for a job well done, we looked in the direction of where the nest used to be and saw a cloud of wasps headed in our direction. Not having planned an escape route if the wasps came after us, we took off through the bean field in a full sprint. As usual in a situation like this, I was at a disadvantage because I was the youngest and in this instance also the slowest. I swear I could hear the beating of the wasp wings as they gained on me. Seeing that I couldn't keep up with my brothers, I knew the wasps were going to have their revenge on me.

In one last ditch attempt to get away from the wasps, I changed direction in hope they would continue straight after my brothers. So instead of continuing to run straight between the rows of bean, I changed direction and started jumping over them. It turned out to be the luckiest thing I ever did because my foot got caught in the beanstalks and I went tumbling to the ground. I hit the ground hard and rolled onto my back. I had not fallen a second too soon. Before I came to a full stop on my back, the cloud of wasps buzzed overhead. A couple of the wasps stopped and lit on the beanstalks above my head as if they knew I was there somewhere among the beanstalks but couldn't find me. I didn't move until I heard my brothers calling me. Cautiously, I raised my head to make sure the wasps were gone. Seeing the coast was clear, I got up and we continued on our merry way home laughing about the close call with the wasps. They told me daddy had told them if we were ever chase by wasps or bees, all we had to do was lay down and they wouldn't be able to find us, and that was what they had done. I said I remembered daddy telling us that to and that was why I had laid down also. I felt too stupid to admit I had tripped instead of remembering daddy's advice. My only solace taken from this experience was I didn't get stung to death by that angry swarm of yellow jacket wasps. That incident may have left me feeling stupid, but when it came to knowing about our African ancestry, I felt I was the most knowledgeable in my peer group.

    For me, there was never a doubt that we were descendants from the folks in Africa. During the hot summer months those of us too young to work ran around barefoot and half-naked, just like the African children we seen on T.V. Our bony little chests and legs were always bared for the world to see. When we played in the front yard where the cars, trucks, and buses passed by throughout the day during the summer, left us playing in clouds of dust. The dust clinging to our faces and clothes made us look like African chilluns. We would be covered from head to toe by the whirling dust the vehicles stirred up every time they passed on the dirt roads. The first time I saw African children in a news clip on television, covered with dirt, half naked, potbellied, and looking frightened, I thought it was about children in Arkansas or Mississippi. Not until the news folks said they were covering the starving conditions of folks in Africa, I forget what part, did I realize that we looked just like they did. So along with the African appearance and daddy teaching us not to be ashamed of our black skin, I had no problems saying I was a descendent of African folks. However, within the community I was one of the minorities in that belief. The majority of the grown-ups in the community had convinced their children that they had no roots, no connection whatsoever with Africa, not even their blackness. They wanted their children to believe that their ancestors came to America on the Nina, Pinta, and Santa Maria with Columbus instead of in the belly of slave ships.

    I never understood why my playmates were so negative toward Africa, and why they were so offended when I called them "black." And believe me, when I say black, I mean they were black. Most of us were just as black as any African I had ever seen on television. Still, they swore up and down that their blackness was a different kind of black from that of Africans because we lived in America. When I would insist that they were descendants of black Africans because we all looked like them, the kids would be ready to fight. They would argue that there was no way they could be related to any African because the African folks were lazy, stupid, and savages because they couldn't speak or write English. The reality my friend's parents kept from them was the majority of the black farmers in the south couldn't speak and write English well either, especially the way it was supposed to be written and spoken, because they were not educated. According to white folks, our lips were too big, and our tongues too thick to pronounce certain words, which is even true today. I couldn't articulate very well what I was trying to say, but I got my point across that there were a lot of black grown-ups who couldn't read or write either, at least not like the white folks did. I would push the issue and ask if they folks could read and write why would they allow white men to cheat them out of their money? Most often than not, the kids would swear both of their parents could read and write just like white folks. They even figured out how much the plantation owner owed them at the end of the share cropping season each year. And their parents knew what was in the white men's money books too. I would say, "Yeah right," and laugh at them because I knew better. I was never ashamed that daddy could barely read or write because I knew it was not his fault. I wasn't too young to know slavery and its legacy was the reason most black folks born and bred in the south couldn't read or write. I ask momma why black folks weren't as smart as white folks when it came to reading, writing, and talking.

The first thing momma told me was to never think it was because we were dumb, because we weren't. She told me there were two main reasons why black folks couldn't read, write, or talk like white folks. First, we had to look at our schooling. The black slaves that was stolen from Africa and brought to America weren't allowed to learn to read or write. Nor were they taught how to speak the language too well, because if the slaves could read and talk right the white people would've thought they were freemen, which would've allowed them to write their own passes which would have allowed them to escape to the north. White folks even forced the slaves to make up their own language if they wanted to talk or write to each other. Most of the English the slaves learned was from po' white trash that work in the cotton fields, right along with the slaves. These po' white folks couldn't speak English much better'n the slaves could. What ended up happening were the slaves mixed their African language with the po' white folks bad English and they came up with the way a lot of us still talk today.

Secondly; after the slaves were freed, the white folks didn't want us to learn to write, read, and talk right because they were scared the black folks would take their jobs. Especially jobs like carpentry, blacksmiths, and trail-drivers. To make sure black folks in the south, and some places up north, didn't learn to write, read, and talk properly, the white people passed laws that took the school money from the black folk school and gave it to the white folk schools. Then the government let them klan devils murder and beat black folks for trying to get educated. Now the white folks want us to believe this Jim Crow junk bout everything being separate but equal. That is the biggest lie the devil ever told. She said it was going to take a long time before we'll be able to read, write, and talk like white folks, but it'll happen sometime in the future. But we have to go to school and get educated, because with an education it makes survival easier. We ain't educated like white folks, and that's why they can read, write, and talk better'n us right now, but our time is coming.

*   *   *   *

I don't know why, but hygiene was not a top priority for me. I wasn't allergic to soap and water I just didn't like taking baths. My older brothers and sisters told me if I could smell myself today that meant other folks smelt me yesterday. I didn't think my body odor was anyone's business but my own until one day I sat beside momma on the front porch and she wrinkled her nose and asked if it was me that smelted like that. I didn't answer because I knew the two-day funk rule was in effect. She laughed and said I smelted like a Billy goat. I didn't mind my brothers and sisters or my friends talking about me being musky because they said I smelled all the time, but hearing it from momma was different. It made me feel I had let her down because she tried to get us kids to wash our armpits, butt, crotch, and feet, on days we knew we weren't going to take a bath. After the episode with momma, I started washing up as it was called almost every day. On days I forgot to wash up my brothers and sisters would remind me of what momma said I smelt like.

*   *   *   *

On hot summer days while fishing, it was common to see water moccasins [snakes] lying on branches hanging over the lake sunning themselves after a long night in their dark musky dens. As long as they didn't bother us, we didn't bother them. It was like we had an understanding that if they didn't invade our space, we wouldn't kill them. I was never afraid of snakes as long as I could see them.

We were told when we went fishing in a boat to stay away from the banks because of the snakes. One day I took two of my nephews fishing in a boat with me. The fish weren't biting much that day so I let the boat drift. Without realizing it, the boat drifted toward the bank of the lake. I was concentrating so hard on catching fish, I didn't notice the big snake laying on a branch directly in the path of the drifting boat. My nephews started hollering there was a snake behind me and I was going to hit it. When I turned to see how much time I had to avoid the snake I discovered I had very little. The branch the snake was laying on was eye level to my face. All I had time to do was tell the kids to get down flat in the boat, and at the same time I laid back in the boat. The boat drifted under the branch, and no more than an inch above my face passed one of the biggest moccasins I had ever seen I my life. It was so close to my face as the boat drifted under the branch it was laying on, I swore I could smell the musky stench of its den.

    Like I said earlier, I wasn't a real religious person, but I said a quick prayer to God to please don't let the snake drop into the boat. If the snake had fallen into the boat, it probably would have fallen right into my face, because that's how close it was. My prayer was answered. After getting far enough away from the snake, I paddled out to the middle of the lake and continued fishing. It was not until I told momma what had happened that I got scared because of what could have happened if the snake had fallen into the boat. My nephews continued to go fishing in the boat with me after the snake incident, but they always let me know when we were drifting too close to the bank of the lake. I never made that mistake while fishing in a boat again, but I continued to share the lake bank with the snakes.

*   *   *   *

    One of the best times growing up was listening to daddy tell amazing stories. It was easy to believe the stories he told because of a true incident that happened when he took in a young female that was having problems at home, which I will tell after the completion of the first three stories. These stories kept us spellbound every time he told them. The first story takes place at a place he called Bob Nob Hill.

    Around 3 a.m. on a Sunday morning, he and a friend named Willie were on their way home after a night of drinking, gambling, and raising hell on Beale Street in Memphis, Tennessee. They were riding along laughing about the women they had met that night when they had a flat tire at the base of Bob Nob Hill. He had heard for years that the place was haunted, but he never paid any attention to it. According to the legend it was a place where, back in the day, the most vicious criminal elements gathered there to drink and gamble. Naturally they would get drunk, get into fights, and kill each other. Their favorite weapons of choice were hooked-bill knives. It was ironic that this particular location would become a killing field. It was a place that was dug deep into the hillside by slaves to hold prayer meeting where the slave masters and slave patrol couldn't see them from the road as they worshiped.

Daddy said when they got out too change the tire Willie realized he had forgotten to put his carbide-light in the car. In the location they were in, the lighting from the moon was not too good, but light enough to get the job done without too much of a problem. After getting the jack and spare out of the trunk, Willie started jacking up the car. Being it was one of the twister type jacks, the process was slow. While watching the car slowly rise, daddy caught movement out of the corner of his eye. He looked up to the top of the hill and a man was standing there looking at them. Upon seeing daddy looking at him, the man came part way down the hill and retreated back into a cove. Daddy said he didn't pay too much attention to the man's presence at first because he thought it was just some guy being nosey. If he wanted to start some mess he would whip his butt and be done with it. The whole time he was thinking this, he was still joking with Willie who was still jacking up the car.

When daddy looked up the hill again, the man had come about halfway down the hill. He stood watching them until daddy turned to face him head-on. The man ran back up the hill to the cove where he had hid previously. Daddy said there was something odd about the man but he couldn't put his finger on it. Willie was in the process of removing the lug nuts. As he was asking Willie how much longer before he would have the tire changed, the man ran all the way to the bottom of the hill and ran around to the opposite side of the hill from where they were. This time it was obvious that the man had no head and he had a long knife in his right hand. Daddy swore he had never been afraid of anything or anyone, but at seeing the headless man the hair stood straight up on back of his neck and chills ran down his spine. He checked quickly to see if Willie had the tire changed, because he knew the headless man would be making another appearance shortly. Sure enough, daddy said he saw the man easing around the base of the hill, staying in the shadows trying to conceal his approach. Upon realizing he wasn't completely concealed, he stopped and pressed himself against the hill out of sight. Daddy said he knew without a doubt that the next time the man showed himself, it was going to be do or die. Knowing the headless man was about to make his move, he asked Willie if he had the spare tire on. Willie said he had the spare tire on, but had only two of the lug nuts on. Daddy told Willie to forget the other three lug nuts because they had to get the hell out of there.

Willie was about to ask why when he saw the man emerge from the shadows and start running toward them with the knife raise. Daddy said he didn't realize how long he had hesitated until he turned to get in the car. Willie had taken off. He had to run to catch up, and just as he jumped into the car, the headless man swung his blade downward and cut his coattail. Daddy said he watched the headless man through the rear window of the car as he made his way back up the hill to wait for his next victim. From that night on, they never stopped at Bob Nob Hill at night for any reason. If they had a flat tire they rode on the rim until they got far enough away from Bob Nob Hill to change the tire.

This second tale was about a disobedient 14-year old young man named Charlie who wouldn't listen to his parents or grandparents. Not only was he disobedient at home, he was already drinking and gambling with grown-ups. Allowing a child to be disobedient in the home in the 1940s was rare, but occasionally you'd see one who was allowed to misbehave for some reason. Charlie's daddy got drunk one night and almost beat the boy to death for losing his smoking pipe, only to find it in the car where he had left it when he came into the house after getting home from a club the previous night. He had beat Charlie so badly the doctor said he would probably suffer brain damage. Whether he suffered brain damage or not was never diagnosed, but that is what his momma and daddy attributed his defiant behavior to.

Knowing he was responsible for his only son's injury, his daddy let Charlie have his way, which everyone believed Charlie were using that guilt to act the way he did. Charlie's grand momma didn't buy his act for a second. She constantly told her son, Charlie's daddy, that what that boy needed was a good whuppin. The guilt his daddy felt was so deep he couldn't bring himself to whup Charlie again.

They would tell him not to stay out late on school nights because they wanted him to do well in school. But convinced school would not get him off the farm, he went wherever he pleased, and came home as late as he pleased. His grand momma Emma became ill and was on her deathbed. She told Charlie that if he continued to disobey his momma and daddy she would pay him a visit from beyond the grave one night. Charlie was a true believer that once you were dead you were done, so after his grand momma died he continued his disobedient ways.

One night Charlie was on his way home from drinking and gambling. He was walking down the same road he walked every night to get home, but this night things were different. When he got close to home, a wiener dog started crossing the road in front of him. Charlie didn't think anything of it although he knew no one on the planation where he lived owned a wiener dog. He waited for the little dog to get across the road but the dog kept going and going. Seeing no end in sight, Charlie ran and jumped over the dog. He did acknowledge to himself that a never-ending dog was odd, but it didn't frighten him. A short distance down the road the dog started to cross the road in front of him again. This time as the dog started crossing the road Charlie was afraid because he now knew something was trying to get his attention. The dog's eyes were blood red and it was growling at him. He didn't waste any time. He ran and jumped over the dog and ran the rest of the way home.

When Charlie got to his house the wiener dog was sitting on

the porch waiting for him. Really afraid now, Charlie didn't know what to do. He tried shooing the dog away but it wouldn't move. Building up the nerve to approach the dog, he tried to kick it to make it move aside so he could get in the house. He told himself if he could get in the house he would be all right. Charlie stared in disbelief when the dog stood up on its' hind legs and transformed itself into his dead grand momma Emma. She broke a switch from one of the trees in the yard and commenced to whip his behind. Charlie's cries woke up his family. They came out and watched as Charlie jumped up and down crying, "I'm sorry grand momma I won't do it again." During the whole time the scene was playing itself out, they could see no one other than Charlie jumping up and down. After that night, Charlie became a model child from that day forward. He obeyed his parents, graduated from high school, and was ordained a minister at the age of twenty-three.

    The third tale was about a homeless woman named Sara, who had two children and nowhere to stay in the dead of winter. Her husband had died in a farming accident and the plantation owner told her since she and her young children, ages 3 and 5, would not be able to work the farm the coming farming season, she had to leave. The house she lived in and the land they sharecropped for the last eight years had been rented out to another family who would be moving in in two days. Although the people in the community felt sorry for her, they didn't have enough room to take her and her children in. A woman on an adjoining planation told her that there was an old vacant house located half a mile down the path from where Dead Man's road ended. They said the white plantation owner would probably let her stay there, but the house was haunted. No one had ever been able to stay the whole night. She was told the reason it was haunted was because the old white folks who died there were protecting a large cache of money that was buried somewhere in the house or on the property. Rumor had it they were descendants of slave owners, and each generation had buried their riches in the house, or somewhere on the property instead of putting it in a bank. They didn't trust banks. The last two family members who died in that haunted house were the last generation of that family tree. Before they died, they sold everything they owned, except the house, and buried it in the house or on the grounds surrounding it. It was estimated that as much as three million dollars was buried there, but no one could find it. Because of the house's reputation, the treasure seekers only searched the house and grounds during the day.

Sara was a deeply religious woman who believed God would provide a place for them to lay their heads. Not wanting to trespass on anyone's property, she asked the owner of the house if it was okay with him before taking up residence in the house for the night. The old white man who owned the house told her if she could spend the night there without being run out as everyone else had, she could stay there as long as she wanted. So, with children in tow and her old tattered bible in hand, Sara moved what belongings she had into the house the following morning. The house was in surprisingly good condition considering no one had lived in it for any length of time recently. The cook stove had been left in the house and the fireplace was in good working condition. Wood for both the kitchen stove and fireplace had been gathered and left in place by the last occupant(s) who attempted to take up residence in the house six months earlier. An old rocking chair was even left sitting by the fireplace.

After making a fire in the fireplace, Sara spent the day cleaning and straightening up around the house, all the while mentally preparing herself for the unknown terror she knew she would be facing come sundown. That evening after sunset she cooked supper and fed the children by candlelight because there was no electricity in the house. Afterward, Sara took out her bible and read to them for a couple of hours by the fireplace before putting them to bed. After putting the children to bed she went back and sat by the fireplace and waited for whatever it was she had to face. Sara was determined to stay the night because she had nowhere else to go. She read her bible until she dozed off while sitting in the rocking chair. She was awakened by the sound of chains rattling in the ceiling above her head. When she looked up, several big sets of slave bracelets attached to chains were descending from the ceiling directly in front of her. The closer they got to the floor, the more noise the chains made. Sara raised her bible and started reading. The chains stopped right in front of the rocking chair and rattled so loudly it hurt Sara's ears, but she never stopped reading her bible. After several minutes the chains disappeared and there were silence.

Knowing that was only a warm up for what was to come, Sara hummed an old Negro spiritual to settle her nerves. About half an hour later there came another noise from the ceiling. This time when Sara looked up there, charging directly at her was one of the biggest bulls she had ever seen in her life. It had blood red eyes and flames were shooting out of its nostrils. She closed her eyes and prayed as she had never prayed before in her life. The bull stopped close enough to Sara's face for her to smell its breath and feel the heat from the flames coming out of its' nostrils. Sara kept her eyes closed as she prayed for fear if she looked the bull in the face she would not be able to stay. She didn't know how long this encounter lasted, but when the bull finally went away, she was drenched with sweat.

Sara didn't know how much more of the haunting she could stand because her nerves were frayed and getting the better of her. She knew the final test of her courage would probably be at the witching hour, which is at midnight. She figured if she could withstand the final test of her will she would probably be okay. Instead of the sound coming from the ceiling as before, it came from the fireplace. A low gravelly voice was telling her to get out of the house or she and her children would die there, as those before her, who had dared to test the will of those in the spiritual world. She did not move and the flames started to rise. Sara watched as the flames rose higher and higher, and the voice got louder and louder. "Get out, or your children will die. Get out, or your children will die. Get out, or your children will die." It was her faith in God that kept her from gathering up her children and leaving the house. All of a sudden a face with horns like the devil shot forward from the flames. The face was so close to Sara's she could smell its fetid breath. The face asked Sara what she wanted from them. Sara could feel the heat from the face's breath on her face as it spoke. She clutched her bible to her chest and said, "In God's name, all I want is to be able to care for my children and keep them safe and warm. I have nothing but the rags on my back and nowhere to live." The horned face told her when she awoke in the morning, to dig deep in the fireplace and she would find what everyone had been seeking. Sara fell asleep from exhaustion where she sat. She awoke early the following morning, fed the children, and dug in the fireplace as the voice had told her to, and buried several feet underneath the ashes and rock floor was an old weathered, black tarp. When she pulled back the tarp covering the treasure, she almost had a heart attack because underneath was more money than she would ever be able to spend in her lifetime. There was money of every note and denomination ever printed in America dating back to the Civil War buried there. Jewels, diamonds and family heirlooms were also buried there. There was even Spanish gold bullion buried there. Sara replaced the tarp back over the treasure, filled in the hole, replaced the rock floor in the fireplace and said nothing to anyone about what she had found. The children were too young to realize the significance of their momma's find and she never explained it until much later.

The owner of the house stopped by the next day to see if she had run off during the night. When he saw she was still there, he was true to his word and told her she could stay as long as she liked. Sara got a job working for a white family as a maid, and stayed in that house until she died. It was not until she was on her deathbed did she tell her children, now in their 30s, where to find their fortune. She told them once they had the money, they had to leave Mississippi or the white folks would take everything from them and leave them penniless. Her two children took the money, heirlooms, and the gold bullion divided it evenly, and was never seen again. Daddy said he was sure her children never had to work another day in their lives. Being she was a woman, no one ever questioned her to whether she had found the buried treasure. And being the house was occupied, people stop coming to the house looking for the loot. The ole house was never haunted again.

I will now relate the story that gave us reasons to believe daddy's ghost stories, although we had been skeptical to believe him in the past. A fourteen year-old girl name Ruby came to live with us because her grand momma could not handle her after her momma died. Her daddy died several years prior to her momma's death. She had only been with us a short time when one morning while we were all scattered around the kitchen eating breakfast. Daddy looked at Ruby and he said, "Your momma came here to check on you last night." Ruby, being the skeptical child that she was, told daddy he couldn't possibly know it was her momma because her momma had died five years before we even moved to Arkansas. Daddy described the exact clothing that her momma was buried in. Ruby looked on in astonishment, as did we all, when daddy told her that her momma knew she was mad at her for dying, but she wanted her to know that she loved and missed her and her sisters and brothers very much. If she could have stayed with them, she would have. She wanted so much to watch them grow into beautiful young women and handsome young men, but God had other plans. She said God had assured her He would never abandon them and neither would she. She wants you to promise to keep her in your heart forever.

Ruby started crying and said that was what she had wanted to know, that her momma still loved her because she and her momma had a fight the night her momma died and she didn't get the chance to ask for her momma's forgiveness. Several days later Ruby moved back home with her grand momma and never left home again until she got married.

Since I'm on ghost stories, I may as well tell my version of the haunted house we lived in when we lived around Cow Bayou. We would lay awake sometimes listening to someone or something, walking around in what sounded like boots in the attic. We knew it was not our imaginations because we all heard it, and when we asked daddy about it, he said there was nothing to be afraid of. Bubba, being the oldest, had to get up in the morning to make fires in the kitchen stove for momma to cook, and in the living room to warm the house during the winter. He kept us spellbound as he told us about the noises that greeted him in the kitchen each morning he got up to make the fires. He never told us he saw anything, but he knew there were always haints around him every morning he got up to make the fires. I personally never saw anything but was scared because of the noises I heard at night and the older children saying the haints were bound to get someone sooner or later, and most of the time it was the little kids they got first.

Where it had been only my imagination that there was someone or something in the house, one morning at breakfast Biddy put a face to what was walking around in the house and attic when he told daddy he had seen a little man with a hat and suit on standing over him last night. Daddy said he knew about the man, but he wasn't going to hurt anyone. He didn't know how to get out of the house to get to the other side. That the man was the one we heard walking around in the attic. Needless to say, I was petrified for weeks because I thought the man wasn't looking for Biddy but me, and that was why he didn't mess with him. I was sure if he came for me, I was a goner. Why I thought that way I don't know, but I tossed and turned night after night scared to death. We stayed in that house a long time, so you can imagine how happy I was when daddy decided to move.

* * * *

In the 1950s interracial relations between black men and white women were taboo in the wonderful state of Arkansas, however, I do remember on one occasion an interracial union was overlooked by the members of the white community, even by the Klu Klux Klan. But there was a major uproar when the black young man who had gone up north for several years announced he was returning home with his white wife before they seen the happy couple.

I don't remember the exact year only that it was in the late 1950s when Sonny Boyd could no longer get along with his daddy and decided to leave home. He hopped trains and traveled around the country before settling in New York. According to his family he got a job working at the dockyard. It was whispered that Sonny was not the brightest bulb in the room. It was also whispered that his whole family was dysfunctional. Supposedly his daddy was sleeping with his daughters and their momma condoned it. I do know Sonny's daddy didn't allow his daughters, four of them, to date my brothers or any of his friends. And I overheard daddy and momma talk about how he never allowed his wife to socialize with any of the women on the surrounding farms. She wasn't even allowed to attend church. So when word spread that Sonny was bringing his white wife home everyone agreed that if anyone was stupid enough to pull that stunt it would be Sonny.

The conversations were always hushed in the black communities because everyone knew the white citizenry was highly upset that a Negro had the audacity to defy their unwritten law against interracial relations. Listening to daddy and momma discuss the issue with other black people on the farm was frightening. The gist of the conversation was always the same.

Daddy and a neighbor name Mr. Anderson were sitting under the shade tree in the back yard sipping lemonade and discussing Sonny's awaited return home with his white wife.

Daddy said, "I always knew that boy was crazy, but I didn't think he was crazy enough to get himself hung on purpose. He knows if he brings that white gal back here to Arkansas they are going to kill him, and probably a couple other Negroes too show they're serious about black men not messing with their women. His daddy ain't helping the situation none because he's telling that boy to go ahead and bring her home because he wants to meet her."

"That boy and his family know how crazy these white folks get even if they think a Negro is messing with a white woman. I heard tell Mr. Ganger, who his family sharecropped with, went to Sonny daddy's house and told him to tell that boy not to bring that white gal here. That if he do, they were going to string him up as soon as he step foot in Wabash. They serious to," Mr. Anderson said.

"The only thing I hope is the woman is worth risking his life for. You know how us black men are when it comes to white women. We will settle for anything if she's white. I mean, every black man I ever seen with a white woman she was one of the ugliest creatures God ever put on earth, but they proud as they want to be because she's white. I told my boys they had better never bring a white girl in my house. If they do, both of them is out the door," daddy said.

"I know what you mean Joe. Them white folks is probably going to hang Sonny's daddy right along with him for allowing that boy to bring that white girl to his house. I feel sorry for Sonny's momma. She will have to find a man willing to help her raise her chilluns after this is over," Mr. Anderson shook his head sadly.

"All I can say is, Sonny and his daddy knows what he's doing is wrong. So whatever happens, Sonny brought it down on them. Another thing, when they do get here you better tell your boys to lay low for a while because them white folks is going to be looking for an excuse to kill any black man they can get they hands on," daddy cautioned.

"Yeah I know. I've already told them boys of mind to be careful about what they do and where they go when Sonny and that white gal gets here, but you know them boys. They will want to go by the house just to see what that white gal look like," Mr. Anderson said.

"Yeah, I know you're right. The only thing my boys talk about is whether she is pretty or not. They don't care that Sonny is going to swing from the highest tree. Maybe they'll see that sleeping with a white girl is not worth it when they see what happens to Sonny. God help us all," daddy said.

As the time approached for Sonny and his bride to arrive to Arkansas the air became so tensed you could feel it. The white folks openly talked about they would be hanging a coon soon. While in the black community, daddies and mommas cautioned their sons to watch for angry mobs of white men when Sonny got home so they could avoid any confrontations with them. The day before Sonny and his bride was supposed to arrive it was the talk of the town. Both sides, black and white, braced themselves for what was going to happen the following day. Knowing white men used occasions like this to take revenge on black people they didn't like, shotguns and rifles were kept at arm's length in black men homes.

Sonny and his white wife arrived home under the cover of darkness, so no one knew when they got to his daddy's house. Sonny's daddy told everyone they never showed up. Everyone relaxed a little when they thought Sonny had gotten cold feet about bringing her to Arkansas. A couple of days after he was supposed to have arrived home, Sonny and his bride made it known they had indeed arrived. They wanted to give everyone a chance to settle down before making their presence known.

After getting a look at Sonny's bride, the anger generated before their arrival faded. She was one the most pathetic looking individual God ever put on the earth. She had dirty, stringy, blonde hair, rotten teeth and was so frail she looked as if she might kick the bucket at any moment. The black men in the neighborhood wondered what he seen in her. The white men joked that they should give Sonny a medal for taking such an ugly white woman off of their hands, but said they still had to leave Arkansas regardless of how ugly she was. So the first interracial couple I seen in Arkansas got the blessing of everyone in the community. Sonny and his bride stayed in Wabash for three days and it was back to New York.

* * * *

Summary

The stories I have related here bring back fond memories in some areas of my childhood, and not so fond memories in others. I think being somewhat protected from the harsh reality of the racist society in which I grew up, it gave me the time I needed to learn to cope with the challenges of life. The stories of my childhood and those told to me by my daddy, I now pass down to future generations. It gives them a measuring stick so they will be able to see how far we have come as a people.

Joyce Ann Wade
Born: March 22, 1952
Place of Birth: Mobile, Alabama

CHAPTER #11
OYCE

I was born March 22, 1952 in Mobile Alabama. I was 8 years old when I started working, chopping and picking cotton. It didn't take long for me to figure out why my older brothers and sisters fussed all the time about having to get up so early every morning to go to the cotton fields of Arkansas and Mississippi. I wasn't the most dedicated worker in the world in the first place, so you can imagine how much I hated working in the heat when it was a hundred degrees or more. Or when, I found myself wading through chest high cotton fields getting wet from chest to toes on those cold chilly mornings while chopping cotton. Because I didn't like working in the fields, I prayed for rain every time I saw a dark cloud in the sky, regardless of its size. I knew the work wasn't going to kill me, I just didn't like farm work.

It wasn't enough that Daddy criticized me because I struggled to keep up with everyone else while chopping cotton, one day daddy made a demand of me that traumatized me for the rest of my cotton picking life. We were about halfway through the cotton-picking season when daddy got tired of me picking less than 200 lbs of cotton a day, which is what everyone else was bringing in and more. He said "Sista", I want you to pick 200 pounds of cotton today or I'm going to whip your butt tonight." I had never even come close to picking that amount of cotton in one day. My best output to that point was 165 lbs in one day, and I thought that was a good day. I averaged about 155 lbs daily. So you can imagine how scared I was because I knew I couldn't do it. Because of the fear of knowing daddy had given me an impossible task, the day flew by and I felt as if I was picking in slow motion. I knew I was picking faster than in the past, but it didn't seem like it. As the end of the cotton-picking day approached, I knew I was going to get a beating because I had not reached the goal daddy had set for me. Knowing I couldn't pick that much cotton on my best day, Bobo and Pon'k helped me bring in 199 pounds. Being that daddy very seldom compromised on any limit he set for us, I thought he was still going to tan my hide because I came up one pound short. To my surprise he forgave the one-pound shortage. I think he let me pass because he knew I had done my best. I just wasn't good at picking cotton, mainly because the boles had sharp pointed ends that would stick in your fingers. Truth be told, I wasn't good at farming, period. After that day he never set a goal he wanted me to reach, but he never told me he wouldn't. This incident proved to daddy that I wasn't as good as my siblings when it came to chopping and picking cotton, and it reinforced my status as daddy's pet. I never reached that 200 lbs. plateau.

*   *   *   *

I don't know why I was daddy's favorite, but I was. I guess it was because I was always around him, and would do things for him all the time. Things like rubbing his head when he would be hung-over after getting drunk the previous night. I would take him water, fix his plate, and cook for him when momma wasn't around. In addition to doing that for him I would go places with him when no else would, usually because he would be drunk. On these occasions daddy scared the life out of me every time I got in the car with him, but I pretended I wasn't afraid. He would try to pass every car on the road, and God forbid if someone tried to pass him. It would be as if the other driver had challenged daddy to a drag race. On one occasion I went to town with daddy and he got so drunk he made me drive the twenty miles home from town. He said he knew I could drive because he had heard about all the boys who were teaching me to drive. Although what he said was true, I had never driven that great of a distance before. Thank God I made it. After that first time it was a piece of cake. I even looked forward to daddy getting drunk when we went to town so I could drive home.

My brothers and sisters knew I was daddy's favorite, so they did mean things to me. Several winters in a row we got snow and ice storms. Will and Pon'k would pull me out onto the snow or ice covered road after these storms because they knew I couldn't walk on the ice like they could and was going to bust my butt. When I did, they laughed their heads off. To rub salt in the wound, after I fell they would drag me on the ice getting my clothes wet. I would tell daddy on them hoping he would whup their butts, but he would only tell them to leave me alone, or tell me to stay in the house so they wouldn't bother me. I don't know how momma felt about me being daddy's favorite child because she never really said anything to me about it. But I do know she didn't love me any less because of it.

* * * *

Our workday didn't end once we left the cotton field. When we got home we would have chores to do, such as washing dishes, working in the garden and cleaning the house. Living in the country, it was next to impossible to keep the house clean. When we weren't tracking dirt into the house, every truck or car that passed the house would stir up clouds of dust that would drift into the house during the summer and cover everything. When it rained I swear my brothers and daddy tracked mud into the house on purpose to make momma and us girls mad, because they knew we were the ones who had to clean the mud off the floors. We knew it was what society expected of females, but it didn't mean I had to like it. Life on the farm for a female was no picnic.

During the winter months it was the boys' job to cut down trees and haul them to the house. Once they got the logs home they had to cut and split them into firewood. Sometimes when they were sawing the logs they would ask me, and my sister Pon'k, to sit on the logs while they sawed them to keep the logs from rolling with the pull of the saw. A lot of times the experience was not fun because our brothers would call us all kind of hurtful names. As for myself, they called me Knotty-Joe-Hog-Head, why I don't have the faintest idea. But it gave them great joy to see how much the name upset me. Most of the time when we had to sit on the logs while our brothers sawed them me and Pon'k ended up helping them take the firewood into the house. Luckily for me, and Pon'k, we didn't have to get up in the morning to make fires in the stoves. The boys took turns making fires in the morning in the kitchen stove so momma could cook breakfast, and to warm the house. The closest we got to making fires was helping our brothers gather the kindling wood and chips they used to start fires with in the morning.

*   *   *   *

When we washed clothes, it was an adventure in itself, which was normally Saturday morning. Can you imagine washing clothes for ten people? It took an hour just to separate the so-called good clothes from the work clothes. The next step was pumping water in buckets and carrying them and pouring it into two number three tin tubs on the back porch until they were full. We used soapy water in one tub to clean the clothes, and the other one to rinse the clothes out. The rub board we used to scrub the dirt out of the clothes was constructed with a flat piece of wood covered with rough ridges made out of tin. Many times in my anger at having to wash so many clothes, I got careless and ended up rubbing skin right off my knuckles. After rinsing the clothes in the clean water we wrung them out by hand and hung them on the clotheslines. To get the white clothes clean we would put them in hot soapy water that was close to boiling and use a flat board in the shape of a boat paddle to poke the clothes clean. Then we would rinse them in cold water. I hated having to handle the hot clothes as we took them out of the hot water. I can't recall how many times I burned my hands while handling those hot soapy clothes. We had to clean the house and wash the clothes, but daddy and the boys usually put the food on the table.

Country people had a unique way of killing chickens on the farm. Daddy or my brothers would take the chicken by the neck and wring it until the head snapped off in their hands. Because of the sudden loss of its head, the chicken would not die right way. It would jump and flop around slinging blood all over the place. Daddy would tell us to grab the chicken while it was still flopping around. Pon'k, and me would be scared of the chickens because every time we reached for them their headless bodies would jump in a different direction. Although I reached the point I could catch the chickens and hold them until they died, I never got used to it. I guess that's where the term "running around like a chicken with its head cut off" came from. While I'm on the subject of chickens, I will relate an incident that got Bobo's butt whupped real good.

One day my brother Bobo, Pon'k and me were sitting on the back porch throwing rocks at momma's baby chickens. That old momma hen put herself between Bobo and her babies, which didn't set too well with Bobo because the hen pecked away ignoring him as he threw the rocks. Bobo started off throwing small rocks at first, but when the old momma hen continued to ignore him he found bigger and bigger rocks. I think Pon'k and me knew what was about to happen when the baby chicks stepped around the momma hen and was now exposed for Bobo to take his best shot at hitting one them. We watched fascinated as Bobo picked up the biggest rock he could find and threw it in the direction of the baby chicks. The closest chick to him didn't stand a chance of surviving when that big rock caught it right upside its head. The poor baby chick fell over and started kicking in its last throes of death. Bobo pleaded with Pon'k not to tell momma, but there were no way she would pass up the chance of watching him get his butt beat. So Pon'k ran in the house and told momma he had killed one of her baby chicks, and she beat his butt real good. Bobo getting his butt whipped didn't bother me either because he shouldn't have killed the baby chick.

* * * *

Me going to church on Sundays, was a regular event, but I wasn't going to get saved. I went to church to play with my friends, where we would end up fighting almost every Sunday morning, or to meet my boyfriends. At one time I called myself having two boyfriends at the same time, Alan and Harry. I was too young and naive to realize that a girl could get herself hurt playing on the emotions of immature boys who were trying to prove their thirteen year old manhood. Every Sunday both of them would be at church and try to talk to me. It wasn't easy the church being so small, but I made sure they never talked to me at the same time. I told each of them that momma and daddy would get mad at me if they saw them messing with me at church, so they had to be cool. And I made sure they never came to my house at the same time.

It worked for a while. I don't know how, but Alan found out that I was messing with Harry. He asked me about it one day while we were playing in the woods adjacent our house. When I confessed it was true, he pulled a switch from one of the trees and whipped me on my legs. If daddy had found out about Alan hitting me he would have hurt that boy bad, so I never told on him. Alan then went by Harry's house and told him to never mess with me again. Alan warned him that if he did he was going to get hurt. All Harry said was "whatever" because he knew he wouldn't be seeing me again anyway because of an earlier incident.

Seeing how mad Alan was after finding out about me and Harry, I was glad he never found out that one night I went to the woods to meet Harry with the intention of spending the night with Harry, but daddy came and got me and took me home before he showed up. Daddy found the biggest belt he could find and whipped me good. "Lord, have mercy! I thought he was going to kill me." I didn't want to see Harry ever again, so when Alan told him to leave me alone it saved me from having to tell Harry I no longer wanted to see him. Shortly after breaking up with Harry, Alan was history also. There was never a shortage of boys. My high school was swarming with hormone raging boys.

*   *   *   *

When we attended Elaine Middle School, Bobo made me carry the brown bag momma always put our lunch in. He didn't want his friends teasing him about the brown greasy bags. So I ended up toting the greasy bags which usually contained biscuit and eggs, fatback and biscuit, or biscuits and sausage. I got tired of always having to carry the bag, so I had to figure out a way to get him to carry it sometimes. I started eating the eggs, fatback, or sausages from between the biscuits and leaving him with only bread for lunch. It took him a few days to realize if he didn't start carrying the bags, bread was all he was going to have for lunch every day. The days he didn't find any meat between the biscuits, he got so mad he wanted to beat my butt. I would tell him if he hit me I was going to tell daddy because he was supposed to keep the lunch for us anyway. He got tired of eating naked biscuits for lunch and started carrying the bags himself, because that was one greedy boy. When I move from middle school to high school my priority changed from brown bags to boys.

While attending Lakeview High School, I made friends with one of the most beautiful people on this earth. Her name was Susan. I guess the reason we were drawn to each other was because we both wanted to be grown, which means we were hot little mommas. We were fifteen years old and in the ninth grade. When me, and Susan would get to school in the morning, we would go into the bathroom before the first bell rang and change clothes with each other. We did this almost every school day. When we passed to the 10th grade, we got bold and started wearing high heels shoes, stockings, and make-up to school every chance we got. Momma would fuss at me for dressing like a fast girl, but I took the criticism in stride because I was determined to get the attention of every boy at school. Susan and me, were so proud of ourselves because the dresses and shoes made us look like grown women. We walked around school during lunch and kept a running tally of how many boys had hit on us. Susan and me, thought we were God's gift to boys. Although we were almost inseparable, I do remember one time me and Susan had a falling out over a teacher name Mr. Key. He was one of the most handsomeness men anyone at Lakeview had ever seen. Every girl in my class had a schoolgirl crush on him. For some reason me and Susan thought we had dibs on him and threatened the other girls in the class with bodily harm if they didn't stop trying to like

Mr. Key. You can imagine the hurt we both felt when Mr. Key said it was nice to have a couple of little girls liking him, but he was involved with a beautiful woman teaching at another school. We took our frustrations at being rejected by Mr. Key out on the boys who tried to talk to us.

Another friend of mine was named Dana. We weren't as close as Susan and me, but I liked her style because she was faster than I was. I wanted to be like Dana because she had a devil be damned attitude, so I let her convince me it was okay to write notes to our boyfriends during class. I should have known it was only a matter of time before the teacher caught me passing notes. I thought it wouldn't matter if I got caught, because I thought I wouldn't be embarrassed if she paraded me up to the head of class to read the note. I was wrong.

One day I got carried away passing notes to David Edward, who I thought was one of the finest boys in the school. He was light skinned and a member of the school's varsity basketball team. My teacher, Mrs. Foster, saw me trying to get another boy to pass the note to him. She walked back to my desk and took the note. I wanted to disappear into thin air because every eye in the class had followed her as she made her way to my desk. After she read the note, the teacher look down at me and said she wanted me to read the note out loud in front of the class so everyone could hear it. I tried to read it real quick sitting there at my desk so I didn't have to see the looks and smirks on my classmates faces, but the teacher made me go up to the front of the class so everyone could see my shame for getting caught passing the note.

As I made my way to the front of the classroom, I felt as if I was walking in quick sand. I imagined it was how folks about to be executed must feel on their way to the electric chair. Before I even started reading the note my classmates were laughing and making fun of me. The note wasn't a long one, only about six lines long, but it felt like I was reading a full-length book because all eyes in the classroom were staring into my mouth, yanking out every word before I even had a chance to finish reading them aloud. I was so mad at that teacher for humiliating me in front of the class. However, her method worked because that stopped me from writing notes to the boys in the classroom. Believe it or not, as traumatic as the incident was, I don't even remember what the note said.

There was one girl in my class named June that most of my classmates avoided because she was mentally challenged. I know it was a mean thing to say, but in those days we called the mentally challenged "retards." June and I became very good friends. I liked her because she was very beautiful and had a good heart. What drew me to her initially was how she handled the criticism hurled at her on a constant basis. When one of the kids called June a retard she would say yes she was and they should thank God that they weren't. Although she handled herself well externally, internally she was always scared that some kids might jump on her for some reason. It was only paranoid feelings on her part because no one wanted to jump her. She didn't understand a lot of things, especially how to do her schoolwork. So I spent a lot of time tutoring her and helping her with her homework. Whenever she saw me playing with other girls she would be afraid that I would no longer want to be her friend. I assured her that I would always be there for her because she was my best friend and always would be.

As I said, June was a beautiful person, she would do anything for anybody, and a lot of the students took advantage her. Everyone knew if they told June they didn't have any money for lunch she would give them some. She always had money because her family owned a farm and was pretty well off. She would try to give me money just for being her friend, but I never accepted it. I let her know that she didn't have to give me anything because I liked her for who she was. I also told her not to give anyone else anything because she couldn't buy friendship or love. I told her if the other kids didn't like her for who she was they didn't like her anyway. I missed her very much when her family sold their farm and moved from Lakeview to Chicago.

Reflecting back to a time when I was still in middle school, at the age of fourteen, I met a boy named John who was much older than I was and we fell in love. The only thing wrong with this relationship was he was much too old for me. He was an eighteen year old high school senior, and I was in the eighth grade. He promised he would never mess with another girl, and that he would wait until I got old enough to marry him. While me, and John were making all these plans for the future, his mother decided to move to St. Louis, Missouri in the middle of the school year. When John came to my house to tell me that they were moving, it broke my heart real bad. I don't remember who cried the most, me or him. He promised he would always love me, and would come visit me whenever he could. The thing that I loved most about John was that he had respect for me. He didn't try to make me do anything I didn't want to do because I was so young. The night before he left he came to say good-bye. When he left that night, my intuition told me I would never see him again. Being as young as I was, I didn't trust my instinct, but as faith would have it my instinct was right because that was the last time I ever saw him. A couple of years after they moved to St. Louis momma told me a neighbor told her that John had gotten killed by a hit and run driver. The neighbor said he was crossing a street when the car hit him and took off. They never caught the driver who hit him. Although we hadn't kept in touch it still hurt me very badly, so bad I cried for days.

*   *   *   *

One of my favorite neighbors ever was named Ms. Lucy, and she had a peach tree in her yard. Every fall she would allow me to eat all the peaches I wanted, but I couldn't pick them myself because I was allergic to the peach fur. Ms. Lucy didn't want me itching from the peach fur, so either she would pick the peaches for me or make some of the other kids pick and wash them for me, which didn't sit too well with them. They threatened to beat me up because they had to pick and wash the peaches for me, but I knew better because Ms. Lucy would have whipped their butts for messing with me. The first time I picked the peaches myself they broke me out on my arms and hands. It took a long time for the ugly red whelps on my arms to clear up and my hand to return to looking normal. I guess Ms. Lucy felt guilty somehow for me breaking out from the peach fur. I told her, as well as momma, that she should not feel guilty because she had no way of knowing I was allergic to peach fur. Ms. Lucy's generosity towards me went farther than the peach tree in her yard. Almost every time she went to the store, she would bring me something. This generosity might also have been because her son liked me and I wasn't showing much interest in him.

Patterson, Ms. Lucy's son, liked me but I liked another boy name Henry. Patterson was a really big boy and a real bully. He could whip any boy on the farm, and usually did if he didn't like them. Patterson said he couldn't see what I saw in Henry because Henry was nothing but a little wimp. One day Patterson was trying to talk to me and I told him to leave me alone because I liked Henry, not him. He talked to me nicely, trying to get me to change my mind about not liking him. When the smooth talk didn't work, he became himself. He ranted and raved for a while, and then told me if I didn't quit Henry he was going to beat both of us up. Patterson said he would hurt Henry real bad. Instead of telling Henry the truth as to why I didn't want to see him anymore, I lied and said I was tired of seeing him. It hurt me to tell Henry that, but I didn't want Patterson to beat him up. I delivered my break up message via telephone.

I was able to avoid him for several days before Henry cornered me at school and said he wasn't going to leave me alone until I told him the truth as to why I quit him. I broke down and cried and told him everything. Henry laughed and said he wasn't scared of Patterson, or any other boy at the school. Henry took me by the hand and dragged me along with him to confront Patterson. We found Patterson beating up a boy on the playground who had refused to give him his lunch money, with his bully buddies cheering him on. Upon seeing us approaching them, Patterson let the boy go and waited for us. He had been laughing while he was beating the boy, but the laughter was replaced with a scowl.

The look on Patterson's face scared me almost to death, but Henry ignored the look and asked Patterson if what I had told him was true. Patterson said yeah, but he didn't really mean anything about it. He was just trying to get in good with me that was all. Henry said good because he wasn't afraid of him or his buddies. After that confrontation, Patterson left us alone. I always wondered why Patterson backed down, because as far as I knew, there was no one in Arkansas who could whup that evil boy.

* * * *

Me, and Pon'k double dated at our junior prom, but I ended up with a friend of mine name Mary Ann. She was standing around looking sad because her date, A. J., had dropped her off at the prom and went and picked up another girl and brought her to the prom also. After arriving with the other girl, A. J. ignored Mary Ann. Although I didn't really want to do it, I encouraged my date to dance with Mary Ann every once in a while to make her feel better. For some stupid reason she would only dance with my date. Doing the prom, my brother Bobo and a friend of his, poured liquor in the punch. One girl, unaware of the liquor being in the punch, drank so much she got tipsy and wasted punch all over her dress. This alerted our teachers that something other than sugar was in the punch. It didn't matter they dumped the little punch that was left because the prom was winding down and most of us were feeling no pain.

I had devised a plan to skip out on Mary Ann so me and my date could be alone after the prom was over. My bonehead date was a friend of A. J's, and he let A. J. talk him into letting Mary Ann tag along with us. A. J. said he would meet us at Oneida after dropping the other girl off at home and would take Mary Ann off of our hands. Oneida was where everyone who didn't want the teachers to see them get wasted met to do just that. A. J. never showed up and we had to listen to her crying and moaning the rest of the night. After the place closed, the other prom dates went to find places to neck or make out. Me, and my date ended up taking Mary Ann home. By the time we dropped her off at her house it was too late for me, and my date to do anything. Daddy had given him a time that he had to have me home. I stayed mad at Mary Ann for a long time after that night, but I never told her I was mad at her.

* * * *

I caught a lot of flak from my brothers and sisters because I could see haints [ghosts], and they couldn't. I remember one late Saturday evening after sunset, daddy told us to go get water for the night. Me, Bobo, and Pon'k, went to the pump to get the water. While they were pumping the water I saw a man [haint] dressed in black coming toward us and I started screaming. We all took off running to the house. Daddy got mad at us and said if we didn't get our butts back out to that pump and bring in the water for the night, he was going to whup us silly. We went back out and got the water, but I don't think they ever forgave me for scaring them. Daddy and Momma could see haints [ghosts] too, so they knew there were always ghosts [haints] around us all the time. The haints never had recognizable faces. You would just see the outline of their bodies.

* * * *

Although I didn't get as many whuppings as my brothers and sisters did, I do remember getting in trouble. I remember one time I had cut off a piece of summer sausage and was about to eat it when I heard momma coming. I hid the piece I had cut in the dish cabinet, but I didn't have time to put the rest of the sausage away. Momma asked me who had taken the summer sausage from the cabinet and cut off a piece. I said, with an honest face, I didn't know. That when I came into the kitchen, it was already laying there. She told me to put the sausage up and not to mess with it. Little, young, and dumb me thought I had pulled the wool over momma's eyes. After she left the room, I got the piece of sausage and started eating it. It was the best summer sausage I had ever eaten. Unknown to me, momma knew I had lied about not cutting off the piece of the sausage. She stood right outside the door and waited until I started eating it. She waited until my mouth was good and full before stepping into the kitchen. Busted, I tried to give her my best puppy-dog-face to show that I was sorry for lying to her, but it didn't work. She got a belt and whupped my butt good. She took the piece of sausage I had left and gave it to Will. I wanted to whup his butt for getting to eat what I had gotten my butt whupped for stealing. So it gave me great pleasure to watch when Will got his just desert when he did something wrong.

* * * *

When Will was a little boy, he had a bad habit of trying to look under women and girls dresses. I don't remember how old he was, but I know he knew what he was doing was wrong. He finally got what was coming to him when Ms. Bea caught him peeping under her dress. Ms. Bea was not a shy woman. She said if it was acceptable for men to pee off the porch, it should be okay for women to do it to. Therefore, it was common knowledge that Ms. Bea would go out on the back porch, pull her drawers to the side, and pee. When we were at her house playing with her children, Will would get under the house every time he saw her on the back porch and wait hoping Ms. Bea would take a whiz so he could peep at her. I don't know how Ms. Bea found out he was always trying to peep at her but she was ready to give him a real show whenever she caught him peeping. A couple of days after she found out Will were peeping at her. We came over to her house to play. Will took up his position under the porch waiting for Ms. Bea to take her daily whiz. Knowing Will was probably under the porch to peep at her, Ms. Bea looked through the cracks until she saw where he was hiding. She watched as Will got closer to get a better view. Ms. Bea positioned herself right over the crack Will was peeping through and she peed through the crack right in his face. To the relief of a lot of girls his peeping days were over.

* * * *

Summary

The hard times we experienced growing up grew us closer together. We depended on each other for comfort and support. We had our disagreements and fights, but in the end it only bought us closer as a family. God has truly blessed us as a family. Looking back over my life, I can see we had the greatest parents in the world. They loved us and prepared us for life.

Wilmer Wade
Born: March 1, 1953
Place of Birth: Mobile, Alabama

Chapter #12
WILL

I was born March 1, 1953 in Mobile, Alabama. My earliest memory is when my sister Betty Ann passed away. I don't know how old I was. I think I was around three years old. I just remember Momma and Daddy sitting on the bed crying, but being as young as I was, I didn't realize the gravity of the situation. I had no concept of what death meant. I don't remember whether we went to the funeral or not, but I knew when Momma and Daddy came home Betty Ann wouldn't be with them. Momma and Daddy was sad for a long time after she died. Even though there were a lot of us kids in the house, Betty Ann's absence left an empty spot that couldn't be filled by anyone else. I can't describe my feelings. It was like my intuition was running on autopilot and I knew things would never be the same without her, but as usual life continued. In no time, for us younger chilluns, it was back too business as usual, being bad and getting our behinds whupped.

*　*　*　*

I used to watch daddy, the other grown-up in the community, my big brother and his friends shoot dice almost every weekend. I watched the money change hands to the happy winners, but it never dawned on me that the loser's emotions took them on a completely different roller coaster ride. The losers got mad sometimes after losing their money, but they never truly showed how much it hurt to lose. So I thought when I started to gamble, I too would lose with dignity and hope I would be the winner the next time I rolled the dice. I knew that when the shooter threw a seven or eleven on the first role, they automatically won whatever the bet was. With my little undeveloped brain working overtime, I knew I would win everyone's money because all I would ever throw would be a seven or eleven. It never crossed my mind that if I didn't shoot first, there was the possibility I would lose my little hard begged for nickel I managed to get from daddy, without getting the chance to roll a seven or an eleven.

One Saturday evening as daddy was sitting up for the weekly crap game, he gave all us children a nickel each. He asked if we wanted to shoot dice. I jumped at the chance to show how grown-up I was and readily let it be known I wanted in the game. Daddy laughed at me for being such a brave little soul. We knelt around the pad daddy had spread out on the floor and rolled one die at a time to see who would get to shoot first. My older sister Sue rolled the highest number the most times so she got to shoot the dice first. Not knowing the consequences of what was about to happen, I took Sue's bet of a nickel. Usually the bets were a penny at a time so we wouldn't lose everything in one roll of the dice, but Sister Sue was a gambler at heart and chose to put her whole nickel on the line. To show I was a gambler too I covered the bet. She shook the dice in her hand like we had watched daddy and the other grown-ups do. She shook them and let them fly. Midway through the roll, the realization that I might lose my money hit me. As I watched the dice roll in slow motion, I prayed they would end up snake eyes, a pair of ones, or craps, three. My mind kept telling me to do like the grown-ups did when they thought the first throw might be a good one and grab the dice before they stopped rolling and make her roll again, but I was frozen in place. When the dice stopped rolling, my heart jumped into my throat as I counted the dots, five on one die and two on the other one. Sue whooped and hollered as she picked up my nickel and said "One nickel down and four to go." She was referring to my other brothers and sisters who wanted to see what it felt like to gamble. I watched in horror as my sister picked up my nickel and put it in her pocket. My hand had reached out involuntarily to stop her from picking up the nickel, but I was too late. I couldn't believe the nickel it had taken me so long to get was gone in one roll of the dice. I asked my sister to give me back my nickel. I said I wasn't playing for keeps. She laughed and said she wasn't giving me anything back, that she had won the nickel fair and square. Realizing she was serious about not giving me my nickel back, I started crying like a baby who had its bottle taken away. Everyone laughed at me but I didn't care, I wanted my nickel back. After tiring of my whining, Daddy told Sue to give me my nickel back and he would give her a nickel to replace it. He then turned to me and said, "Boy don't you never play dice again. If you can't stand to lose, you can't be a gambler." I didn't care what daddy said, I was happy to have my nickel back. It was a long time before I got the nerve to gamble again. I guess I was around seven years old when I learned that gambling was not for me. I went from risking my money gambling, to risking my life riding with daddy.

* * * *

Daddy had a reputation of having a lead foot because he always drove so fast. Momma said he was always in too big of a hurry to get to where he was going, which most of time was no place important. I didn't care. I rode with him every chance I got, even though I would be scared half to death most of time as we sped down the dirt and gravel roads. However, I did like the take off because daddy would stomp down on the accelerator and make the rear tires spin causing the car to fishtail as we took off throwing dirt and gravel everywhere and onto whatever, or whoever, was behind us. When we were hauling butt down the roads, I never knew how fast we would be going but the rocks and gravel would be flying from under the tires hitting everything on the side of the road as we passed. When people were walking down the road and saw daddy coming, they would get off of the road to make sure they weren't hit by flying rocks. During the summer when the roads were dry, when I looked behind the car, there would be such a big cloud of dust you couldn't see anything. When we passed a car going in the opposite direction, the car would disappear in that cloud of dust almost instantly. It was only because momma complained about how dangerous it was to be speeding on loose gravel that made me afraid when we were on the dirt or gravel road because she said it was on gravel and dirt roads where most people were killed in accidents. On the highway I wasn't afraid at all because the ride was smooth regardless of how fast we were going. Momma always said daddy couldn't drive and was going to kill us. I think because momma was always complaining about his driving is why daddy drove especially crazy when she rode with him. After each ride, momma would swear she would never ride with him again. Daddy would laugh as momma got out of the car, as if scaring her was one of his favorite past times.

 Although momma was sacred to ride with daddy, it didn't seem to bother the little old ladies in the community who he would drive to town every day. When momma would try and convince them daddy couldn't drive, they blew it off as her being jealous because daddy was kind enough to help them out. It wouldn't be just a couple of ladies, sometimes he would have to make a couple of trips to get them all to town and back home. It didn't stop momma from waiting to hear the news that daddy had run in to an oncoming car, or run into the lake killing himself and all who would be in the car with him. The neighbors thought it was rather amusing that the only people who didn't think daddy could drive was his own family members. They made sure he always had enough gas to take them where they wanted to go. Daddy's driving wasn't the only thing that got under momma's skin.

 Another one of momma's biggest complaints about daddy, besides not being able to drive, was his gambling and selling moonshine whiskey. Daddy would go out gambling on a Friday night and wouldn't come home sometimes until Sunday afternoon. He would come home happy sometimes because he was the big winner, and other times he came with his head hanging because he lost every dime to his name. It seemed to me daddy lost more times than he won. This is where the moonshine whiskey comes into play. To make up for the money he would lose gambling, daddy would make up selling moonshine whiskey. He had stashes of moonshine whiskey buried in numerous locations in the cotton field. Moonshine was good for whatever ails you, let daddy tell it.

Momma told daddy that moonshine whiskey was going to be the death of him if he didn't get out of the business and if he didn't stop drinking it. Daddy always told her if she and the kids wanted to continue eating and having a roof over their heads, she had better stay out of his business. I remember once we had a long rain spell and daddy them couldn't work in the fields for thirteen days in a row because the fields were too muddy to work in. It was at this time I thought momma might be right about moonshine whiskey killing daddy, because he got drunk every day of the thirteen days he didn't work. While he was passed out, momma had to sell the whiskey for him. So that meant we had to go to the various locations in the cotton fields and bring the whiskey for momma to sell. She would be fussing the whole time she was taking the money from daddy's customers, which were quite a few. I don't remember if daddy was making the bootleg whiskey or buying it from someone else and reselling it.

*　*　*　*

When it came to women, daddy was one of the smoothest talking dudes in the world. In no time flat, he would have the average woman he was talking to eating out of his hands. His greatest weapon was the ability to make women believe him when he told them how beautiful they were, even though some of them were dog butt ugly. When the women would question his sincerity, he would explain his philosophy that everything God makes is beautiful, and being that women were His most important creation they were all beautiful, after all they were chosen to replenish the earth. Therefore, there were no doubt in his mind they were His most beautiful creation. He said men who looked at a woman's physical appearance missed the most important part of her beauty, which was her ability to keep the world from dying and filling it with love. They would get all giggly and do whatever he asked of them. Of course momma said those stupid women who believed his bull crap deserved to be pitied instead of criticized. I used to go to town with daddy and we would end up at Jim Café where I would watch as he gave his "woman you are beautiful" speech and would then spend his last dime to impress the lady. When I asked him why he would spend his last dime on a lady he didn't know and then leave the club, he would laugh and say he was making plans for when he met her again. Daddy told me if I was to be successful with women, I would never tell a woman she is ugly, no matter how ugly she happens to be.

* * * *

Almost every Sunday momma would cook a special dinner after church, especially if the preacher was going to stop by, usually chicken. Momma would tell us to catch a couple of chickens from the yard for dinner. I loved catching the chickens. I would pick out the fattest one of the bunch and I wouldn't give up until I had that sucker on the table. It was a real treat when momma would bring lunch to us out in the cotton field and it would be the left over chicken from Sunday's dinner. I also loved when momma brought neck bones, pinto beans, corn bread, and peach pie to the cotton fields for dinner. When momma brought our dinner to the cotton fields, it was always good and hot. Otherwise, we were stuck with cold bologna and crackers.

I worked hard when I was a kid in the cotton fields of Arkansas and Mississippi. Very seldom did daddy give us any of the money we earned. At the end of the week or day, the foreman would pay daddy the money the farm owner owed us as the head of the household. When daddy wasn't with us, the foreman paid our wages to the oldest boy who was working with us. All we ever asked for was enough money to get a couple of pieces of penny candy or a couple of two-cent cookies. We also asked for money to go to the picture show. It cost ten cents to go to the movies. I can't remember going too often, and I don't remember momma and daddy never taking us to the movies. I really can't remember daddy or momma really taking us anywhere as a family other than to town every once in a while. Maybe there were too many of us to take anyplace at one time.

* * * *

When I started the eleventh grade at Lakeview High School, I tried out for my high school basketball team without telling momma and daddy. I didn't tell daddy because I didn't think he would allow me to skip work, or other things he wanted me to do around the house when I got out of school, to practice. I made up excuses as to why I was always late getting home from school. When the basketball season started, I told daddy and momma I was going to watch the games. I don't remember how he found out, but when he did daddy didn't like it one bit. He said I had too much work to do in the field and around the house to be playing a foolish game. Daddy said, "Boy, you got things to do at home. You don't have time for this nonsense." After much pleading by me and momma, he finally gave in and allowed me to play. He still didn't like it, but gave in and didn't bother me about playing basketball again. Momma said daddy did not really like me playing basketball, but he was proud when people told him I was pretty good at the game. I think daddy went to one basketball game. Momma never went to a game as far as I can remember.

The greatest game of my high school basketball career was the night we defeated our biggest rival, Miller High School. We had never beaten them in the history of our school existence, so we went into the game that night not really expecting to change that history, although we had only loss one game up to that point. We knew we had a pretty good team, but doubted we could hang with them because they had a lot more athletes to choose from. The guys who couldn't even make that team could start at most other schools, so we made a pledge with each other going into the game that we would at least let them know they had been in a game. Coach kept telling us if we believed in ourselves, and each other, we could do the impossible. We all had the same reaction, "yeah right."

When the game started, we played with more energy than we had played with all season. This was our twelfth game of the season, and because this was our biggest rival, the gym was packed. We traded basket for basket throughout the first half. The two stars of our team were having incredible games. At halftime we led by one point, but we weren't fooling ourselves. We knew during the second half they were going to throw everything but the toilet bowl at us. Coach was so proud of how well we played the first half I think he wouldn't have minded if we lost the game. Of course he didn't tell us that. He said the night was our night. We were David, and we were going to slay Goliath.

When the second half started, we took up right where we left off. I did the rebounding and played defense against their best player. The battle swayed back and forth throughout the game. With eight seconds left on the clock, Miller went up by one point. We advanced the ball to half court and coach called a time out. He drew up a play for our best shooter to get the ball to try and win it at the buzzer. My job was to try and put back a desperation offensive rebound if we missed the shot. The ball was in-bounded to the designated player, but he was doubled teamed immediately with the guy who was supposed to be guarding me. I had scored only one point all night, and didn't expect the ball to come to me. In desperation he passed the ball to me. I found myself wide open at the free throw line. Everyone in the gym was yelling shoot, shoot, shoot, I was told after the game, but I don't remember hearing the yelling. I just knew if I didn't get the shot off we were going to lose and everyone and their mother would dog me out for not shooting the ball, so I let it fly. The motion as I released the ball felt so good, I knew the ball had a chance of going in. Everyone in the gym followed the flight of the ball with open mouths. As the ball whisked through the basket, the buzzer sounded, and pandemonium erupted throughout the gym. The Lakeview High School Basketball team had made history. We had beaten the unbeatable team in our district. I was carried from the gym on the shoulders of my teammates. It didn't matter the star of our team had scored 30 + points and I had scored a total of three points. I rode that emotional wave for the remainder of my high school basketball career. We didn't win state or anything while I played at Lakeview, but beating Miller High School was the highlight of my career, and a night I will never forget. It didn't even bother me that kids at school teased me saying they saw daddy at a game using a popcorn bag as a handkerchief.

* * * *

One Friday night daddy let me use the car to go to the club where all the teenagers hung out. It was fun having my own ride for a change. Girls who wouldn't even talk to me before came up to me asking if I would take them out sometime. I picked up a couple of my buddies on the way to the club and was thrilled to death to see the envious looks on their faces as the girls talked to me about taking them out, because I told them my daddy had told me I could use the car anytime I wanted to. Later that night, after I had dropped my buddies off and was heading home, I went over the railroad tracks at too high a rate of speed and the car slammed to the ground knocking the muffler loose from the manifold. I was too scared to tell daddy what had happened when I got home. Besides, it was after twelve midnight and I didn't dare wake him up at that time of night. I would wake up early that morning and tell him about it before he started the car. As all best laid plans goes, it didn't. I overslept. Daddy got up that Saturday morning and started the car. You can imagine how loud the engine was without the muffler. He was mad as he crawled under the car to repair the muffler. Momma came into my room and asked me what I had done to the car. I told her it was an accident. She told me to tell that to my daddy. I went out to where he was working on the car and told him I didn't want to wake him last night, and had intended to tell him about it before he started the car that morning. Daddy said angrily, "Boy, if you were serious about telling me what happened you would have gotten your sorry butt up and told me before I started the car this morning. I don't believe you for one damn instant. Don't you ever ask to borrow my car again." Unfortunately for me, my newfound status of driving a car turned back to bumming a ride. The girls who had talked to me the previous weekend because they thought I would be driving my daddy's car stopped talking to me again. My buddies were happy that we were back on even ground again. In one night my bragging rights among my buddies were gone.

* * * *

Once there was this woman we called Mrs. Bea. She told momma she had caught me trying to look up her dress. I told momma I was under the porch when Ms. Bea took a pee, but I wasn't peeping at her. I was under the porch looking for worms to go fishing. I knew I was wasting my breath defending myself because back then, parents always took the word of a grown-up over that of a child. To further debunk my claim of innocence, my sister Oyce confirmed Ms. Bea story although she didn't see anything. So, as a result of the testimony against me momma wore me out.

* * * *

Once there was a couple who said they were mommas' momma and daddy but I don't remember their names. The woman said they had given momma up at birth because they had so many children they couldn't afford to keep them all. So they gave her to the family who raised her. They knew when and where momma was born, and that her daddy had been killed in a job related accident. The man said they just wanted her to know the truth about who she was, and to know they never stopped loving her. They told her if there was anything they could do to make up for abandoning her, to let them know. Momma told them even if they were her parents they didn't owe her anything because the only momma she knew loved her, and had taken good care of her. In the end momma said they were full of B.S. and didn't have anything else to do with them. When they called she refused to talk to them on the phone, and when they came by the house she refused to let them in the house to talk to her. They eventually got the message that momma didn't want anything to do with them and stopped coming around.

* * * *

The last person in the world I wanted to whip my butt was

daddy, so when momma would catch me messing up, all she had to say was if you don't stop it I'm going to tell your daddy on you. However, when I did something that I knew I was going to get a spanking for, I would try and get momma to do it. It worked on some occasions but most of the time she didn't feel like it. I would pray all day long that something happened that would either make momma forget to tell daddy what I had done, or daddy would be too tired to whip me that day. I knew I was hoping in vain because daddy never got too tired to whip butts.

* * * *

Summary

The family wasn't as large as when my older brothers and sisters were all at home. When I came along most of my older brothers and sisters was married and had families of their own. Also, I didn't have it as hard as they did in the cotton fields. Doing family reunions, and when they come home to visit, you can see the love and respect we have for each other. God continue to bless us one and all.

Mary Frances Wade Jones Garner
Born: October 1, 1954
Place of Birth: Yazoo, Mississippi

CHAPTER #13
PON'K

I was born October 1, 1954 in Yazoo, Mississippi. I am the thirteenth child in the clan. I don't know if I had it easier than my siblings before me, but I do know we didn't have much while I was growing up. Although momma and Daddy didn't have a lot of material things to give to us kids as we were growing up but they gave us love, direction, the knowledge of what it took to survive, the will to work, and the fortitude to do the right thing. I have very fond memories of momma and daddy while growing up.

I loved to listen to momma and Daddy's stories about what it was like when they were children growing up in Corinth, Mississippi. I would sit spellbound while they told of a time in America when black folks were still treated like slaves, although the chains had been removed. The majority of black folks freed from slavery had no land or homes to call their own, so they ended up back on the plantations where they had been enslaved. Although they were now being paid for their labor, it wasn't enough to survive on. After all those years since slavery ended, they found themselves still in the clutches of the white plantation owners. And they still experienced the same indignities of beatings, hangings, no right to vote, and denied education that our ancestors faced while enslaved.

White men raped black women and young black girls whenever they wanted to and nothing was ever done to them. They went to black men's houses and dragged them into the front yard and hung them for anything they were accused of, whether the charge was true or not. Most of the charges were disrespecting or messing with a white woman. They said the only solace they had was the church. So every Sunday their parents dragged them off to church to praise God for giving them the ability to continue day after day, and reassure them that better days were ahead for them, when they too would be treated as human beings.

On the domestic side, they didn't have water pumps so they had to draw water from a well or the nearest river. They had to make their own soap to use to wash clothes or to bathe with. One of momma's daily chores was milking the cows and gathering the eggs from the hen house. Momma would laugh at how mad she would get when the cows managed to kick over a bucket full of milk, or she would go into the hen house to gather the eggs without knowing one of the hens had started to sit. She explained that when a hen started to sit meant she was bringing forth baby chicks, and they would peck anyone who stuck their hand into their nest to protect the eggs. Momma had to walk about three miles to and from school. Fortunately for her, momma never had to endure the rigors of chopping and picking cotton. Because of a back injury she suffered earlier in her childhood, she never had to worry about having to pick cotton. The bending over was too hard on her back. Her momma didn't even let her chop cotton because of the fear that the constant walking might hurt her back also.

Daddy said when he was about ten years old he had to plow the fields with mules in the spring for planting season, and during the summer to keep the weed from killing the cotton. He would talk about when the mules got ornery he would hit them with some type of board or something like his daddy had told him to. I don't remember what he said he used, but it sounded cruel to me. Daddy said he had to walk about two miles to school during the two years he attended school. When he started plowing with the mules he didn't chop cotton, but during the fall he was out there with his cotton sack with everyone else picking it. The reason I loved to hear these stories was because they assured me that I could overcome almost anything I would ever face in my life. Simply because they fought and suffered for the rights of black people, I wouldn't have to start from scratch as I paved the way for my children. I was thankful they laid the foundation for me to build upon.

* * * *

Momma and Daddy's belief in God, daddy later in life, carried over from their childhood into their adult lives because I could hear daddy and momma saying their prayers every night before going to bed, asking God to protect them and the children while they go forth into this cruel and uncaring world. Daddy would say his prayers so loud we could hear him throughout the house. Momma was much quieter while saying her prayers, but you could hear her. It was more of a whisper than a shout like daddy. I would thank God I didn't have the burden of feeding, clothing, and caring for us, simply because of the number of us in the family. When I said my prayers before going to bed at night, I would put in a special request to God that He hear my momma and daddy's prayers.

* * * *

We did a lot of moving around when we were kids. Every time we got comfortable and made friends at one school it was time to pull up the stakes and move again. We would start the friend making process all over again in another town and another school. We attended schools in Marianna, Moro, Anna Strong, Wabash, and Lakeview, all in Arkansas. The enduring memory of attending all those different schools was our fellow students were the same as us, black and poor, regardless of where we attended school.

Me, and my brother Will first started school when we lived on Cow Bayou, in Marianna, Arkansas and finished our schooling at Lakeview, Arkansas where we graduated. It didn't matter that our ages were different they put us in the same grade. That was fine with me because I didn't want to be in a classroom with a bunch of kids I didn't know. When lunchtime rolled around at Wabash Elementary School, it was like eating with the Beverly Hillbillies. Our daily diets consisted of one of the following delicacies; fried rabbit, fried squirrel, fried pork, fried eggs, all stuffed between grease soaked bread, and carried to school in a greasy brown paper bag. Those of us who bought our lunches to school in those greasy, brown paper bags were very conscious of the image we presented, and were embarrassed. We preferred the peanut butter and jelly, or bologna sandwiches like the well to do kids brought to school for their lunch, because the sandwiches looked neat and made the kids eating them looked sophisticated. They didn't have to wipe their hands on their clothes or the grass after finishing their meal to keep the grease from getting on their school papers. I wouldn't eat because I was too shy. I couldn't handle the idea of the other kids looking into my mouth as I chewed on rabbits and squirrels.

    Sister Oyce made our mealtime adventure even more embarrassing on some occasions because she would eat the eggs and meat out of the bread before lunchtime, and leave nothing but the greasy bread in the bag. You can imagine our surprise when we would sit down with our group, reach into our greasy bag, and pull out the greasy biscuit with no meat in it. The other kids would laugh at us because of the confused looks on our faces as we stared at the naked bread. Bobo and Will would be too embarrassed to eat the bread without any meat. Not having meat to eat with the bread did not bother me because as I said earlier, I didn't eat my lunch anyway.

    The lunches momma fixed for us to take to school was not to embarrass us or show how poor we were, because the majority of our fellow classmates were in the same boat with us, but to ensure we didn't go hungry. Our parents loved us very much and did whatever it took to keep us fed. I can never remember being really hungry or going without food for any length of time. It was just that we didn't always want what momma had to offer. Our dear momma always cooked three meals a day, and every now and then she would throw in something sweet in between meals. Along with our own stock of chickens, hogs, and canned goods, daddy was one of the best hunters, and fishermen in Arkansas, so he kept food on the table. I thank God for our parents and the way they raised us. Still it was embarrassing to carry that greasy, brown paper bag to school before we started eating in a school cafeteria.

When we moved around the Lake and started going to Lakeview Elementary School we went from carrying our lunches to school in brown greasy paper bags to going to the school cafeteria. Being we were living below the poverty line our lunches were free. I thought not having to deal with the homemade lunches I would be more willing to eat. However, that wasn't the case. Every day when it was time for us to go to lunch, I would start crying because I was ashamed to eat lunch in front of a lot of people. So after getting my tray of food, I would find Will and sit beside him during lunch, but I wouldn't touch the food. I'd sit next to him crying and looking into his face. And because I was ashamed to eat in front of the other kids, I didn't want him to eat either. He'd say I was being silly, and would gulp down whatever was on his plate and whatever was on mine's. I would just sit there and watch. I wouldn't eat the food, but I always saved my carton of white milk to take home to momma. I never missed a day bringing my milk home. Momma always smiled and said, "thank you baby." I guess that's why I kept on taking the milk home.

While attending Lakeview School, 4th or 5th grade, I had this teacher named Ms. Alexander. She was the meanest teacher in the world. I guess she didn't like me for some reason because one day she whipped me on my legs for no apparent reason. After she finished whipping me, my legs started turning real dark from the broken blood vessels caused by the switch. And by the time I made it home, my legs were black and blue and swollen. I thought daddy and momma was going to go to the school and fuss at Ms. Alexander, but all they said was she didn't whip you for nothing. All they did was rub some kind of grease on my legs and that was the end of that. I never found out why she whipped me. I didn't hate Ms. Alexander for what she did to me because we were taught not to hate anyone, but if something bad had happened to her, I wouldn't have lost any sleep because of it.

I remember this one teacher named Mr. Patterson. He had a habit of throwing whatever he got his hands on, a shoe, an eraser, or a writing tablet, at the student that was acting up in his classroom. His favorite saying was "I'll beat your back off." Some of the kids misbehaved on purpose just to get him upset so he would throw something at them.

At one time there were six of us Wade kids in the same classroom, but different grades. The school was the classic "one room" schoolhouse. I don't remember where we were living at the time. My classmates thought it was funny. They used to say there were enough kids in our family to form our own basketball or baseball team. During this time in our lives, we had to do our homework before it got dark, otherwise we would've had to do it by the glow of the oil lamps because we didn't have electricity. You should have guessed by now that since we had no electricity we didn't have fans in the summer to keep cool. We would raise the windows, day and night, to catch what breezes we could. We made cardboard fans to fan ourselves, but they weren't much help. At night after the sun went down the house would cool somewhat. Later on in the night it would be rather cool if you didn't have to cover up to keep the mosquitoes from draining your body of it much needed blood supply. So we spent our nights between trying to keep cool while we slept and denying the mosquitoes the blood they sought. The mosquitoes ended up winning because they knew it was only a matter of time before we would fall asleep and automatically kick the covers off because it would be so hot. Anyway, the light from the lamps was so dim it's a miracle we didn't go blind. When we didn't have oil for the lamps we had to do our homework and reading assignment by candlelight. Another miracle was we didn't develop lung cancer from the smoke we inhale from the burning oil lamps and candles.

I remember while living in Wabash, Arkansas, Bobo, Oyce and me missed the school bus on purpose on one occasion because we had thrown our school shoes on top of the house. We pretended to look high and low for them knowing we were going to miss the bus, which meant we would have to miss school, or so we thought. After missing the school bus, we made plans on how we were going to spend this free day from school. We were sure our plan had worked to perfection. To our disappointment, and horror daddy made us put on our brogan work shoes and walk to school, which was several miles away from where we lived. Needless to say, we were teased by the students at school that day because the majority of the kids knew we were wearing work shoes. I don't remember ever missing the bus again after that, for any reason, other than being sick.

As kids we even found time to have fun together, when we weren't fighting. We girls played baseball and basketball with our brothers. However, most of the time when their buddies came over to play, they wouldn't let us girls play with them, talking about we might get hurt. At times like these they were just being male chauvinist pigs. When we didn't have baseballs or rubber balls to play ball with, we would use the heads of our dolls, mainly because the boys had already ripped the heads off while ignoring our protests. We also wrestle, went fishing, swimming, and swinging out over the water of the Cow Bayou Lake. We never gave it a second thought that we might fall and break our necks if the vines broke over the ground, or drown if we happened to fall in the lake because we couldn't swim very well, which eventually happened to a couple of my brothers and two of their friends. They lived to tell the tale. I was disappointed I wasn't there to enjoy the moment. The ignorance of taking chances and not being concerned about the dangers they posed was the bliss of being a youth.

*   *   *   *

One of my fondest memories growing up was the time me and my sister Oyce needed new dresses for a banquet we were to attend at Lakeview High School, in Lakeview, Arkansas. We moped around the house like we had lost our best friends, because we knew the other students would laugh and make fun of us if we had to wear the same old dresses we wore to school during the school year to the banquet. As the time got closer and closer to banquet time, we started losing hope that we would be getting new dresses for the banquet. So we picked out what we thought were the best looking dresses we had in our po wardrobe and hoped for a miracle.

I don't know where they got the money, but to our delight and surprise, momma and daddy came up with the money somehow and bought two dresses for us to wear to the banquet. You would think we were the two happiest girls in Lakeview, Arkansas. We had brand new dresses and didn't have to wear our old dresses. Although I was happy to get the dress, my selfishness kept me from being completely satisfied with it. I had seen a pretty powder blue dress in town that I wanted, and it only cost $3.00 more than the dress I got.

Don't get me wrong, they were pretty dresses, but they were made just alike and I didn't want to go to the banquet looking like Oyce's twin sister. The only difference in the dresses was the color. Mine's was pink and Joyce's was yellow. But when you're broke and po' you play the hand you're dealt, so I went to the banquet determined to make the best of it, regardless of what our classmates had to say about us being dressed alike.

When Oyce and I showed up at the banquet looking like the mismatched color twins, we thought we would be teased to no end. As it turned out, everyone thought it was an excellent idea that we had decided to wear identically made dresses in different colors. We had a really good time.

After the banquet was over I felt guilty for trying to be choosy about what dress momma and daddy had bought for me to wear to the banquet. I knew I should have been thankful for any kind of dress they could afford to get me because it meant I was blessed.

* * * *

Other memorable events were the times daddy would take us to basketball games at Lakeview High School to watch our brother Will play. Although we liked watching Will play, the highlight of these basketball game excursions was daddy would always buy us popcorn and a soda. I would clap along with everyone else when Will did well, but my mind would be on half time when we would make our way to the snack stand. Daddy was so proud to be sitting in the stands watching his son run up and down the basketball court. You could see in his eyes that he wished he had been in the position to show the world what he could do as an athlete in baseball. I believed he wanted Gene, our younger brother, to follow in Will's footsteps, but basketball was not Gene's gift.

Although I enjoyed these outings with daddy at the basketball games, there was a few times I wished daddy would've taken a handkerchief to the games with him. I would be jumping up and down enjoying the game and I would hear daddy blowing his nose. Knowing he didn't have a handkerchief with him, I would turn around to see what he was using for a rag. To my amazement he would be blowing his nose into the empty popcorn bag and wiping his nose on the sleeve of his shirt. My schoolmates would have a field day the following day at school talking about it. Some of my classmates would save their popcorn bags from the night before and tell me to give it to daddy so he would have something to blow his nose with at the next game. I took everything that was said about daddy in stride, because I wanted to attend all the basketball games I could and he was the one who was going to take me to see them. I don't remember how many games daddy attended but it was considerably more than what Will remember him attending.

* * * *

I don't think I appreciated daddy more than when I got sick and had to go to the doctor, or had a toothache and needed to go to the dentist. At times like these he would hold my little hands and assure me that everything was going to be all right. The fear that I felt gripping me on the way to the doctor or dentist office, making me think the end for me was near would slowly disappear. His assurances didn't stop once I got out of the car, it continued once I was in the doctor or dentist office. He would have the doctor or dentist assure me that if they did anything to hurt me, daddy would be there to take care of the problem.

* * * *

When I got pregnant at sixteen I just knew my life was over. At first when the morning sickness started, I didn't know what was wrong with me. I kept saying it must have been something I ate, but as the baby started to grow inside of me I had to face reality. I pictured myself homeless and hungry, with a newborn infant in my arms, because I knew momma and daddy were going to kill me, revive me, and then kick me out of the house. I hid my pregnancy for as long as I could before telling momma. I begged her not to tell daddy because I was afraid he would beat the living daylight out of me, pregnant or not.

I started wearing loose fitting clothes so no one could tell I was pregnant, but because of the morning sickness momma let me stay home from school quite often. My staying home sick all the time was not lost on daddy. I overheard him ask momma why I was missing so much school. Momma told him he would have to ask me. As was daddy's custom, he never asked what was on his mind right away, especially if he thought it was going to be bad news. Every time he came near me after I overheard their conversation, I stiffened in anticipation of that dreaded question he was going to ask me. I was so stressed out waiting for daddy to ask me if I was pregnant, I started wondering if I would lose my baby because of it. Well, several days later he finally asked me if I was in the family way. Although I was scared to death, I admitted that I was. I then waited for him to berate me for being stupid, and then beat me silly. To my surprise all he said was we would get through it as a family, and walked away. I was so relieved and grateful that momma and daddy still loved me after what I had done. I didn't realize I was crying until the salty tears ran into my mouth. To show he meant what he had said, daddy took me to the doctor for my prenatal care until the baby was born. And my dear momma made sure I was okay, and she counseled me on what to expect once the baby was born. I thank God and my lucky stars for having parents that loved me.

After the baby was born, a girl, momma and daddy couldn't get enough of her. Daddy acted like a first time daddy when he would take me and the baby to the clinic for checkups.

Since I hadn't finished high school, I wondered if I would have to stay home and take care of the baby after it was born. Momma and daddy had already decided before the baby was born that I would resume my education after giving birth. So a short time after giving birth, I was back in school and a short time later I had my high school diploma. Momma and daddy did such a good job of helping me to raise Shell, she started calling them momma and daddy instead of grand momma and granddaddy. That was fine with me because I wouldn't have made it without their help. Again, I felt blessed to have parents who loved me and my baby. Meanwhile, my favorite brother almost caused me to have a miscarriage.

    Bobo had to be the craziest boy in all of Arkansas, or he honestly didn't realize my condition while I was pregnant. He still wanted to horseplay with me although he knew I was with child. I don't know how far along I was, but one day while in his playful mood, he picked me up and body slammed me to the ground. He got scared when I told him I was going to tell daddy he had slammed me to the ground and may have hurt my baby. He pleaded with me not to tell daddy what he had done, and promised he would never hurt me again. I told him I wouldn't tell on him this time, but I almost changed my mind later because I was in pain all that night. The pain was so bad I thought I might lose the baby. The following day, the pain subsided to the point I was able to keep my promise not to tell daddy on him.

    Bobo kept his promise that he would never physically hurt me again. However, he never said anything about not scaring the mess out of me. One day while I was washing dishes, he snuck up behind me and tapped me on the shoulder. I turned to see who it was and came face to face with a person in an ugly Halloween mask. It scared me so bad I almost fainted. Bobo laughed as if it was the funniest thing he had ever seen in his life. He kept saying, "I got you, I got you." What he didn't know was he almost scared that baby right out of me. I knew my baby was going to be a strong child because it had survived the stress I went through trying to hide my pregnancy from daddy, me being body slammed, and being scared half to death by Bobo. Healthy and strong she was.

* * * *

All we children in the Wade household entered the workforce at a young age. We started working in the family garden around the age of five. I know the first thing that comes to everyone's mind today is how much could there be to do in a garden? In 1959 our garden was almost the size of a small cotton field. We had rows upon rows of beans, okra, tomatoes, cucumbers, squash, watermelons, corn, greens, beets, cabbage, and anything else that could be grown in a garden. So chopping weeds in the garden was almost a full time job. I remember saying I might as well be working in the fields, at least I would be getting paid for the work. But when winter rolled around during mealtime, we were thankful for the stuff we grew in the garden.

At age six I got my wish about working for wages, that was when I started chopping cotton for three dollars a day from 6 a.m. to 6 p.m., $15.00 a week. Transportation to and from the fields was limited when daddy's car was broke down. We had to catch a ride to and from the fields anyway we could. If we were lucky we would get a ride on the back of a truck driven by one of the local foreman on the farm where we were working that day, however, most of the time we would find ourselves piling into daddy's car. Those that couldn't fit into the car would find themselves piling into the trunk. Being we always left home to go to the fields before sun-up, often these rides were bone chilling cold.

When the cotton was at its highest height and dew fell that night, I would get wet from my chest down to my feet. It was the same every morning the dew fell that night. I would look at the field with the leaves dripping with dew and it would look like a swimming pool to me because I knew it was only a matter of time before I would be wet from chest to feet. Like someone testing the water before getting into the pool, I would shake some dew off the first stalks of cotton on my row to get a feel of how cold the plunge was going to be. I knew it was senseless to try and avoid the water that had collected on the leaves, but I did anyway. With each step I felt the water soaking my clothes. As a child I had nothing for the men and boys to ogle at, but the older girls and women performed the first wet T-shirt contest although they had no intention of doing so. Lord, help the girl or woman who wore a white shirt or blouse and wasn't wearing a bra. The men and boys would almost break their necks trying to get a peek at her breasts. How soon I would dry out depended on how fast the sun heated up the air, and the dew on the leaves of the cotton dried up. Usually it was just before lunchtime before my clothes dried. My clothes and shoes would be as wet as if I had been swimming in them.

Some of the fields we chopped in had these vines that were called morning glories. They would be so thick and spread out you couldn't tell where their roots were, so we would have to kick them around until we found the root to cut it. While kicking these vines, they would wrap around my ankles and cause bruises. My ankles stayed sore whenever we had to work in these types of fields. After cotton-chopping time in the summer was over, it was cotton-picking time in the fall.

At age six you weren't expected to pick too much cotton because you were at that learning stage. However, the following year at age seven I was picking as much as a hundred pounds of cotton a day and each succeeding year the amount increased until I reached the maximum I would be able to pick. My older brothers and sisters were picking between 250 and 350 pounds depending on their ages, except for Oyce who never could pick cotton worth a darn. We would get to the field before sun up and leave after the sun went down, upholding that saying of the slaves of working from "can't see to can't see". For some reason, I thought when I started working the field I wouldn't have to work in the garden, but when we got off work from the fields, we had to work in the garden. The food was good after harvesting, but we hated the growing, caring, and gathering process. In addition to working in the garden, we had our regular chores of gathering wood for the cook stove and living room stove used for heating the house in the winter. Chopping cotton and chopping in the garden during the summer, to picking cotton and canning the vegetables from the garden during the fall, was the natural order of us children on the farm. Another order on the farm was gathering every bow of cotton possible, which had us in the cotton fields as late as December.

Wintertime in the cotton fields was a time of dread for me. Dread because it would be so cold while we were "strapping" the cotton. This was the cotton that bloomed late and we were allowed to strip the stalk, bows and all. Sometimes it would be after Christmas in December before we got it all in. Many days we went to the field with ice and snow on the ground. Daddy would have to make a fire so we could keep our hands and feet warm enough to continue work because the ragged gloves and sock weren't thick enough to keep our feet and hands warm. I remember many days crying because I was freezing, but had to suck it up and get that cotton. Year round, the lunch we carried to the fields with us to eat consisted of either wieners, fried chicken, or treet canned luncheon meat, augmented with either crackers, cookies, bread, or honey buns, and water. Every once in a while we would have a soda to wash down the cold food.

In addition to growing our own vegetables, daddy and my brothers kept the family supplied with meat and fish. Year round we cleaned fish, rabbits, chickens, squirrels, coons, possums, and turtles. Each winter there were hog killing rituals throughout the community. Families would take turns slaughtering hogs. This ritual was carried out at least twice during the winter months. It was the women and girls job to clean the chit'lings and cook the cracklings, which was the hog's skin and first layer of fat. From the cracklings we got the grease or lard we would use for cooking. The men and boys would grind certain portions of the hog to make sausages. The remainder of the meat momma and daddy would sugar cure and place in the smokehouse. Sometime I would feel kind of sorry for the hogs because I would remember all the times I had to chase them back into their pen when they were little pigs and got out. Interacting with the animals over a period of time, you would get somewhat attached to them, which wasn't a good idea on a farm because you knew you were going to end up eating the animal you considered your pet. Only the dogs and cats were safe from this fate.

* * * *

When I was growing up there was no washer and dryer. We had to pump the water, carry it, pour it in the big number three tin washtub that contained the washing powder and use a rubboard to get the dirt out of the clothes. After getting the dirt out of the clothes, we then had to put them in another number three tub to be rinsed, which we had to pump the water and carry it and pour it in the tub. Then we would have to wring them out by hand and hang them on the clothes-line, which was normally three strands of wire stretched between two poles about twenty feet apart. If it happened to rain and dirt splashed up on the clothes, or we happened to get some of the clothes dirty while playing around them, usually by pulling them off the line, we had to wash them again. When we had to wash white clothes, we had to make a fire under the big black pot daddy used at hog killing time to clean the hog. Sometimes the water would be so hot it would almost scald your hands. Talking about some fussing sisters when it came time to wash the white clothes. We were thankful momma and daddy couldn't hear what we were thinking. We had to ask God for forgiveness before we started washing the clothes so we wouldn't go to hell, because He knew the fussing and cussing was coming. Most of the cussing came from my older sisters.

We also didn't have electric or gas stoves, so we had to sit on the logs to keep them from turning while my brothers sawed them into pieces small enough to fit in the big cast iron stoves momma used to cook on, or the tin heater stove used for heating the house during the winter. While sitting on the wood, my brothers would tease us by calling us silly names. They called me "Willie the Wild Woman," and my sister Oyce "Notty Joe Hog Head." The only reason I can think as to why they call us those awful names was because they were low down bullies. But we got back at them occasionally because when momma was sick, Oyce and I had to cook, and man was it bad. We would laugh because daddy would make them eat it.

* * * *

To use the toilet, we had to take a stroll down the path to the outhouse. You can imagine what it was like if you had to go late at night in the dead of winter. We became experts at taking the one-minute whiz or dump. It didn't help that daddy used to tell us scary ghost stories that always happened at night. So whenever one of us had to use the outhouse at night, we became real close siblings and kept each other company while we did our business. During the summer, the stench would get so bad daddy would have to pour lime on the feces to kill the smell. The only good thing about having an outhouse was when it got full, daddy would throw lime in the hole, fill it in with dirt, and pack it down so no one would fall into it, and dig another hole and move the outhouse over to the new location. I don't remember how long it took us to fill one of the holes up, but I do remember daddy and my brothers moving the outhouse a couple of times.

* * * *

Our wardrobe consisted of two sets of clothing. One set was for school, our good clothes, maybe two or three dresses, and the other set was to work and play in. There were more work clothes than any other kind because I was the thirteenth child of the brood, which meant there were lots of hand-me-downs. We would have two pairs of shoes, one for school and the other for work and play. We didn't get new shoes until we needed new shoes. Daddy had a bad habit of putting cardboard paper in the bottom of our shoes when the sole got holes in them, and he wired the soles together when they busted loose. We didn't have a summer wardrobe and a winter wardrobe. You wore whatever clothes you happened to have at the time. So it was common for us girls to have to wear thin summer dresses to school in the winter. Those cold north winds would blow right through our coats and that thin material as if we were walking around buck-naked. I would almost freeze to death going to and from school during those cold winter days. It is amazing we didn't catch pneumonia and die from exposure. The boys didn't care what they looked like, so they would wear two pairs of pants and two shirts with their coats to keep warm when they didn't have long drawers to wear.

*   *   *   *

The next few incidents I'm going to share are about me and my sister Oyce. This is therapeutic because it allows me to let off the last remaining little steam left over from our childhood, because she was always getting me into trouble. We got into a fight about something at church once, and I ended up dragging her out the back door of the church by the hair over the ice-covered ground. I also locked her in the outhouse once. I knew she was afraid of the wasps, and since the outhouse was full of them, I wanted to punish her for always getting me into trouble with momma and daddy. While banging on the door for me to let her out, it disturbed the wasp nest and they stung her in her face. Because of Oyce's screams I quickly unlatched the door so she could get out. Momma, hearing Oyce screaming, came out and asked me what had happened to my sister. I said I didn't know, and I in turn asked Oyce what was wrong with her. Of course she told momma I had locked her in the toilet. Her face swelled to the point she could hardly see out of her eyes. Being the sarcastic children that we were we couldn't pass up the opportunity to call her little china girl. As my older siblings have said, we called everyone Chinese if their faces were swollen for any reason. Momma whipped my butt good and made me Oyce's maid until the swelling went down, but it was worth it. Although it was wrong to lock Oyce in the outhouse, I did it for revenge. A few days earlier my dear sister Oyce was the cause of me getting one of the worst beatings in my life.

On that hot summer day while picking cotton, Daddy had let Oyce go to get a drink of water, so I asked if I could go get a drink also. Naturally he said, "Yea, go ahead but don't take too long." When I got to where daddy left the water, Oyce was playing with the jug. I asked her to give me the jug so I could get a drink of the water. She said no I couldn't have any. While we were wrestling over the jug we ended up knocking it over and spilling the whole contents of the jug before I could get a drink. Knowing that she was going to get in trouble for her part in the wasting of the water, Oyce ran ahead of me and told daddy someone had drank all our water. When I got back I told the truth as to what had happened and how we had accidentally wasted the water. Daddy went to confirm that the water had been wasted. When he got back I told him that it was Oyce's fault that we wasted the water not mine's, but since she was his favorite child, he had pity on her. She had to be punished since she was there when the water was wasted so he whipped her a little bit, but when he tore into me, he beat me really bad. He whipped us with cotton stalks complete with cotton bows still on them.

Daddy used a small stalk of cotton when he whipped Oyce, but when it was my turn to be punished I swear he pulled up two of the biggest stalks he could find. The stalks were about two feet long when he started whipping me. When he got through, they were worn down to snubs. Daddy was always petting Oyce and believed everything she told him no matter what it was. So I took joy in beating up on her and doing bad things to her every chance I got. Unfortunately, Oyce wasn't the only reason I got whippings. I would get my butt whipped for mumbling protests under my breath when it was my turn to wash the dishes, clean the house, wash the clothes, and for writing dirty little rhymes about other people mommas, so I didn't need her help in getting my butt whipped.

Another thing that bothered me about my sister Oyce was she was always scaring us, by claiming to see haints and hearing things outside the house in the middle of the night. And when someone we knew died, she would keep me awake all night crying because she thought the dead person was going to come and get her.

As an example, since we didn't have indoor plumbing, we had to bring water into the house at night for drinking and for momma to use for cooking the following morning. This particular evening we didn't pump any water. In our hearts we knew daddy was going to whip our butts and make us go and pump some and bring it into the house. But we held on to the hope that daddy would get mad and would go and get the water himself, or make the older boys go get it. We thought the gods were with us because daddy didn't realize there was no water in the house until after it had gotten dark outside. Normally he didn't make us girls go outside after it got dark, so we were feeling pretty good about ourselves. Needless to say, the ploy didn't work this time. Daddy made Bobo go with us. He was madder than a freshly whipped slave because he had to go with us.

We made our way to the water pump, shaking like the leaves on the trees because of all the ghosts stories daddy always told. Every haint daddy ever encountered was during the hours of darkness. While we were pumping the water, Oyce stood around as usual, doing nothing but staring into the darkness. The only thing Bobo and I were thinking about was filling the buckets and getting them back to the house as soon as possible. We hadn't even filled the first bucket when Oyce starting hollering and screaming that she saw a man that only she could see, coming after us. We didn't hesitate. We hauled butt for the safety of the house. As we were going up the steps, daddy heard the commotion and met us on the porch and asked us what was going on. When we told him Oyce had seen a haint coming for us, he grabbed a belt and started popping our behinds and told us not to come back to the house until we had the water.

Shaking with fear, we went back to the pump and this time we brought both buckets filled with water back to the house. As faith would have it, we would rather face all the haints in Arkansas than to disobey daddy. If Oyce saw anything on our second trip to the pump, she kept that knowledge to herself. And although Oyce was the cause of our panic run to the house, daddy blamed me and Bobo, saying we know that girl is always seeing things, that we should've ignored her. I wanted to ask daddy how I could ignore her when he was always saying she could see haints just like he could. To ask that would have been disrespectful and would have earned me a butt whupping. At least Oyce's haint sightings never cost us any friends. They were just as skeptical about her ability to see things as we were.

*   *   *   *

We had so many neighbors and friends because of the constant moving all the time. I can't even remember most of them. Some of the neighbors I remember are Mr. Job and Mrs. Bea, Mr. Horse and Mrs. Lucy, Mr. Joe Cox, Mr. Charlie and Mrs. Lilly, Ms. Thelma, Mr. Art and Mrs. James. These are just a few of the village parents who helped raise us, and provided us with peers to interact with. Some people might call it having other kids to fight and have fun with, even on church grounds.

On one such occasion when we were living, I believe on Cow Bayou, my brother Will told me to hit Ms. Lucy's daughter, Rose, in the back of her head for no reason and he would help me whup her. Being gullible, I believed him, so I gave her a good whack while her back was turned. Needless to say all he did was laugh while that girl tore my behind up. The fights didn't stop us from playing together. It was just a part of growing up. Beside, all us kids worked along side of each other in the cotton fields, went to school together, and visited each other on a daily basis. My brothers, Bubba, Deedie, Biddy, Bobo, and Will would go to Ms. Bea's house at night to watch television because we didn't own one. Oyce and I wanted to go with them to watch television, but we knew on the way home they were going to run home and we couldn't keep up. I think they did it on purpose because they didn't want us tagging along because we were afraid of the dark. We had to settle for watching television during the day.

*   *   *   *

When we moved to Lakeview, Arkansas, my best friends were Jessie and Dorothy. We were friends all through elementary and high school. Of the two, Jessie was my favorite because she was the only one who would spend the night at my house and me at hers. I remember Jessie getting into a fight on the school bus with a boy named T. J., and he bit her while he was beating her up.

I felt sorry for her because none of her brothers and sisters would help her. I would have helped her, but T.J. would've beaten me up too.

*   *   *   *

In my mind as a child, my eldest sister Sue was a lowdown witch. Whenever momma and daddy would leave to go someplace, they would leave her in charge. They would instruct her that when they got back to the house, it had better be clean, and our hair combed. She would assure them that the house would be clean, and our hair combed upon their return. Momma and daddy said she was a good girl because they could depend on her to do what they asked of her. Sue would wait until momma and daddy were out of sight, and would then start bossing us around. If we didn't mind her, she would whip us as if we were her children. Me, and Oyce had to clean the house while she laid on the couch watching television. Every once in a while, while we would still be cleaning the house, she would order us to bring her a cool drink of water. We would go out to the pump and get the water, but it was never cool enough for her. So she would make us go back to the pump again and again until she was satisfied with the coolness of the water. After the house was clean, the real torture began.

Sue would make us sit side by side while she combed our hair. To us it was torture because she called us nappy headed and tried her best to pull our brains out through the top of our heads. We would beg her to wet our hair to soften it, but she would only laugh and continue pulling at our brains. And to insult us, she would say we should have hair like Betty Ann, because she didn't have nappy hair like ours. She told us Betty Ann had what the folks in the community called good hair, and she was pretty. I always pointed out to Sister Sue that Betty Ann was no longer with us. My reward for pointing that little fact out to her resulted in more pain.

The only way I could get back at Sister Sue was to spy on her and her boyfriends. And whenever they kissed, I would tell momma and daddy about it. After one such episode of my spying,

Sue started calling me Nosey Rosey. I didn't care because she shouldn't have been so mean to us. I never stopped spying on her and them nasty old boys that came to see her either. I wished she was more like my oldest brother.

My oldest brother Bubba wasn't as mean as Sue, but he always teased me about liking boys I didn't like. He loved to tease me about one boy in particular, name Vandy Johnson. He would say "Pon'k loves that little long head Vandy boy," and I would cry. I knew Vandy liked me but I didn't like him, and because of Bubba's teasing, I ended up hating him.

* * * *

Being so far down the line of siblings, I didn't get the chance to be the boss that often, but when I did, I took full advantage of it. My chance at being lady boss came in the form of being momma's enforcer. Whenever she was sick or didn't feel like disciplining my baby brother Gene after he had messed up, she would delegate her authority to me. As cruel as it sounds, it made my day when I got the chance to whip his butt. He would get all huffy and say he was going to get me back when he got bigger. I would tell him if he even thought about touching me, I would tell daddy he was going to fight me for doing what momma told me to do, and that would give him second thoughts. Sometimes Gene deserved to get his butt whipped, like the time he quit his job and lied to daddy about it.

Gene and one our nephews quit their job because they were tired of working. They told the boss they had to go to Memphis for some reason. The only thing they were doing was riding on the side of tractors praying weed killer to kill the weeds in the fields. I don't remember how old they were, but it didn't matter. When Daddy found out about what they had done, he reached up in a tree and broke off the biggest limb he could handle and beat them really bad. The beating must've worked because they never quit another job until they left home.

* * * *

Although I didn't have a lot of material things while I was growing up, it was a happy childhood. It is well documented that a lot of folks with wealth and fame are some of the unhappiest people in the world. They are living lives without any joy or peace. I'm thankful we were all healthy. And the strength we grew from each other is something no amount of money could ever buy.

In case my brother Deedie forgot to tell about the time he had escaped a whipping, but ended up getting whipped anyway I thought I would remind him here. Daddy had whipped some serious butt for some reason. We got so many whippings, it is impossible to remember what it was for this time, but as daddy was leaving the room Deedie came from his hiding place and said "Daddy, here I am." I'm sure you know what happened to him. (Smile)

* * * *

Bobo may have been the craziest, but he was my favorite brother. I guess it was because my other brothers were so much older than I was. I really missed Bobo when he joined the Job Corp with Deedie and Biddy. I remember when we lived around the lake we used to wade across this little stream of water about knee deep. I don't remember where we were going, but I would cry every time we got to the stream because I was afraid to cross it by myself. Bobo was the only one that would take the time to help me across the stream. However, being scared of the water never stopped me from tagging along because I knew Bobo was going to help me across.

* * * *

One day I was playing at Mrs. Bea's house with Kate, Will and Loren. We had filled an old tub with water. I don't know why, but my friend Kate and I sat down in the water with our clothes on. Pretending to be fast little girls, we decided to pull our dresses up high so that Will and Loren could see our thighs. We raised our dress-tails way up to our behind just to show off. I showed my butt because Loren, and me, called ourselves real life boyfriend and girlfriend. I thought me and Loren would be girlfriend and boyfriend forever. I liked him, but as with every other friend I had made up to that point in my life, I had to say good-bye because we moved. I think I was about 5 years old.

*   *   *   *

    Daddy used to go somewhere on a wagon or in a truck every weekend, and would ask us if we wanted to ride along with him. When he drove a truck we would sit on the tailgate of the truck. If it were a wagon he was driving, we would bounce along in the bed of the wagon. When he asked who all wanted to go with him I always said I did, but I didn't want to go. To try and get out of going on the ride I would ask momma if she needed me to stay and help with cleaning the house or something. She always said she didn't need help with anything, to go ahead and have a good time. I don't know why I went through this crazy ritual every time I volunteered to go on these rides. I would end up sitting in the back of the truck or wagon crying my eyes out, wishing I could have stayed at home with momma. Of course my brothers and sisters wished I stayed home because they didn't want to hear me bawling. Daddy said he wanted me to tag along so I could get over my shyness. The weirdest part of this crazy ritual was, if daddy said I couldn't go with them I would cry. Luckily, I out grew that stage in my life.

*   *   *   *

    I stayed with Sue once when she lived around the Lake behind Toney's corner store down under the hill. I was her live-in babysitter. So she never had to worry about her kids when she went out on weekends. I really liked staying with her. She was real good to me then. I guess she was making up for the past for how she treated me, Oyce and the other younger kids.

    While still living with Sue, there was a boy called Little

Pinky who hung around us all the time. He was called Little Pinky because he was a Jr. and his daddy was called Big Pinky. I never knew their real names. Big Pinky was a habitual criminal, and had spent the majority of his adult life in prison starting at age thirteen. Little Pinky was on his way to being like his daddy. At that time he was known to be a petty thief, liar, cheat, and gambler. Everyone felt it was only a matter of time before he joined his daddy in the big house. He tried to like me, but I didn't like him at all because he was too grown, too mean, and just plain lowdown. But I did use him to learn to drive a car. It made him mad that I would not go alone with him while he was teaching me to drive. I always took a girlfriend with me. I couldn't stand him, mostly because he was always bragging about how he had spent time in prison helping his daddy work off his latest sentence.

One time Little Pinky tried to show out in front of his friends and got mad because I said I didn't like him. I was leaving the store and a lot of people were outside in the store yard laughing, drinking and having fun. The boy, Tudy, who I did like, was in the yard also. Everyone in the yard knew I liked him, and since he was in the yard, Little Pinky tried to make him mad. Little Pinky grabbed my arm trying to pull me up against him. I pushed him away. Since he knew people were watching us he had to try and make himself look good. He had a monkey wrench in his hand and he hit me on the shoulder with it, not hard, but it looked as if it was because at the same time he hit me, he pushed me and I fell and rolled down the hill, but I wasn't hurt. Everyone told him if he touched me again they were going to tell my daddy what he had done. Not even Little Pinky wanted Joe Wade after his butt. The fall and embarrassment was worth it because he never bothered me again after that incident.

I guess Tudy didn't like me as much as I liked him because he didn't do or say anything when Little Pinky hit me. Tudy's friends called him a coward and a punk for not taking up for me. I guess he figured there was no reason for the both of us getting our butts whupped. Little Pinky was known to kick serious behind.

* * * *

Learning to ride a bicycle was harder for me than learning to drive a car. Every time I got on a bike I would fall over in the middle of the highway, or in the yard depending where I was riding. I would run off the roads into the bean and cotton fields because I didn't know how to steer to keep the wheels straight. One time I was riding a bike I fell on the highway and skinned my ankle, my knee, my elbow, and my shoulder, all on the left side of my body. As usual I cried, but I always got back on the bike again. It took a long time and a lot of falling before I finally learned to ride a bicycle, but ride I did.

* * * *

We were living around the Lake off highway 20 when we got our first telephone. Back then everybody was on a party line and anyone could listen in on other people conversations. One day I picked up the phone and two white women were talking about somebody had killed that Nigger. The other one said, "Yea, they killed Dr. Martin Luther King." I didn't really understand at the time what they were talking about, but I soon found out because everything was going crazy. Black folks were rioting and burning stuff up all over the country. When momma explained to me what Dr. King was about. I knew that a good God fearing man had been killed for trying to do some good in this crazy world. Trying to make things right for people of all color that were underprivileged and mistreated was frowned upon by some of the racist white people in America. I didn't fully understand why, but I was mad right along with the grown-ups. I talked about how those mean white people hated to see a black man do anything good for his people or America. I felt better after letting off steam about what had happened to Dr. King.

The conversations on the party line were not always serious. I loved to pick up the phone and listen to the older boys talk dirty to their girlfriends, or some woman or man fussing and cussing about their spouses cheating on them. The party line was my Peyton Place, especially when I listened in on white folks. I thought they were the funniest talking people in the world. There was nothing funny when I would overhear white people talking about us being lazy and no good while working us like dogs, and cheating us to boot. It was a sad day for me when the party line went the way of the dinosaurs. Before it went the way of the dinosaurs, I'm sure someone listened in on my conversations also.

There was an almost grown boy named Roosevelt, who everyone called Snake, that liked me. He was so black and ugly I couldn't stand him. He would call me all the time. Oyce fooled me once about who was on the phone. Since I didn't know Snake's real name at the time, when I ask Oyce who it was, she said it was some boy named Roosevelt. I answered the phone, which made Snake very happy. Although I didn't like him, I never hung up in his face unless he made me mad. At other times she simply said she didn't know who it was on the phone. It tickled Sister Oyce to no end when she would trick me into answering the phone when she knew it was Snake. Sometimes when he called, Will would answer the phone and try to get me to talk to him, but I would refuse to talk to Snake if I knew it was him on the phone. No matter how much I tried to ignore him, Snake never gave up and he kept right on calling. On one occasion, Will came over to the bed and pushed my face down into the bed and made me talk to Snake because he was tired of answering the phone. I was the happiest girl in the world when snake found himself a girl that liked him, and he gave up on me.

* * * *

I used to be really nosey when I was young. One day an old lady stopped by our house to talk to momma about our next-door neighbors, Miss. Dole and her husband. I don't know what the woman told momma, but it made her mad. I thought momma told the lady what she was talking about was between her and Miss Dole. When I asked her later what the lady had said that made her say it was between her and Miss Dole. Momma said she told the lady it was between her and God. I don't remember momma getting upset often, but on this occasion she was mad about whatever had been said. Momma always seemed happy, even when everyone knew she was going through hard times in her life. Sometimes I would see that she had been crying, but she never complained to anyone in the house as far as I know. I never found out what the lady had said to momma that had gotten her so upset, because she refused to discuss it with anyone.

* * * *

As if we didn't have enough cotton in Arkansas to keep us busy, we went to my oldest sister, Mag house in Tiptonville, Tennessee to chop cotton a couple of summers. This particular summer we went it was daddy, me, and Margaret. Daddy and Margaret stayed over at Mag's house and I had to stay with Mag's friend. She lived next door. Everyone told me that the old lady was a witch. I didn't know if she was or not, but I was really scared. I would be so glad when morning came so I could get up and out of that house, at least for a while. I never got over being scared of staying in that house. I knew I was being silly because the lady never did anything to me, and she treated me okay. I chose to believe the folklore rather than what was obvious right before my eyes.

One night Mag's house caught fire, or something had cause a lot of smoke. It woke them up and they had to get out of the house. I didn't even know about it until the next morning because I was staying at her neighbor's house. Mag's sons told me what happened the next day. They said the smoke must have woken daddy up first. He got out of bed, grabbed Margaret and ran out of the house leaving everyone else inside. Daddy said he hollered for everyone to get out of the house on his way to the door. No one remembered him saying anything. They said him, and Margaret were standing out in the front yard, daddy was in his shirt and under-shorts, holding Margaret's hand with their suitcases under his arm when everyone else came running out of the house. It had to be smoke because I don't remember Mag's house burning down. I used to hate going up there to work.

Mag's sons couldn't get along with Margaret because she

would never wash the dishes, or do anything else around the house for that matter. One day one of Mag's son was outside throwing darts at a dartboard hanging on a tree. Margaret came outside and started meddling with him by putting her hand in front of the dartboard. He kept telling her to move her hand but she refused. Getting mad he threw the dart and it stuck her in the hand. He was so pleased with himself, he didn't mind that he got the mess beat out of him.

The times we went to Tennessee to work and stayed with Mag daddy would tell her she should be ashamed of herself for having El Tharp, her husband, getting up at night fixing the babies bottles. Daddy said El Tharp would be up in his under- shorts and he would be shaking like a leaf in the wind because it would be so cold in the house. Mag said, "Hell daddy, I get up all time of night fixing bottles in the cold. Why should things be any different for men?" Daddy said because they were men, and that was all the difference that was needed. Mag said momma had spoiled him and that was why he was a male chauvinist pig. Daddy laughed and said that was why God put women on earth, to serve man.

I remember overhearing daddy and Mag talking one night about Lenora, an older sister who lived in Alabama. I don't know what started the conversation, but Mag said Lenora had never cared for momma because she felt momma didn't love her. Mag said she told Lenora she should be ashamed of herself because she knew momma loved all of her children. Mag said she loved momma because she was the momma who raised her, and the momma who treated them right. She said she didn't know why Lenora felt as she did because she knew it wasn't true. When I asked her why Lenora felt that way, she told me it was none of my business. She told me to stop eavesdropping on her conversation with other people. If she wanted me to know about anything she had to say about anyone she would let me know. I didn't hold my breath waiting for her to tell me anything because I knew she wouldn't.

* * * *

For my Junior Prom, Sue bought me a pretty blue dress. It had puffed sleeves from my elbow up to my shoulder. The dress had long sleeves and was made on an empire style with little green flowers going around the waist part of the dress. She put some false hair on my head and I really looked pretty. I really enjoyed my prom night. Bobo and one of his friends snuck into our prom some kind of way, and both said they didn't know who I was from the back. I guess they had never seen me looking decent.

* * * *

When Will and me got old enough to baby-sit, that's all we did. One night Will was keeping one of our nephews, his name was Vincent, and he was crying a lot. So Will kept giving him some kind of medicine that would make babies sleep. The medicine was supposed be used to stop a baby's stomachs from hurting. Every time Vincent would wake up, Will would give him some more of the medicine and he would go right back to sleep. I told Will he had better stop giving that baby so much of that stuff before it killed him. I am happy to report Vincent survived.

I kept one of Sue's friend's little girl. The baby's name was Doris. I never will forget babysitting this little girl. Me, and the baby fell asleep, and somehow the baby ended up at the head part of the bed, up by my head, and she messed in my hair. I don't mean a little turd. No. I mean the soft mushy kind that went all the way to my scalp. I couldn't believe what had happened. I smelled the odor of the dukey coming from my head, and reached up to confirm what had happened. When I looked at my hand covered with feces I ran to the bathroom. I washed and washed my hair. I didn't think the smell was ever going to come out. Of course after a while the stench was not in my hair, but in my imagination. I don't believe I ever kept Doris again.

* * * *

When I was 17 years old I was taking sewing classes up in Helena in a building on the bank of the Mississippi river. Daddy would drop me off every morning and spend the whole day in Jim's Café drinking until I got out of class. By the time I got out of class, he'd be so drunk he could hardly stand. However, by the grace of God, he always managed to drive to Helena Crossing where there was hardly any traffic where he would turn the wheel over to me. Because of my inexperience behind the wheel of a car, he never allowed me to drive in traffic. My heart would be in my throat all the way home. As scared as I was while driving, it's a miracle I didn't kill us. There were many times when meeting oncoming traffic, I thought we were goners. The highway we took home was just wide enough for two cars to pass without one having to get off onto the shoulder of the road. Sometimes the cars would pass so close the drivers could reach out and shake hands. I kept thinking one of these days we're going to meet a drunk or a fool and that would be the end of us, but we never did thank "God."

* * * *

We lived on a place called the Mud Line. We had to turn off the highway and go about a mile and a half down a dirt road to get to our house. I'm only guessing because I'm terrible when it comes to estimating. Anyway, at night when there was no moon, it would be pitch black. One of Will's friends, Sam Hilburn, told me and my sister Oyce one day that somebody had told him that a greasy man was going around looking in peoples windows at night under the cover of darkness and if he could see you he would get you. So every night me and Oyce would get blankets and cover the windows in our bedroom so the greasy man couldn't see us. We should have known the rumor wasn't true because no one outside our circle of friends ever mentioned this supposedly peeping tom/killer. Still, we were so scared we wouldn't get up for anything at night, not even get up to go to the bathroom.

When daddy overheard me and Oyce talking about how scared we were the man might get us, he told us not to be because if he caught any man peeping through his windows he would end up with buck shots in his behind. Knowing daddy didn't make idle threats, the fear left us. We never covered the windows again knowing daddy was standing guard over us.

* * * *

When Gene was the baby me, and Oyce would argue over who was going to rinse the mess out of Gene's cloth diapers. I don't know what possessed either of us to want to handle dukey diapers. Momma laughed at us. I guess she was thankful to have the dukey sisters to clean Gene's smelly diapers.

* * * *

One time Oyce was cooking something that smelled pretty good, so I asked her what she was cooking. She said butter beans with fatback and said I could have some when they got done. I said I didn't want any of those old butter beans. I just didn't want to admit that she was a good cook. When the butter beans were done, my sarcasm left and I had three helping and wanted more. Momma laughed and said she was glad I didn't want any of those old butter beans because I may have hurt myself. It was the same when momma would take leftover biscuits and rice and make a bread pudding or a rice pudding. I would eat until I thought I would bust. She would also take leftover mashed potatoes and make fried potatoes patties. They were simple recipes, but boy was the food good. I mean really good.

* * * *

When we were living on Cow Bayou Teenie took me to town in Marianna. I had on a purple wide tail dress. I used to wear wide tail dresses all the time. I guess momma thought I was cute in them because I overheard her tell Teenie the dress showed off my big pretty legs. Anyway me, and Teenie was walking down the street. She had bought me some shades (sunglasses) and an ice cream cone. Because of the heat, the ice cream started melting and was running down my hand onto my dress and everything else. I didn't care because it had been a long time since I had gone anywhere. Unless you have been closed in for an extended period of time, it's hard to imagine what a relief it is to finally go somewhere where you can feel free. That's what I was feeling that day in town with Teenie, freedom.

* * * *

During the summer we would go pick blackberries and momma would make blackberry dumpling for us. At other times, we'd eat them with carnation milk and sugar. When momma wasn't making blackberry dumplings or creating goodies from leftovers, she could be found in the kitchen baking cakes. She would let me scrape the sides of her cake bowls when she finished pouring the cake mixture in the pans. I loved momma's homemade cakes. Even her frosting for the cakes was homemade. Egg whites and pineapple, or egg whites and coconut and you would have a delicious frosting. While scraping the bowls, I would eat the raw cake batter. Sometimes the bowl would be so clean I don't think momma needed to wash them. It was good to be a kid in momma's kitchen.

* * * *

Summary

Although I criticize my siblings on occasion, I could not love them more. Growing up in a large family was truly enjoyable because no matter what came our way at least one of us had experienced it somewhere along the way and gave guidance to those going through the same thing. I wouldn't change my experiences for anything, because what we had, and have, is a blessing from God.

Margaret Wade
Born: April 29, 1959
Place of Birth: Wabash, Arkansas

CHAPTER #14
MARGARET

I was born April 29, 1959, in Wabash, Arkansas. Being I was the youngest girl, I guess daddy had settled down in his old age, because I didn't have a hard time growing up. Momma and daddy gave me almost anything I asked for. The only time I ever had to pick or chop cotton was when we needed money to go the basketball games to watch my brother Will play at Lakeview, High School. Other than that I never had to go to the fields. However, like all my brothers and sisters, I did feel the wrath of daddy's form of discipline for being disobedient. At age 14 I thought I was grown enough to challenge his authority.

One day after school my boyfriend was playing basketball in our front yard and daddy came to the door and said, "Sister, come in the house and wash the dishes." I said, "I'm coming daddy, shoot, can't nobody even play." I then continued to ignore daddy's order to come in the house and wash dishes, trying to show off in front of my boyfriend and the other kids playing in the yard. Daddy came to the door again a short time later and told me again to come into the house and wash the dishes. I said, "Shoot daddy, I said I was coming." Realizing I had said this in a disrespectful manner, I turned to say I was on my way, but I didn't get a chance. As I turned to say I'm coming, I saw this big black-hand coming at me. I didn't have time to react to the blow. All I could do was brace myself for the impact. The slap caught me upside the head and knocked me to my knees. I don't know which hurt the most, the slap or the embarrassment of getting my behind knocked off with my boyfriend watching. From that day forward,

I never disrespected daddy again.

Another incident that happened while showing disrespect to my elder was with Pon'k. She was so mean and hateful when she was pregnant. I remember one Saturday morning she was mopping the floor and I walked across it. Pon'k told me to get off the floor. I made a snide remark like I wasn't stud'n her. I knew how hard it was to keep those floors clean, especially while walking on them when they were still wet, but I didn't care because I didn't have to do the sweeping and mopping. On numerous occasions I got in the way while Pon'k and Oyce was sweeping or mopping. My instinct to survive kicked in and told me to turn around and look, because I knew by the look on Pon'k's face I had pushed her beyond her tolerance level. As I turned and looked, Pon'k threw a big pop (soda) bottle at me, and it came within millimeters of hitting me on the side of my head. Seeing she was looking for something else to throw at me, I went outside and didn't come back in the house until momma them got home.

* * * *

One night I was sitting on the night pot taking a number two and reading the newspaper. I looked up when I heard a noise outside the window. Not seeing anything at the window, I didn't pay much attention to it. So I went back to reading my newspaper. When I heard the noise again, I looked up and there stood two dark figures staring at me through the window. When I jumped up to run, they started beating on the window. At the time I didn't know that the two dark figures were Pon'k and Gene.

Anyway, I took off running holding the pot under my behind. I ran to the back of the room and realized the only way out of the room was the direction from which I had just run. Being too scared to risk going past the window to get to the living room, I started jumping up and down crying, still holding the pot under my behind. In my state of panic, I didn't realize the content in the pot was jumping up and down too, so you know what that meant. I had dukey all over my behind. I was so mad at Pon'k and Gene when they came into the house laughing at me, I wanted to beat the mess out of the both of them. Not so much for scaring me, they did that all the time, but because of the embarrassment I felt having to clean my butt as if I was a baby who had crapped on herself. I knew whupping them was out of the question because I couldn't fight worth a darn and would have gotten the tar beaten out of me. So, all I could do was get mad.

* * * *

One of my girlfriends and me were female party animals. We went out every weekend to display our curves and womanly charm for the drooling boys and men who frequented the clubs. It was a real ego boost for us to have the grown men competing with the boys for our affection. When we really turned on the charm, we would have the grown men acting like immature little boys, but we had to be careful with them because it didn't take much to make them mad. When that happened, we would get out of the club, and the next weekend we would completely ignore them. Lucky for us, the week between clubs visit always gave them time to cool off before they saw us again. As far as the boys were concerned, we didn't care if they got mad or not. They knew if they touched us, we would tell our daddies and they would get in trouble with their parents. In the south, boys were taught that they didn't fight girls. It was a miracle we didn't get our butts whipped, because we were cruel to a lot of guys.

There was a worn path between my friend's house and ours. It was on that path we would meet every Friday and Saturday night after getting dressed to decide who was going to drive to the club that night. Since meeting on that path had been our regular weekend routine for a couple of years, I had no reason to expect anything out of the ordinary to happen that would scare the living crap out of us, but as daddy always told us, we should be prepared for the unexpected. One Saturday night while making our rendezvous to decide who would drive to the club that night, we were caught totally unprepared by two pranksters. Those pranksters were my baby brother and one of our nephews.

Knowing my friend and me met on that path every Friday

and Saturday night, Gene and our nephew decided to have a little fun at our expense. I noticed they weren't in the house watching television as usual when I left the house, but it didn't dawn on me that their absence may have meant they were out to scare us. They had eased out the back door with white sheets while I was putting on the finishing touches to my make-up. They found the darkest spot they could at the point where my friend and I always met. As we approached each other, our minds were on what unlucky boy or man was going to have to go through if they wanted to talk to us. When we reached that rendezvous point, Gene and our nephew stood up with the white sheet over their heads saying "BOO! I'm going to get you." One of the sheets came in my direction and the other one went after my friend.

My friend started screaming and running backward. The heel of her foot caught in the grass because she had veered off the path, and she tripped and fell. She turned onto her belly and started crawling to get away from what she thought was a ghost. She was crying uncontrollably and calling on Jesus to save her. Our nephew realized it was time to put an end to the prank when he smelled the odor of fresh pee coming from her clothing. At this point our nephew took off the sheet and tried to calm her down by telling her it was him. He reached down to help her to her feet, but she was so scared she hadn't heard a thing he said, nor did she see the hand of comfort he offered her.

Gene was the butt head who had come toward me with arms raised booing and carrying on. He scared me so bad I couldn't move. I just stood there shaking and praying that the ghost would see how scared I was and would leave me alone. It was not until Gene took the sheet off of his head and started laughing that I realized what was going on. I wanted to whip his butt. Meanwhile, my poor friend had gotten to her feet but she was still shaking like a leaf on a tree. She called Gene and our nephew dirty dogs for scaring us so bad, and swore she would get even with them one day. My friend went home, washed up again, changed clothes, and we were on our way to do what we did best, play with the boys and men toys at the club. Nothing could dampen our party spirits for long, not even that frightening episode.

When I was younger and not quite the fox I became when I was running with my older friends, I used to go out for reasons other than teasing boys and men at the club. My goal every weekend was to set up an observation post to observe who was cheating on whom, so I could go back and tell their boyfriends, or girlfriends on them. I was an equal opportunity tattletale. My personal target every weekend was Pon'k's boyfriend. I knew he was a dog so I made sure I went out of my way to see whom he would be messing with at the club every weekend, so I could go back and tell Pon'k whom he was with. For reasons unknown to me, no matter how many times I told Pon'k I'd seen him with another girl she either didn't believe me or allowed him to lie his way out of his situation. It took a while, but I got tired of Pon'k not believing me when I told her what her boyfriend was doing. It didn't mean I stopped spying on him, it just means I just stopped telling Pon'k what he was doing. I hoped in the end I would get something on him that I could use to blackmail him in the future.

Although I had close girlfriends, when it came to boys, it was every girl for herself and the love of God for us all. Usually the standard agreement between girlfriends was they would never mess with each other's boyfriend. I broke that long-standing agreement when I started messing around with one of my girlfriend's boyfriend. Her name was Ann. I'm not sure I believed Greg when he said he no longer wanted to be with Ann because she said she wasn't sure if she wanted to be with him anymore. In my heart, I knew that boy was lying because he was the only thing Ann talked about when we were together. Even with the knowledge about how she felt about Greg, I allowed him to convince me there would be no fallout by me messing around with him. At first Ann didn't know I was messing with Greg, and I wasn't about to tell her. I told him if what he said about Ann not wanting him anymore was true, he should be the one to tell her he liked me more than he did her, not me. He wimped out, saying she was bound to find out sooner or later anyway. As fate would have it, she found out sooner rather than later, like the following Saturday after me and the cheating dog had our little conversation.

While I was getting ready to go out Ann called and ask me who I was going out with. I told her I was going to go out alone, because I didn't know how long I would be staying at the club and didn't want to have to rush anyone when I got ready to leave. She said ok, and changed the subject to talking about Greg. Ann got all giggly and said she could hardly wait for Greg to pick her up because she had a big surprise for him. I didn't doubt he was on his way to pick her up because he hadn't called me and said he wasn't. After hanging up the phone to finish getting dressed, a pang of jealousy shot though my body. I knew it was stupid to be jealous of Ann when it was her boyfriend I was messing with, but I couldn't help it. I was on my way out the door for a solo night on the town when Greg pulled up in front of my house. I asked him why he was at my house because I had talked to Ann earlier and she said he was picking her up to take to her to the club in Oneida. He said he had told Ann that he wasn't going anywhere so he could be with me. I told Greg I didn't like sneaking around behind Ann's back like that. If he really liked me he would tell her about us. He said he would in time, but the timing wasn't right yet. In the meantime, he wanted to show me a good time. Instead of getting in the car right away, I asked him what he was going to say to Ann when she showed up at the club. He said we weren't going to Oneida. We were going to the club in Elaine. We both knew it was no guarantee she wouldn't show up in Elaine sometime during the evening. We all bar hopped between the two clubs most every Saturday night. He said if I felt guilty about being with him, he would go and pick Ann up. We ended up going out together instead of him and Ann.

    We both knew Ann would make a scene if she showed up at the club in Elaine. So we were both nervous about what was going to happen if she showed up. Greg pretended he wasn't nervous but I knew better because he was wiggling like a worm on an ant pile. There were only two clubs in the community for teenagers to go, so it was only a matter of time before she showed up. When Ann didn't find Greg at the club in Oneida, she headed for Elaine. When Ann pulled into the parking lot, she saw Greg and me sitting in his car. We hadn't even gotten out of the car yet.

She walked over to the car, called me a backstabbing wench, and asked Greg if she could talk to him alone. Greg got out of the car and they walked a short distance from the car to talk. I got out and waited beside the car. I tried to eavesdrop on their conversation but I couldn't hear what was being said, but I could tell she was giving him a piece of her mind. The discussion ended abruptly when Ann slapped Greg across the face and stormed toward the club. When he got back to the car I asked him what she had said. He said, "Nothing, let go." Not wanting any more drama that night, we left the club and went and park in Lover's Lane for a while before he took me home.

    I called Ann a couple of days later to tell her how me, and Greg got together in the first place, but she wouldn't talk to me. She didn't talk to me for about three weeks because of Greg. When she did decide to call and ask me to bury the hatchet, she had an ulterior motive. She acted as if all was forgiven, but she tried to get back at me for messing with Greg. She told her brother Lamont, who was supposed to be my real boyfriend, that I was cheating on him while he was gone. Lamont went to work on his aunt's farm for the summer somewhere in Texas. His aunt and her husband owned their own farm, and had horses they would let him ride. He went to visit them every other summer. Ann, on the other hand, couldn't stand animals and wouldn't go to visit her aunt unless the whole family went together.

    Lamont was really mad but he didn't ask me anything directly about what Ann had told him. He tried to trick me into confessing that I was messing around with another boy while he was gone by asking me a lot of indirect questions surrounding what Ann had told him. Did you meet any new friends while I was gone? Did you go to the clubs with anyone other than Ann? What boys were hitting on you while I was gone? Are you interested in any other boys?   Either he forgot, or was too stupid to realize that I was Joe Wade's daughter. Meaning he couldn't fool me when it came to bull crap. And as far as what happened between Greg and me, when he realized I wasn't giving up anything, he went back to Ann, who was more than willing to take him back.

* * * *

When I was in the tenth grade, I was the official snitch for Coach Calderon. He always left me in charge of the classroom and during gym class, because he knew I would tell on everyone who didn't do what he had instructed them to do. The boys I just loved telling on were Ed Lee and his friends, especially when we were in P.E. class. Coach Calderon believed in physical exercise and would punish anyone who he felt was a slacker. Although everyone knew Coach Calderon felt that way, Ed Lee and his boys wouldn't do anything when coach wasn't in the gym, until I told them I was going to tell on them. They would do some of the exercises he told them to do so they would be able to tell coach they did something. Whenever coach came back to the gym or in the classroom the next day, I would tell coach they didn't do half of what he had told them to do. To my delight and satisfaction, coach would make them do double of whatever exercises they were supposed to have done the day before. Their tongues would be dragging the floor when coach got through with them.

Of course Ed Lee and his boys tried to figure out a way to get back at me. They knew it wouldn't do any good to tell coach, or any other teacher, that I was a slacker when they were not in the room because I was the one always left in charge. The only way they could get back at me was to spread lies on me. The biggest lie they told was when they spread a rumor that they saw me and coach on the stage behind the curtain in the school gym kissing. The kids in my class teased me about the rumor although they knew it was a lie. Ed Lee and his friends only made it harder on themselves, because after they started that lie, they never did anything coach told them to do as far as I was concerned, and coach always believed me. Who knows, coach may have had a small vendetta to settle himself with Ed Lee and his little lying bunch of misfits. Anyway, they regretted the day they started that rumor.

* * * *

One night me, and Oyce decided to pay Pon'k a visit at her house. As we walked along the road, we were talking about vampires. I don't know why we were talking about vampires because we were two of the scariest girls in all of Lakeview, Arkansas. We both pretended that what we were talking about had no effect on us, but the truth be told, I was tense inside while looking around to make sure there weren't any vampires in the vicinity.

Unknown to us, a boy we called Duck had ran down the road ahead of us and hid in the bushes on the side of the road. I don't know how he knew we were going to Pon'k's house, but apparently he did. He put a sheet over his head and waited patiently for us to arrive at his location. Me, and Oyce were strolling along still chatting away when we made it to where Duck was hiding in the bushes. When we got even with him, he started making strange noises in a very low voice, and started shaking the bushes lightly to coincide with the noise he was making. The noises were so low we weren't sure if we had heard anything at all, but we did notice the bushes moving slightly, although there was hardly a breeze at all. We stopped in our tracks to listen, thinking it was probably an animal of some sort. We stared in to the dark bushes but couldn't see anything. Duck then performed his grand finale. He made a loud guttering noise and rose from the shadows of the bushes with arms raised, reaching toward us. The sheet was flowing down his back resembling a vampire's cape. Oyce screamed that there was something in the bushes and took off. She ran off and left me, not even looking back to see if I was okay. I looked at the figure as it rose from the shadows and was too scared to move. I watched as what I thought was death coming to get me. I closed my eyes to accept my fate when I heard Duck laughing at me. When I opened my eyes and saw it was Duck, it felt like the weight of the world was lifted from my shoulders. Through tears of fright and relief, I got so mad at Duck. If I had been a boy, I would've whupped his behind for scaring me silly.

I don't know how far Oyce ran before realizing she would have to explain to daddy why she had run off and left her sister knowing her life may be in danger. Duck was walking with me still laughing because he had scared us when we met Oyce coming back to see if I was okay. She had found a big stick to use on whatever had gotten me. It was my turn to laugh when I told her I was going to tell everyone how she had ran off and left me so the vampire could get me while she got away. Oyce threatened to whip Duck's butt with the stick for scaring us. Duck had fun telling that story for at least a month.

I never figured out why I always froze when something, or someone, scared me. Everyone told me I had better learn to haul butt if anything was trying to hurt me. Luckily, I was only subjected to pranks.

*   *   *   *

Summary

Like I said, I didn't have it hard at all but being a member of the Wade family is beyond description. Although most of my older siblings was grown and gone when I was growing up, they encouraged me to do the right thing doing family reunions, or when they came home to visit. Being a part of this large family is the greatest thing that could happen to me. I love them all.

Eugene Wade
Born: November 6, 1963
Place of Birth: Wabash, Arkansas

CHAPTER #15
EUGENE (GENE)

I was born November 6, 1963 in Wabash, Arkansas. I was the last child born to the union of Joe & Zelma Wade. Like my sister Margaret, I didn't have it as bad as my older brothers and sisters while growing up, but I do have a story to tell.

One morning when I was around the age of five, momma had cooked breakfast for the family, and we had finished eating. While my older brothers and sisters gathered their school supplies, and whatever else they may need for school that day, I took one last trip to the kitchen to see what was left from the hardy feast momma had prepared for breakfast. If you grew up with the brothers and sisters I had you knew the chances of any food being left over was practically zero. After finding nothing on the stove, that's usually was where momma would put whatever was left over after each meal, and finding nothing on the stove, I checked the plates that was left on the table. Sure enough there were pieces of fatback and biscuits left on a couple of my sister's plates. Let it be known I said sisters, not brothers because my brothers would have eaten me along with their food if I got in the way. Anyway, I started making my way around the table eating from the plates that had meat and bread on them. I was so happy at finding additional food to eat I didn't even notice when daddy walked into the kitchen.

He asked me what I was doing. I looked at him scared to death because he had that, I'm going to whup your behind if you don't give me the right answer look on his face. I didn't know what to say. He asked me again why I was eating scraps from the plates. When I still didn't answer daddy reached over and slapped the-you-know-what out of me. Unknown to daddy, as he raise his hand to hit me again momma had walked up behind him. Before he could deliver the second blow momma was on him like white on rice. I'm standing there crying, not only because of the slap but because my momma and daddy was fighting. Daddy grabbed momma around the neck as tight as possible without really hurting her. He just wanted her to stop hitting him. Realizing she couldn't win the fight, momma calmed down. Daddy told her that I had just finished eating. He said he knew damn well I wasn't still hungry. I was just being piggish. Momma said she didn't care if I was hungry or not. As long as he lived he had better not ever hit me again for wanting something to eat, or she would kill him. After momma said that daddy let go of her neck and walked out of the kitchen without saying a word. After daddy left the kitchen momma came to me and kissed me and asked me if I was okay. I said yeah. She then asked me if I was still hungry, if so she would make something else for me to eat. Because of what had happened between momma and daddy I had lost my appetite, so I said no. Even if I had still been hungry, I wasn't about to cause another episode like the one I had just witnessed. The truth be told, I wasn't hungry in the first place. Like daddy said, I was just being greedy. Momma told daddy I was just being a kid. Although it was a frightening experience watching them fight one thing became very clear at that morning. I knew no matter what happened momma had my back. It was well known if you hit "Joe Wade" and he didn't rearrange your face, you were special. What I didn't know was, it frightened daddy to even think about the possibility of momma leaving him. He loved her more than he did himself. And he knew no other woman in her right mind would put up with his drinking, gambling, and womanizing ways. This was the only time I ever witnessed momma totally losing her composure.

    I also remember how my older brothers and sisters took great pride in watching me cry when they would tell me that I wasn't really a Wade, that someone left me on the front porch and momma took me in. She didn't have me as she did the rest them. It didn't matter that momma would tell me my brothers and sisters was just playing with me, that she had me the same way as she did everyone else, I would still bawl like a baby whenever they teased me like that. That was really cruel. I mean, "Low down" cruel!

* * * *

One of nephews, and one of my nieces, started Kindergarten the same year as I did. Will was two years older than me, and Barbara was one year older than me. When we were told to stand and tell everyone our names we really screwed our names up. Will said his name was Willy Joe Wade. Barbara said her name was Barbara Wade, and I said my name was Eugene Love. Will and Barbara last name is Love. My last name is Wade. How we managed to turn our last names around I don't know, but the names got straightened out eventually.

I ended up being the teacher's pet. She would carry me around on her hip, and give me candy. She even let me stay up during naptime while all the other kids were asleep. I guess the reason she like me was I would tell on the other kids whenever they did something wrong. Yes, I was a snitch. There was this one kid named Buster Brown who cussed all the time. When I wanted special treatment I would tell the teacher Buster was cussing again and she would put me on her hip to get me away from Buster because he was a bad influence on me. I don't remember her name, but I do know I loved that woman.

My first day in the 1st grade was one of pure terror. I was afraid and didn't want to leave the nest. I wanted to stay warm and secure in the arms of that beautiful, wonderful, woman I had known all my life, "momma." I don't know what I was afraid of. My older brothers and sisters were attending school and nothing ever happened to them. Then again, it may have been because my older brothers and sisters told me the first day I left home to go to school full time, they were all going to move and not let me know where they had moved to. Momma assured me this wasn't true, but my young mind wondered if she was just saying that to get me out of the house. I didn't dare ask daddy because if it was a question he felt was stupid he would probably smack me.

The first day of school, I got up and ate breakfast. Afterward, momma washed my hands face and put on everyone's favorite skin lotion on my arms and face, "Royale Crown Hair Dressing." After getting dressed it was time to get my hair comb. Momma would have a big glob of Royale Crown Hair dressing in one hand and my biggest enemy in the other, that old time country comb. I swore the thing took great pleasure in biting into my scalp and trying to pull my brains out through the top of my head. Momma would talk to me while combing my hair to get me to calm down. I wasn't having any of it. As soon she got within combing distance I started squirming and crying. It got to the point where she had to hold me between her legs with my hands clamped at my side. It was the only way she could get me to stay still long enough to comb my hair. I must have had the nappiest hair in the world. We went through this ritual every morning during both my kindergarten and first year of school. I never could understand why my hair was so nappy. Momma would wash it and grease it, but nothing she tried would soften my hair for any length of time. The only thing momma could do was hold me down and pop them naps.

When we lived on the Mudline, the house was so far back in the woods the school bus didn't run by our house and daddy had to be at work before we got dressed for school, so daddy made arrangements for us to catch a ride with this lady who lived even farther back in the woods than we did. Every morning she passed our house on her way to work for some white woman somewhere around the Lake. Anyway, we would pile on the back of her truck and she would drop us off at the designated spot on the side of the road to catch the school bus. It had to be at least a good two country miles from our house to where we had to catch the bus. During the summer months we would be dusty from head to toe getting on the bus. In the wintertime we would be frozen half to death by the time we got on the bus. There were times when the woman didn't have time, or had trouble with her truck, to pick us up. Those days we had to walk that two country miles to the bus stop. It wasn't too bad during the summer months, but during the winter there were days that were really, really cold. I remember a few days these white people who live somewhere in our vicinity would let us pile into their car and they would drop us off at the bus stop.

Another incident that stands out in my mind was my 8th grade school year. Will sent momma some money to buy my school clothes. Instead of going and getting the clothes herself, she gave the money to Sue to go for her. When Sue came back with the clothes, I was so glad to get the new clothes I didn't bother to try them on before school started. She said since me and my nephew was the same size the clothes would fit. When I got dressed that first day of school, I put on my new pants and discovered they were all high water. They didn't go past my ankle. I truly believe Sue brought my pants too short on purpose because, as she said, her son and I wore the same size pants, but his pants fit fine. So day after day I went to school with those high water pants on, mad at her. Then there came a ray of hope several months before school finished that I would have at least one pair of pants for school that would fit when my brother Biddy sent me a pair of pants from California. The first day of school after receiving the pants from Biddy, I put the pants on and the cuff of the pants went all the way onto the floor. I had to roll them up. So the remainder of the school year I went to school wearing pants too short or too long. That was one of the worst years of my life.

When I was in high school, my classmates said I was square because I wouldn't smoke weed with them. Every chance they got, my friends smoked that nasty stuff. I couldn't stand the smell of it. Besides, my biggest deterrent was daddy. He scared me when he said he would beat us to death if he ever heard that we were smoking, or using any kind of dope. It didn't take too much convincing on my part because my older brothers and sisters told me that daddy had killed a man and went to prison for it when he was a young man. My friends would grab me and hold me up against the wall in the bathroom and would take turns blowing the smoke in my face, but I still wouldn't smoke with them. Eventually they gave up. What they didn't know was my fear of daddy was far stronger than any high I could get from drugs. With all his faults, and there were many, daddy did a good job disciplining us.

* * * *

While I was growing up in Arkansas, there was no law against contributing alcohol to the delinquency of a minor. If there had been such a law, half the daddies in Arkansas would have been thrown in jail because to them it was a rite of passage that a boy be able to handle his liquor. Daddy was no different than those other daddies who provided alcohol to their sons at an early age. Therefore, I was quite young when daddy would take me with him to the liquor store. I don't remember exactly what age I was, but I remember going into the liquor stores. Not only did I go into the liquor stores with daddy, he would tell me to pick out what I wanted to drink. Being as young as I was, I had no idea what kind of liquor I should be getting. Daddy would laughed and buy something that was sweet and not too strong for me. I don't remember any of the brand names just that the liquor was always sweet.

Going into the liquor stores and being asked to pick out what I wanted to drink sticks in my mind because l knew, even at that age, that it wasn't natural for a child my age to be drinking alcohol. Momma had instilled in us that children who drank alcohol were bad children and were going straight to hell when they die. Although I believed her, my fear of disobeying daddy was a lot stronger than my fear of going to hell. If he said drink, I drank. I didn't want daddy to be the one that sent me to hell with bruises all over my butt. So I would ride along in the car beside daddy, sipping from my own personal bottle as if I was a miniature man. Needless to say, I'd be so drunk when we got home momma would have to put me to bed. Momma would be so mad at daddy for getting me drunk, but he always had an explanation for why he did what he did. He would say Zell, the boy is alright. You know I wouldn't do anything to hurt him, besides the boy is going to have to learn how to handle his liquor when he grows up. Momma would say she agreed with him about me being able to handle my liquor when I grew up, however, she felt they should wait until I grew up before force feeding me alcohol. Daddy assured her it was never too early to start teaching a boy to be a man. In the face of this assurance momma always gave in to his reasoning, but she continued to tell me I was going to hell if I kept drinking. I think momma just got tired of arguing with daddy all the time about giving me liquor to drink and hoped I would get so sick it would turn me against drinking booze. Unfortunately, I never got that sick. It is important that I point out daddy giving me booze was not an everyday occurrence. It sticks out in my mind because I was sure I was going to die at an early age and when I died, I was going straight to hell. I believed everything momma told me because I knew she was the only one in the house who never told a lie.

* * * *

As I stated above, when we moved on the Mudline the first few days was a wilderness adventure. The house we moved into was so far back in the woods we had to pump in sunshine. There were no lights or running water. And momma didn't have any gas to cook with. She had to cook on a wood stove. There was not a single light pole anywhere to be found. Since we didn't have any neighbors, the only sounds we heard at night were the howling of the wolves and the barking of wild dogs. The occasional growling of what we believed to be cougars, and the sounds of whatever else was living out there in those deep, dark woods. Our only source of lights was the candles momma brought with her.

On dark nights daddy would gather us around him and tell ghost stories he was told while he was growing up, and some of his own. We would sit there for 1 to 2 hours spellbound, listening to all this stuff about ghosts and hauntings. We would look around the room from time to time to see if any of the ghosts he was talking about was paying us a visit. After insuring he had scared the mess out of us he would say, "Ok, I guess I'll go to bed now, and y'all kids need to do the same because we have a lot to do tomorrow." Me, and my sisters would look at each other with terror in our eyes. We would then look at momma waiting for her to tell us not to worry about what daddy had told us about ghosts because they were only stories. I wanted to believe the stories daddy told wasn't true, but I had a question for momma to. Why were daddy's ghost stories not true but hers' were? She didn't talk about her contacts with people in the spiritual world too often, but on occasions she told some pretty scary tales herself. The question was never asked, so we would go to bed shaking from head to toe. I would get in bed and not move from that spot until morning. Sometimes I would have to use the night pot so bad that my insides hurt, but the thought of ghosts getting me if I got out of bed gave me the strength to hold out. Because every time I thought about getting out of bed to relieve myself I would hear "Al gee gee" from somewhere in the house and that would kill the desire to do anything. Some nights I thought I would die before it was time to get up for the day's chores, but I manage to hold it in.

However, it is not because of the location where we lived, the ghost stories daddy told, or the hot and cold days we had to bum a ride to the bus stop that causes me to remember the place so well. It was on the Mudline that a pretty teenage girl name Emma came to live with us for a while. Daddy called her a high yeller gal, and said if he was ten days younger he would make her his second wife. I was so in love with her. I followed her around the house like a lovesick puppy, and when she would take a bath I would peep in on her. During these episodes of voyeurism I would fantasize about what it would be like to go with her, not that I knew what going with her meant. I had heard my older sisters and brothers talking about that what you did when you liked somebody. I made up my mind one day that the next time she took a bath I would make my move.

It never occurred to me that she knew I was always peeping in on her when she was taking a bath, and never hid her nakedness from me because I was just a little boy who posed no threat to her. She must have thought it was cute to have a little boy lusting after her. Anyway, several days later she was taking a bath. When I walked into the room she was standing in the tub bucked naked with her back to me. I figured it was now or never. While she was bent over washing her feet, I unzipped my pants and pulled out my little wiener and walked up behind her as if I was going to do something. I didn't even know where I was supposed to put it, but I thought she would be so impressed she would show me. She looked around and saw me holding my little thing and laughed at me. She told me to take my little mannish self somewhere and leave her alone. I just knew she was teasing me and didn't really mean for me to leave her alone, so I reached out to touch her while still holding myself at the ready. She slapped my hand away, and knocked the hell out of me, right upside the head. She hit me so hard I fell to the floor as if she had shot me. I don't know what hurt the most, her rejection of me, or the pop upside the head. I ran outside crying, and hid from everyone until I stopped crying. After that incident, my love for her vanished, and I never peeped at her taking a bath again. I never told anyone what happened that day, and was grateful neither did she.

* * * *

My brother Deedie was a ladies man. I don't know what it was about him that the girls liked, but whatever it was, they liked it. He would bring them to the house while momma and daddy were gone. I was too young to be serious about girls, but I was curious about what Deedie and the girls did when they ran me out of the house. I was sure I knew what they did, but I had never actually watched them do it. He had some of the prettiest girlfriends on the farm. One day he brought a pretty girl to the house, and as usual he gave me a quarter and told me to get lost. I usually took the quarter and walked down to the corner store and bought some candy, and by the time I got back to the house they would be finished doing their business. This day I put my quarter in my pocket, went outside and waited for them to start doing their thing.

I gave them about ten minutes alone before peeping in the window to see what they were doing. The window was too high for me to stand flat-footed and see through it, so I had to stand on the butane tank sitting adjacent the window in order to be tall enough see through the window. My eyes bulged at what I saw. Deedie had the girls blouse open and he was feeling her up. She had her hand someplace it shouldn't have been and they were both breathing real hard. I laughed at the funny noises they were making. I started waving my hands in front of the window and calling his name, Deedie, Deedie, Deedie. At first they ignored me, or they didn't hear me calling his name. When he didn't notice me waving and calling his name, I tapped lightly on the windowpane. The girl was the first one to notice me through the window. She screamed and pulled her blouse closed pointing at the window. Deedie motioned for me to leave, but I was enjoying myself too much. He came outside and told me to get lost or he was going to beat my butt. I jumped off the butane tank and took off across the cotton field, although I knew he wasn't going to chase me because the girl was still in the house. After Deedie went back into the house, I climbed back on top of the butane tank and watched as the girl refused to let Deedie touch her again. He got mad and took her home. He promised me he was going to get me for what I had done. I told him if he touched me I was going to tell momma and daddy what he was doing when they weren't at home. After that day he always made sure I was gone before he made his move. I never got a chance to interrupt him again, but I ruined that day for him, and it was a long time before he forgave me for it.

    Deedie had one girlfriend I thought was the most beautiful girl in the world. I don't remember her name, but I do know she was one of Deedie's prettiest girlfriends. It didn't matter to me she was my brother's girl. I was crazy about her. Being as young as I was, I'm sure she was just playing with my mind when one night while we were outside playing she let me kiss her, or tried to. I was so scared I missed her lips and kissed her on the nose. She thought that was the funniest thing in the world. She said it was alright, that I would kiss many girls in my lifetime. I was so embarrass, I never tried to kiss her again. If Deedie had found out what I was doing with my little mannish self, he would have whup my butt.

*   *   *   *

I had a bad habit of beating up on one of my younger nephews. I don't know why, it just seemed like the thing to do. Normally after I beat him up, he would go crying to his momma. I should have known if I kept beating on him he would eventually get the better of me one day, which he did. On this particular day I was throwing clods of dirt at him, but I couldn't hit him because he kept dodging my throws. He would then run around the corner of the house and stick his tongue out at me. I got bored and went to tell him I didn't want to play anymore. What I didn't know was he was waiting for his chance to unload on me.

Confident that he didn't have the guts to hit me, I stepped around the corner of the house to tell him I quit. He had picked up the biggest clod of dirt he could find and was easing his way to the corner of the house so he could throw it at me. When I stepped around the corner of the house, it caught him by surprise. So it was an automatic defensive reaction that he threw the clod of dirt at me at point blank range. I could see the big clod of dirt coming straight at me, but because of the short distance, I didn't have time to get out of the way. The clod hit me in my right eye. It hurt so bad I fell to the ground hollering, crying, and holding my eye. Upon seeing me hitting the ground and holding my eye crying he took off and ran into the house, as if no one would find out it was him who hit me.

Daddy heard the commotion going on and came outside to see what was going on. Upon seeing me lying on the ground screaming in pain he came over and asked me what happened. Usually, daddy wasn't very sympathetic when we got hurt while throwing things at each other because we all had the same opportunity to be the victor. This time, upon seeing the size of the knot on my head, and seeing my eye was starting to swell shut, he was concerned. I told him who had thrown the clod of dirt that hit me in the eye. I never mentioned I had been throwing clods of dirt at my nephew.

Daddy called my nephew outside and asked him why he had hit me in the eye with such a big clod of dirt. My nephew told daddy that I had been throwing clods of dirt at him and when I came around the corner of the house, I had scared him and he just threw the clod of dirt in self-defense. Unfortunately for my nephew, daddy didn't believe a word he said. Daddy reached up in the tree that was in the front yard and pulled down a small limb and whipped my nephew until all that was left of the limb was a short piece that barely fit into his hand. When we talked about the incident the next day, my nephew swore daddy had flown up into that tree like he was superman. Both my eyes swelled up and turned black and blue. When I told my nephew he should apologize for hitting me in the eye with the clod of dirt, he said I got what I deserved for always beating him up. He never hit me in the face with anything again. Hitting me in the eye with that clod of dirt was the last time daddy ever had to whip my nephew's butt for anything else ever again! I should also mention that I had a new found respect for my nephew because he assured me the butt whupping he got for hitting me in the eye was worth it, and he wouldn't hesitate to pop me in my eye again if I kept messing with him. We continued to throw clod of dirt at each other, but the facial area was off limits.

* * * *

  Daddy would take me with him to this lady's house every now and then that lived way back in the woods to buy chickens. It wasn't a pleasant trip most of the time, because I would end up in the chicken coop to catch the chickens daddy would buy. When we got there the lady would lead us out to the chicken coop and let daddy pick out the ones he wanted. Usually the coop contained about a hundred chickens, so you can imagine how much fun it was catching the chickens daddy had pointed out, which was my job. I always dreaded when daddy finished picking out the chickens he wanted, usually about ten, because it was then time to go in the coop and catch them.
  I would be so scared of those chickens because when daddy herded them toward me so I could catch the ones he had pointed out, they would be squawking and flying over my head. I would be ducking every time one flew over my head and daddy would get mad at me and start hollering at me to catch the damn

chickens. He would point out the ones he wanted me to catch as the chicken came in my direction. Knowing daddy had lost patients with me, it was my behind or the chickens, so I would snatch them out of the air if I had to. As I caught them, I would tie a string around their legs that was tied to a post of the coop to keep them from rejoining the rest of the chickens. Around and around daddy herded them, until we had the number of chickens daddy wanted to buy. I would like to say at this point my job was done, other than loading them into the trunk of the car, but it wasn't.

    I would untie the string from the post and drag the flopping, squawking chickens out of the pen. Then one by one, daddy would grab the chickens by the neck and wring their necks until their heads popped off. The woman was never too happy about this because the headless chickens would be flopping and slinging blood all over the place, which she said drew foxes to her chicken coop. To ensure no more blood than necessary was slung around the yard, after each chicken head pooped off, it was my job to catch it and hold them until they died. I would be so scared as I chased the headless chicken flopping around the yard. As always, I was more afraid of daddy whipping my butt than of a dying chicken, so I held each one until it died. We would then throw them in a Kroger sack and put the sack in the trunk of the car. When we got home with the chicken momma would already have hot water boiling in the big black pot so we could pluck them.

    Sometimes daddy would take my nephew with us to get the chickens, but he was so scared of the chickens he would be useless. However, for kicks daddy would put him in the chicken coop with me and stand outside laughing at my nephew ducking, dodging, and squealing louder than the chickens were squawking. After having his fun, he would tell my nephew to get his sorry butt out of the coop and wait in the car. He told him to wait in the car because my nephew would not touch the headless chickens after daddy popped their heads off either. On the way home daddy would look at my scared nephew and tell him although he wouldn't touch the chickens while they were alive, he had no trouble eating them once they were cooked, with his scary black self.

    My nephew may have been afraid of chickens, but he was

not afraid of taking chances that may get him thrown in jail. He was the biggest negative influence in my life. He was a born thief and con man. Instead of me being the leader because I was the oldest, and was the captain of the Lakeview varsity basketball team, as well as Prom King, I was always the follower because he was the mastermind behind everything we did.

While we were living on highway 20, there was a corner store about a quarter of a mile down the road from our house. The clerk had a bad habit of leaving money lying on the counter in front of the cash register instead of putting it in the cash drawer. He changed that habit very quickly when me, and my nephew started going to the store, because the money started disappearing. He never caught my nephew stealing the money, but he had his suspicions. My nephew was so bold he never even left the store after taking the money. Our normal routine was I would be the one to buy something from the person working behind the counter to keep the person busy while my nephew would steal the money or whatever he could get his hands on. The first few times he stole items from the store I was really scared. I just knew the white storeowner would catch us and tell daddy he caught us stealing. If that happened, daddy would have beaten me within an inch of my life. However, as time passed and we never got caught, I got comfortable stealing from the store too. We always bought meat because the clerk had to leave the counter to cut the meat. It was while he was cutting the meat that we would steal him blind. We always paid for our meat to give the impression that we had done nothing wrong. We would then walk out of the store pleased as could be. If they had looked inside our shirts, we would have been locked up for a long time, because you would be surprised how much stuff we could stick inside our shirts without it showing.

Another thing I let my nephew talk me into was taking daddy's car without permission every once in a while after he went to sleep at night. I'm sure daddy knew that we were taking the car he just didn't say anything. He had to know because we never had money for gas, and his tires went bald sooner than they should have for the number of miles he put on the car. Although he never said anything to us, I would be deathly afraid he was going to confront us at any moment. He never did.

Every night we took daddy's car we would drive down to the drag strip and watch the boys who families had money race those fancy new cars. The drag strip was a mile long straight strip of highway along highway 20. I would be so jealous of them. I dreamed of someday owning one of the fastest cars in Arkansas. What we did was challenge the boys who cars were no faster than daddy's, but no one wanted to risk tearing up their families old jalopies. There was only one time a boy who was driving his daddy's car was not afraid to race us. He was like my nephew, willing to suffer the consequences if he wrecked his daddy's car. My nephew really wanted to race this boy because he would tease him saying he knew Joe Wade's old car couldn't out run a ten speed bike. Believe it or not we won the race, but it took such a toll on the engine we never raced again. However, to show off for the girls that would be there, my nephew would step on the gas burning rubber and driving real fast for a short distance. I would be terrified he was going to wreck the car one of these nights, but I always went with him like the dummy I was. Because I was afraid to speed when I drove, my nephew would never let me drive. I didn't really mind because I remembered how mad daddy got when a friend of his wrecked his car, even though it wasn't his fault.

Daddy bought a new car, actually used, but new to us, and he was showing it to a friend. He was telling his friend about how powerful the car engine was. Daddy said she would flat out get up and go. Daddy's friend said he was full of it, because the car didn't look like it had much power at all. To prove it, daddy told the man he could test-drive the car himself. Me, and my cousin was sitting around listening to the conversation. The man asked us if we wanted to ride with him. It was always a thrill for us when we got a chance to ride in any car, so we jumped in before he could change his mind. We hadn't gone very far when something happened to the steering system. He was turning the steering wheel this way and that but the car kept going in whatever direction it wanted. Naturally he lost control of the car. He was fussing and cussing because he couldn't control the car and we were wondering what was going to happen if he didn't get control of it back. The last thing I heard him say before the car ran into the brick pillar on the bridge a short distance from our house was s**t. I ended up with a big knot on my head from banging it on the dashboard. My cousin got a cut lip somehow. Luckily, we weren't going too fast. Daddy fussed and cussed and swore if the man who sold him the car didn't make things right he was going to stomp a mud hole in his a**. Daddy had his friend tow the car to the man he had bought the car from and threatened to whup his behind if he didn't give him a better car. I don't remember what kind it was but the man gave daddy another car at a discounted price, at least that's what he said.

* * * *

In Joe Wade's house, no one was allowed to sleep in late, even on weekends. Daddy would wake us up every morning around 6:30 a.m. His reasoning was we never knew when someone might need us for some work that needed to be done. "I'm tired because I was out partying late last night" was never an acceptable excuse, it was viewed as a personal problem that had nothing to do with being able to go to work. "I don't want to go to work because I'm tired. Or its Saturday" was the one statement that you never wanted to say in his presence, because he would offer to help you pack your bags to get out of his house.

It was while we were living on the Mudline daddy started teaching us to make our own money by picking up pecans, discarded bottles, and anything else that could be sold to make money. That was also the time I started considering myself a hunter and a fisherman. The difference between my hunting and fishing and that of my older brothers was I did it for fun, not for survival. I never experienced the things my older brothers and sisters did, but we all had the same great teachers, "Joseph Harrison Wade & Zelma Maedella Wade." Daddy's method of teaching us changed with the time, but with the same results. Momma's love, warmth, and caring for us never changed from the youngest child to the oldest. Being I am the youngest, I was the last of our generation to help bridge the way for the next generation of the Wade family.

Being the youngest of the family, I did not experience the hardships in which my older brothers and sisters talk about. However, I do have memories of what daddy was like when it came to discipline and the expectations of everyone carrying their own weight. Daddy refused to buy my clothes when he felt that I was old enough to work and buy my own. He got me, and one of my nephews a job working from 7 to 4 with an old white man killing grass. All we had to do was ride on the tractor and spray weed killer on the grass, but after a while we didn't want to do that. It was hot on that tractor and we were tired of having to get up every morning at six o'clock. Every morning daddy would wake us up at 6 a.m., momma would feed us, and it was off to work on that hot, hot tractor. Well one Friday my nephew and I decided we had had enough of that type of work for the summer. We devised a plan to get fired from the job and not tell anyone. We didn't take into consideration that daddy was going to personally check to see why the old white man stopped picking us up for work. Anyway, after getting paid that Friday, we told that old white man we would not be working with him anymore because we had to go to Memphis to buy school clothes. I don't think he really cared that we quit because he could see that we didn't want to be there. My nephew and I made a pact that we would suffer whatever the consequences would be together. Probably the most stupid pack we had ever made in our lives.

We got up as usual the following Monday morning, got dressed, ate breakfast and acted like we were waiting for the white man to pick us up for work. When the man didn't show up, I heard daddy say to momma, "I wonder why Mr. George didn't pick these boys up for work this morning." We said "oh, oh," but he said nothing to me directly. So I thought we might get away with it. But after the man didn't pick us up on Tuesday, daddy got suspicious. Since he had gotten us the job, and daddy knew we hadn't missed work in the past, he went to the man's house and asked him why he had not come to pick us up for work the last couple of days, and the old white man told daddy what we had told him. Daddy came back home and asked me why the man had not come to pick us up. I said I thought the job was finished and we weren't needed anymore. I was so scared I couldn't move. While daddy was talking to me, my nephew ran out to the outhouse to hide. The last thing I remember was daddy jumping up in the tree in the yard and pulling off the biggest limb he could find. The next thing I remember was him telling my nephew that it would do him no good to hide in the outhouse because he would be waiting for him when he came out. When my nephew finally came out of the outhouse daddy was waiting as promised. I don't think I have to tell anyone what happened.

As I said above, I didn't have it as hard as my older brothers and sisters did when it came to working in the cotton fields. The only time I had to go to the cotton fields was when I needed money to go to the basketball games, which was fifty cents. All I needed to pick was 25 pounds of cotton to buy the ticket and have enough money left for popcorn and a soda, but sometime I didn't even pick that much. I remember on one occasion I was going to come up short of my 25 pounds goal, so I devised a plan to reach it. I took a couple bricks and place them in the cotton sack to get my 25 pounds. If daddy had found out what I had done, he would have whipped me good.

One summer I went to the cotton fields with my sister Pon'k to chop cotton. I had no idea what I was supposed to do. I was told I was going to chop cotton, and that is what I did. I started chopping down the cotton instead of the weeds growing around it. When Pon'k asked me what I was doing, I said chopping cotton. She laughed and showed me what I was supposed to do. She showed me how to thin out the cotton leaving four or five stalks and cutting the weeds from around them. I found this process harder than I thought it would be. I was so slow Pon'k practically chopped both her row and mine. She continued to chopping both her row and mine the remainder of the summer. Not once did she get mad at my ineptitude and leave me on my own, although I was a pain in the butt sometimes. That one summer was my only experience chopping cotton. Needless to say, because I didn't have to work like my brothers and sisters I never learned to carry my own weight until later in life.

* * * *

Momma was a real religious woman and did her best to keep her pastor happy by doing anything he wanted her to do in the church and inviting him to Sunday dinner every once in a while. Meanwhile, daddy had no patience for preachers because he felt the majority of them couldn't save their own souls let alone anyone else's, but he did believe in God because he prayed every night before going to bed. Well one Sunday momma had cooked an awesome dinner because her pastor had told her he would stop by for supper, and while he was there, he would bless the house and all who delved within it.

I walked around the kitchen looking at all that delicious food drooling like a rapid dog. The longer I smelled the food the hungrier I got, but momma said we couldn't eat until the preacher came. Daddy came home from wherever he had gone and asked momma why no one was eating. When she told him that she was waiting for the pastor to arrive before serving dinner, he got mad. He told her he would not allow his children to go hungry waiting on some snake oil preacher to stop by whenever he got ready to show up. Momma told daddy it was bad luck to talk about a man of God that way. If he didn't change his ways, he was going straight to hell. Daddy said he would probably see that damn preacher there right beside him, in the meantime to go ahead and feed the children. The preacher could eat whatever was left when he got there. We children could care less about that preacher. We almost hurt ourselves getting in the kitchen to all that good food. I don't even remember whether the preacher ever showed up at the house or not, because after I finished eating I was out the door. I do know if he didn't show it was because of daddy. Momma was really mad at daddy for overriding her authority, but his word was law in our house.

* * * *

One of the most hurtful and disappointing episodes in my

life was the time I went to town with daddy and he bought a shiny new red and black bicycle. I was grinning from ear to ear when daddy put the bike into the trunk of the car. When we got on the road, I thought we were on our way home, so I was thinking of all the fun I was going to have while riding my brand new bicycle. I was going to be the envy of the neighborhood. Little did I know my happiness was going to be squashed a short time later.

As I said, I thought we were on our way home. Instead we made a stop at some woman's house just outside of town. When we pulled into the yard of the house, a woman and a boy about my age came out to greet us. Daddy and the woman talked a while and then the unthinkable happened. He opened the trunk of the car and gave the bike to that boy. My heart sank and tears stung my eyes. On his way in the house with the woman, daddy told me to stay in the yard until he got ready to go. I went and sat in the car and watched the boy grinning and riding up and down the road on what I thought was my new bicycle. I started crying and couldn't stop until I saw daddy coming out of the house. I never understood how he could buy something I always wanted and give it to another boy. At that moment, I didn't think I could ever love that man again in my life. He got in the car and asked me what was wrong with me. Although I said nothing, I'm sure he knew how disappointed I was that the bike he had bought was not for me. To confirm my suspicions that daddy knew that he had hurt me when he gave that boy the bike. He said the next bike he bought would be mine. He then told me not to say anything to anyone about the bicycle. Abiding by daddy's wishes, I never said anything to anyone about that painful episode in my life.

* * * *

My brother Bobo was involved in an incident with a white man named Preacher. The way Bobo tells the story is probably true, but I want to tell the story the way I heard it and believed while I was growing up. One day Bobo was walking by Preacher's house and he was standing on the front porch. Knowing that most of the black kids in the neighborhood were afraid of dogs, he sic his dog on Bobo. Instead of running like all the other black kids did, Bobo stopped and took his knife out of his pocket, braced himself, and waited for the dog to attack him. The dog, seeing that Bobo wasn't going to run from him, pulled up short of its target and stood his ground growling. Preacher, seeing Bobo with the raised knife, started calling for the dog to get back in the yard. He told Bobo he had better not hurt his dog. Bobo told Preacher he could sic his dog on him if he wanted to but the dog would never bite anyone else, and after he was through with the dog he would be waiting for his white butt. The dog had more sense than Preacher gave him credit for. The dog growled for a little while, then turned around and went back into the yard. Preacher said he should get his gun and shoot him. Bobo told him that was the only way he could keep him off his behind if he ever sic that dog on him again. Preacher called Bobo a crazy negra and told him to get from in front of his house. Preacher pretended not to be afraid, but he knew Bobo meant every word he said.

* * * *

My brothers and sisters always talked about the haunted houses they used to live in before I was born. I felt I had missed out on something special by not being able to share in those stories. However, I did have one ghostly story that I was able to share with the group when I was around sixteen. I went with my friend James to see a girl he liked that lived in Snow Lake. Snow Lake was about an hour drive from Lakeview. Lakeview, Arkansas, is where we were living at the time. We stayed at her house as late as her parents would allow, and we took off for home.

On the way back home from the girl's house, we were cruising down the road listening to the radio and lying about how many girls we had slept with, when far up ahead there appeared to be someone in the middle of the road. I don't know how far out in front of the car the headlights shone, but it was far enough for us to see the outline of a person. Since the image was so far ahead of us, we didn't pay too much attention to it because if it was a person, they had plenty of time to get out of the road before we reached him. As we got closer and closer to the image, we realized that there was something about this image that didn't look right. We couldn't make out a face, and we couldn't see any arms or legs. The image was floating in the air as if it was hanging by strings. It looked like a white sheet or a torn white dress blowing in the wind. James asked what we were going to do. Being we were both scared half to death, I told him to run the bastard down! My eyes were big as silver dollars when James stepped on the gas and attempted to run over whatever it was that was in the road. When we reached the point of impact with the image, it disappeared. Like a puff of smoke, poof it was gone. I looked back and there was nothing, or anyone, in the road. Me, and James rode the rest of the way home in silence. We didn't tell anyone about our ghostly experience along that stretch of road until one of the older men in the neighborhood said a woman had been killed along that road, and every now and then she reappeared looking for the person who had killed her. The man said we had been lucky because normally when she appeared on the road at least half the people who saw her wrecked their cars and died at the scene. Being this stretch of road where we saw the ghost was on the other side of Elaine where we hung out it was of little concern to us. James never did tell that girl the truth about why he never came to see her again at night. He told her he was afraid of her parents. Because of the ghostly encounter, neither one of us ever went back to Snow Lake, Arkansas during the hours of darkness.

* * * *

We lived in this one house around the Lake that was right down the street from Mr. Ernest Toney's store/nightclub called "Mr. Toney's. I believe it was the only black owned store in Phillips County. It was just an average big wooden structure like all the white owned stores, but I loved that store. Us kids would find pop bottles and run down to Mr. Toney's store where he paid us two cents for it. We would promptly spend our earning on penny candy. The other thing I liked was listening to Mr. Toney and his friend talk about sports. It didn't matter if the sport was basketball or baseball they were all experts on who was the best. If it was basketball season they knew who was going to win the NBA championship. If it was baseball season they all knew who was going to win the World Series. If it was football they knew who would win the super bowl. The two guys Mr. Toney argued with the most about sports were Mr. Manuel and Mr. Aubrey. I would sit and listen to them for hours on end on weekends. I just knew there were no other men in the world who knew more about sport than they did, except daddy when he decided to put his two-cent in. It never dawn on me that most of their prediction on who would win was hardly ever right. But it sounded like they knew what they were talking about and that was good enough for me.

Another reason I had all the respect in the world for Mr. Toney was he let Teenie and her three kids live in the house behind the store when she didn't have anywhere to live. Sometime when I would visit Teenie, Mr. Toney would let us clean up around the store and pay us a whole five-cent each. That five-cent would keep me supplied with candy most of the weekend. I don't remember how long she stayed there but it was good while it lasted.

On the club scene in the rear of the store is where momma, daddy and my older brother and sisters went to get their party on. Daddy and my older brothers and sisters went on Fridays and Saturdays night. Momma went occasionally on Saturday nights, and would complain every Sunday about how crazy the people who frequented club was, because every Saturday night there would be at least one fight before the night was over. I think daddy was glad momma didn't like the clubs too much because it gave him the opportunity to mess around with other women. Of course I never said anything like that to him, the consequences would have been too severe. I knew when momma went to the club on Saturdays because the following Sunday morning I would have a big honey bun waiting for me that momma had bought for me, no doubt right before coming home from the club/store.

* * * *

The only time I can remember being somewhat disrespectful

to daddy and didn't lose any teeth was after he had said "yas'suh" to a young white man half his age. We had stopped at a corner store to get a couple of soda waters. After paying for the sodas the white boy said something like "y'all come back," to which daddy had responded with the "yas'suh." When we got in the car, I asked him rather rudely why he always let them white boys disrespect him. He ignored the tone of my voice and said I would understand some day why black men acted the way they did around white folks. I made a pledge to myself that day that I would never say "yas'suh or nos'suh" to any white man younger than I was, even if he was my boss.

* * * *

Summary

Being the youngest child in the clan, I missed out on growing up with the majority of my older siblings. They had grown up, moved out, and had families of their own. They would give me advice whenever they came home but I didn't always listen until life kicked me in the face. The love we have for each other is beyond reproach. I didn't have it as hard as they did when I was growing up, but I did my part to make the family proud.

Acknowledgments

My father in heaven, without Your love and guidance we would not have been able to reach this dream, for we are nothing without you.

My wife, Sun, of forty-four years, without your love and caring heart this book could not have been possible. You are the wind beneath my wings that keeps me aloft, and looking forward to the future.

My children, Ardella, Ronda, Robert Jr., and Zelma, who taught me what it was to be a father, and gave me their unconditional love. You never doubted that I had the ability to make this dream come true. I love you individually and collectively because each of you is unique in your own way.

My grandchildren, Carlos Jr. Sierra, Brandon, Robert III, Jerry, RJ, Ross, and Raigan: I love you all.

My brothers and sisters, because they contributed the stories of their childhoods that made this book a reality. I know momma and daddy is looking down on us from god's heavenly throne saying, "Thank you Lord, because with Your help and guidance, our children have made us proud.

A special thank you to our dearly departed brother, Charles, who passed on to be with momma and daddy in heaven before this book was published, but left with us the story of his childhood to pass on to his children and grandchildren. We love you and miss you dearly.

Families

Vera Magaline Wade Tharp – Husband: El Tharp
    Children: Linda, Margaret, Vivian, Fred Jr.
        Don (deceased), Edward (deceased)
        Barry, Melissa, Charles, Fredrick
        Cherry (deceased), Othena, Artena

    Grandchildren: Sebrina, Eric, Tarveras, Borus, Raomona, Walter, Keith, Tonya, Sammy, Timothy, Tina, Tammy, Thomas, Roderick, Shanna, Lovita, Aunaray, Erik, Shanee, Jecari, Jefaar, Mark Jr., Kiana, Charles Jr., Ashanti, Ariana, Isiah, Vanessa, Ashleigh, Chanti, Darius, Tamar, Carlos, Ishamel.

Lenora Wade – Did not contribute to the book

Joe Nathan – None (Deceased)

Annie Ruth Wilson – Husband: George Sr.
    Children: George Jr. – Annales
            Gregg – Kiana
            Chad – Tyjai, Tayrem, Jaxson, Tyler
            Yolanda – None
            Dr. Loretta Wilson-Wade, D.D.S. – Brandon

Myrtle Christine Blakeley – Widower
    Children: Will Love – Shelton, Melody, Patrick
            Barbara – Deshonda,
            Peggy – Markel, Bliss, Jimmy Jr.

Charles T. Wade – Wife: Maxine
    Children: Gwendolyn – Robert [AJ], Jasmin, Cachet
            Vincent – Aston, Renae, Danielle
            Charles – Charles Jr., Sierra, Chistian, Charis,

Simmone, Chance
Keith – Rell, Keith Jr., Carishay, Kayla
Carla – Karl
Justin – unk
Siarrah – Marichal, [Momma & Poppa]
Welton – Mariah, Zariah

Glenda Sue Wade – No husband
Children: Troy – E Pluribus, Reeshamah, Monique, Jackie, Mario
Jacqueline – Cartrelle
Vickey – Nailah, Nigel
Donnell – Aaron, Andrew, Donnell Jr., Ciera, Valley, Herbert
Stephanie – Genise, Denisha
Belinda – Alexis, Alex, Alana

Sammy Wade – Wife: Sue Ellen
Children: Kitonia – Kenvadus, Aliyah, Nykira, Jordan
Leshonda – Kyleigh, Bailey
Sammy Jr. – Lepri, Ramzia, Emontae
Frenika – None

Musa Akil Saeed – Wife: Betty
Children: Baruti
Paki – Jayln, Jayson, Xavier, Chase

Robert M. Wade – Wife: Sun Hui
Children: Ardella – Carlos Jr., Brandon
Ronda – Robert II, Ross
Robert Jr. – Robert III, Jerry, Raigan
Zelma – Sierra, Amber
Adopted daughter Jacqueline Huether - Jaevonne

Joyce Ann Wade – Husband: Lester (Deceased)
Children: Rosemary – Preston
Veda – Raheim Jr., Musahasi

Deetra – Secoyia, India
Fredrick – Rollie
Lakeshia – Khloe, Makiyia, Malachi
Veonda – Kydarrion, Jadarrion, Amaya, Jassiah

Wilmer Wade – Wife: Jean Harlene
    Children: Wilmer Jr. – None
              Donnica – None

Mary F. Wade Garner – Husband: Tuti
    Children: Demeter – Asia, Stormee, Khayos
              Larry – Shamya, Tayshun
              Rhonda – Zakariya, Zaiben
              Larita – Shania, Brittani & Brandi, Messiah, Keashia
              Kevin – Kadevin, Maryha, Kennedy
              Kionna – Darrell

Betty Ann – Passed at nine months of age

Margaret Wade – Husband: Not married
    Children: Derrick –Vaysha
              Derius – None
              Daysha – None

Eugene Wade – Wife: Patricia
    Children: Eugene Jr. – None
              Delila – Darius

This book is a brief oral history account of an African American family who survive the harsh conditions of sharecropping and being farm hands in the cotton fields during the 1940s thru the 1970s in the south. Though some of the memories are dimmed by time, the brothers and sisters telling their stories give accounts of the hardship they endured while growing up as children in the cotton fields in the south to the best of their recollection. It is told through the eyes of 13 of the 14 children who started work at six or seven years of age chopping cotton for $1.50 per day working from 6am to 6pm. They tell what it was like to pick cotton from "Can't see to can't see" for .02 cents a pound, and how they took pride in who could pick the most because it was an honest days' work. They tell of sibling interaction that was sometime cruel. They tell of the whuppings they received at the hands of their momma and daddy, but acknowledge the whuppings, on most occasions, were well deserved. They tell of taking apples and pears from neighboring yards, watermelons from neighbor's watermelon patches without permission. They tell about experiencing racism first hand, and not understanding why things in the south was the way they were. Most importantly, they tell of a momma and daddy who loved, nurtured, disciplined, and directed their lives to become good citizens. Parents that regardless of the circumstances held their heads high and demanded that their children do the same. This is their story.

The Ends

www.ingramcontent.com/pod-product-compliance
Lightning Source LLC
Chambersburg PA
CBHW070736170426
43200CB00007B/542